Unhitched

Judith Stacey

Unhitched

Love, Marriage, and Family Values from
West Hollywood to Western China

New York University Press • *New York and London*

NEW YORK UNIVERSITY PRESS
New York and London
www.nyupress.org

First published in paperback in 2012.

References to Internet websites (URLs) were accurate at the time of writing.
Neither the author nor New York University Press is responsible for URLs
that may have expired or changed since the manuscript was prepared.

Library of Congress Cataloging-in-Publication Data
Stacey, Judith.
Unhitched : love, marriage, and family values from West Hollywood to
western China / Judith Stacey.
p.   cm. — (NYU series in social and cultural analysis)
Includes bibliographical references and index.
ISBN 978-0-8147-3785-9 (pb : alk. paper) —
ISBN 978-0-8147-8382-5 (cl : alk. paper) —
ISBN 978-0-8147-8383-2 (ebook : alk. paper)
1. Gay parents — Case studies. 2. Same-sex marriage — Case studies.
3. Marriage — Case studies. 4. Families — Case studies.   I. Title.
HQ75.27.S73 2011
306.8109 — dc22   2010048298

New York University Press books are printed on acid-free paper,
and their binding materials are chosen for strength and durability.
We strive to use environmentally responsible suppliers and materials
to the greatest extent possible in publishing our books.

Manufactured in the United States of America

c 10 9 8 7 6 5 4 3 2 1

Do you [Adam] take [Eve] to be your wife—to live together after God's
ordinance—in the holy estate of matrimony? Will you love her, comfort her,
honor and keep her, in sickness and in health, for richer, for poorer, for better,
for worse, in sadness and in joy, to cherish and continually bestow upon her
your heart's deepest devotion, forsaking all others, keep yourself only unto her
as long as you both shall live?

—traditional Western wedding vows

Contents

Acknowledgments

Is it my imagination, or does the effusiveness of a book's acknowledgments tend to shrink with the seniority of its author? I remember noticing this pattern several decades ago when I set out to compose paragraphs of public gratitude to the many people who had helped me complete my own first book. At the time, I took the terse acknowledgments offered by many seasoned authors to be a sign of professional arrogance. Success at publishing, I thought, had dulled their appreciation of how much of it depends upon the kindness, wisdom, and contributions of others.

Now that the shoe is on my other, decidedly senior foot, however, I too feel inclined to issue thanks in terms as simple and straightforward as my first book's were florid. This book draws upon debts accrued over more than a decade that I spent in various research, writing, and teaching projects in three continents that I did not intend to join in one book. It's worrying to realize that I cannot possibly remember everyone who made this work possible. I can only hope that this book's readers and its many benefactors will interpret my brevity and amnesia with more sympathy than I once granted to senior colleagues.

My greatest debt is to the gracious individuals, families, and communities in California, South Africa, and China who welcomed me into their lives and to the countless colleagues, friends, hosts, contacts, and guides who helped me locate, visit, and interpret them. A special shout-out here is due to the Pop Luck Club in Los Angeles, to Shireen Hassim, Lynne Aschman, Ndabenhle Ndaba, and Ann Marie Wolpe in South Africa, and to Wang Zheng, Eric Zhang, Li Ying, and Najinamu in China. This book also draws from two prior collaborative research and writing projects with Tim Biblarz and one with Tey Meadow. I wholeheartedly thank both Tim and Tey for incomparable intellectual and personal companionship. Arlene Stein, Jeffrey Weeks, and Harvey Molotch gave spirit-boosting, insightful responses to a draft of the manuscript. Many others read particular portions, discussed ideas, suggested readings, and encouraged me along the way. For intellectual, professional, and personal contributions at various points, I thank Lynne Aschman, David Bilchitz, Edwin Cameron, Jackie Cock, Raewyn Connell, Stephanie Coontz, Kent Diebolt, Ruth Dixon-Mueller, Martha Ertman, Eric Fassin, Doug Foster, Beth Goldblatt, Shireen Hassim, Melanie Heath, Fred Hertz, Carole Joffe, Jonathan Ned Katz, Don Kulick, Suzanne Levine, Emily Martin, Zethu Matebeni, Likthapta Mbatha, Tey Meadow, Ashley Mears, Sheila Meintjes, Zanele Muholi, Kelly Musick, Barry O'Neill, Graeme Reid, Vernon Rosario, Sasha Roseneil, Debby Rosenfelt, Gail Saliterman, Steve Seidman, Jake Stacey-Schreier, Peggy Swain, Barrie Thorne, Pierre de Vos, Nina Wakeford, Judy Walkowitz, Danny Walkowitz, and Michael Yarborough.

I am immensely grateful for institutional support and faculty research grants from my current and prior universities, NYU and USC, and for the gift of several indispensible periods of field research and writing enabled by a fellowship from the National Endowment for the Humanities in 2001–2002, a Visiting Scholar residency at the Russell Sage Foundation in 2005–2006, and a luxurious month as a Resident Scholar at the Rockefeller Foundation Bellagio Study and Conference Center in 2006. In the summer of 2007, Shireen Hassim and Sheila Meintjes graciously sponsored me as a Visiting Scholar in the Political Studies Department at the University of Witwatersrand, where I completed the South African field research.

Jean Casella provided invaluable early editorial advice on how to combine and convert three distinct scholarly projects into a coherent book for a much broader readership. Then gifted poet, friend, editor, and wordsmith extraordinaire Martine Bellen tried to teach me how to "relax" my prose without collapsing my intellectual principles. I also thank Rebecca DiBennardo, Marin Gerber, Billy Koeblitz, and James Thing for superb, tireless assistance with laborious research, bibliography, and manuscript preparation tasks. Finally, at NYU Press I am grateful for wise guidance and support from my editor, Eric Zinner, and his assistant, Ciara McLaughlin. Eric gets an extra gold star for finding such a golden, elegant image to adorn the book's cover and Ciara for refining the title that the image illustrates. I am also lucky to join the lengthy roster of NYU Press authors indebted to the incomparable manuscript production process directed by Despina Papazoglou Gimbel, and I thank Andrew Katz for his careful copyediting.

Chapters of this book include revised versions of material from some of my previously published articles. Portions of chapters 1 and 2 first appeared in "The Families of Man: Gay Male Intimacy and Kinship in a Global Metropolis," *Signs* 30 (3) (2005): 1911–1935; "Cruising to Familyland: Gay Hypergamy and Rainbow Kinship," *Current Sociology* 52 (2) (March 2004):

181–197; "Gay Parenthood and the Decline of Paternity as We Knew It," *Sexualities* 9 (1) (2006): 27–55; Judith Stacey and Timothy Biblarz, "(How) Does the Sexual Orientation of Parents Matter?" *American Sociological Review* 66 (2) (April 2001): 159–183; and Timothy Biblarz and Judith Stacey, "How Does the Gender of Parents Matter?" *Journal of Marriage and the Family* 72 (1) (February 2010). Chapter 3 is a revised version of Judith Stacey and Tey Meadow, "New Slants on the Slippery Slope: The Politics of Polygamy and Gay Family Rights in South Africa and the U.S.," *Politics and Society* 37 (2) (2009): 167–202. Chapter 5 is a revised version of "Unhitching the Horse from the Carriage: Love and Marriage among the Mosuo, co-published by *Journal of Law and Family Studies* 11 (2) (2009) and *Utah Law Review* 2009 (2).

Introduction

Tolstoy Was Wrong

Love and marriage, love and marriage
Go together like a horse and carriage
This I tell you, brother
You can't have one without the other
> —"Love and Marriage," lyrics by Sammy Cahn,
> recorded by Frank Sinatra, 1955

WHEN "FRANKIE," A New Jersey hero, recorded the song "Love and Marriage" in 1955, he was crooning for me and my gals, and we sure did soak it up. Coming of age in a white ethnic, lower-middle-class New Jersey town, we were part of the first generation of kids to encounter the magic box of television, which fed us a steady diet of fifties family fables—*Father Knows Best, Leave It to Beaver, Ozzie and Harriet,* and my personal favorite, *I Remember Mama.* In the mid-fifties, my gal pack and I jumped rope chanting the popular jingle, "First comes love, then comes marriage, then comes [Judy] with a baby carriage." The post-war era was a time when such platitudes were uncontroversial and almost as empirically accurate as they were morally prescriptive, a time when in the eyes of many voters, divorce rendered presidential candidate Adlai Stevenson unfit for office, and marital infidelity turned Hollywood heartthrob Ingrid Bergman, the Swedish star of *Casablanca,* into a pariah denounced on the floor of the U.S. Senate as "Hollywood's apostle of degradation."[1] Those were the days, of course, when any sort of love other than heterosexual monogamy dared not yet whisper its name, and nobody would have thought to specify the sexual orientation of the imaginary blissful couple that the song and the jump-rope jingle celebrated.

Baby, carriage, and all sure have come a long way down and around since then. Paths between love, marriage, and babies have multiplied, divided,

1

A Palin family tableau at the Republican nominating convention.

inverted, eroded, and confounded. Divorced candidates, even conservative Republicans, now routinely run for the highest offices without apology, or public mention. No fifties rope jumper, seventies feminist, or family sociologist, like me, could possibly have imagined a world in which an unwed pregnant teenager could perch with her boyfriend amidst the proud family tableau on the dais at the Republican presidential convention while her mother, a right-wing governor, accepted the party's nomination for vice president of the United States. But that, of course, was what happened when Sarah Palin became Republican John McCain's running mate in 2008.

During the same decades that divorce, adultery, and unwed maternity were becoming unremarkable, rising percentages of Americans began to freely fall in and out of love without bothering to marry or parent at all. In 1950, married couples anchored four out of five households, but now the majority of domiciles shelter unmarried adults living with or without other grown-ups or children.[2] Instead of *Leave It to Beaver* or *Father Knows Best*, viewers can set their TV dials to a dizzying array of niche-market, domestic sitcoms, series, and "reality" shows that range from *The Good Wife*,

Desperate Housewives, and reruns of *Sex and the City, Six Feet Under*, and *Friends* to *Big Love, The L Word, Noah's Arc*, and reportedly soon even a CBS reality program, *Arranged Marriage*.

Meanwhile, love, marriage, and baby carriages are all the rage among lesbians, gay men, and transgendered people. The drive for same-sex marriage became the centerfold campaign of a vigorous gay rights movement. More than eighteen thousand lesbian and gay couples sprinted to tie the knot in California during the five months of 2008 after the state's supreme court opened the constitutional gates to the altar to them and before passage of Proposition 8 slammed the gates shut once again.[3] The families of former vice president Cheney's lesbian daughter and donor-insemination mom Mary Cheney and of queer sex columnist and gay adoptive dad Dan Savage can vie with thousands like theirs for a vacation berth on Rosie O'Donnell's "Family Cruise" or at "Family Week" in Provincetown. On board or at the beach, gay parents can park their kids in Camp COLAGE (Children of Lesbians and Gays Everywhere), while the grown-ups sample film screenings that feature all manner of queer families, like *Transamerica,*

After fifty years together, pathbreaking lesbian and feminist activist couple Del Martin and Phyllis Lyon are the first same-sex couple to legally wed in San Francisco, on June 16, 2008. Del Martin died two months later, on August 27, 2008. Reprinted by permission of Liz Mangelsdorf.

the critically acclaimed feature about a male-to-female trans-parent who sets out to meet the son she unknowingly sired when she was a male.

And yet, despite these mind-bending changes, the word *family* continues to conjure an image of a married, monogamous, heterosexual pair and their progeny. This is still the model of a "normal family," not only in the world of soccer moms and Joe six-packs and among politicians across the ideological spectrum who bid to win their votes but even among some family researchers who should know better. As the popular rubric "alternative families" makes clear, this "normal family" remains the standard against which all other forms of intimacy and kinship are compared and usually found lacking. Citizens and scholars alike widely presume that the "normal family" is not only superior to all others but close to universal historically and cross-culturally, a quasi-natural institution, virtually the core definition of family.[4]

Certainly, a married papa and mama with their children is the image most often brought to mind by the memorable opening lines of *Anna Karenina*: "Happy families are all alike; every unhappy family is unhappy in its own way."[5] But it should be pretty obvious by now that Tolstoy was wrong. Or rather, he was a great fiction writer. In no place or time have all happy families been alike. Across centuries, continents, and cultures, happy (and unhappy) kinds of family and kinship always have differed wildly. They continue to do so today. This book takes issue with the singular view of a proper happy family embedded in the popular songs and chants of my fifties childhood and in the ideology of family values that has become bipartisan political orthodoxy in the United States over the past few decades.

Of course, this is by no means the first book, or even my own first book, to challenge that view.[6] By now a voluminous literature, including fine recent books like Stephanie Coontz's *Marriage, a History*, Andrew Cherlin's *The Marriage-Go-Round*, Barbara Risman's *Families as They Really Are*, and Nancy Polikoff's *Beyond (Straight and Gay) Marriage*, has expertly exposed the fallacies of the one-size-fits-all vision of happy families that undergirds and distorts a great deal of public family policy today. Nor is this book unique in debunking three influential tenets of the contemporary marriage promotion movement: first, that marriage is a universal and necessary institution; second, that the ideal family structure for raising children is a married man and woman and their biological or adopted children; and third, that children generally, and boys particularly, need both a father and a mother to turn out well.[7] However, in this book I trek a different, less-traveled road to the Rome of family diversity. I do not enter the fray over the causes and consequences of "divorce culture," "fatherlessness," the campaign for same-sex marriage, gay parenthood, or other divisive issues in the family wars. Instead, I offer readers an ethnographic introduction to happy (and unhappy) instances of a few of the contemporary world's newest, oldest, and least "familiar" species of family life and of the social, political, and economic conditions that buttress and batter them. When we understand how and why different sorts of families foster different patterns of happiness and unhappiness for their members, we will better grasp the inescapable challenges and trade-offs that our quests for intimacy and kinship must navigate in the modern world.

Domesticity Is Rarely an Aphrodisiac

Of course, it's true that all societies depend mightily on families to feed and form children and to sustain, and restrain, adults. As *Civilization and Its Discontents,* Freud's gloomy rumination on the human condition, underscored long ago, just as individuals toggle uncomfortably between the competing demands of id and superego, all human societies contend with irreconcilable tensions between the domains of eros and domesticity. We might think of families serving as culture's counterpart to the ego in these duels. Every culture develops family and kinship forms to negotiate inescapable human conflicts between unruly romantic and sexual desires, on the one hand, and timeless human (and social) needs for durable, dependable, intimate relationships and care, on the other. All societies devise families to confront this universal quandary, but the families they design are by no means all alike. Even a cursory scan through the historical and anthropological record reveals that the nuclear family that most Americans think of as normal—one spawned when reciprocal romantic love inspires one man and one woman to exchange vows to forsake all others before they begin inviting visits from the stork—is quite the cultural exception rather than the rule.

Sammy Cahn's pop lyrical conceit that "love and marriage go together like a horse and carriage" would seem ludicrous, or perhaps literally assbackward, to most inhabitants of traditional societies. The reality, succinctly captured by Stephanie Coontz in the subtitle, *How Love Conquered Marriage,* of her superb history of the institution, is that romantic love and erotic attractions rarely enter into the calculus of traditional, marital matchmaking.[8] Rather, "first comes marriage," as the title of a contemporary

7

advice book that offers relationship wisdom from the still-vital tradition of Indian arranged marriage customs insists.[9]

Just this premise inspired a more savvy set of lyrics in *Fiddler on the Roof*, the 1960s smash Broadway musical that dramatized the clash between traditional and modern family values in a Jewish shtetl in Tsarist Russia. Tevye the milkman, the paternal protagonist of the play, flummoxes his wife, Golde, by asking if she loves him. "*Do I love you?*" his exasperated helpmeet warbles: "For twenty-five years I've washed your clothes / Cooked your meals, cleaned your house / Given you children, milked the cow / After twenty-five years, why talk about love right now?" But Tevye persists until Golde concedes, "Do I love him? / For twenty-five years I've lived with him, / Fought with him, starved with him / Twenty-five years my bed is his / If that's not love, what is?"[10]

Few married women living in traditional cultures then or now would define love much differently. Through most of human history, and still throughout much of the world, romantic love has occupied a realm outside of marriage, reserved chiefly for those men and members of the aristocracy who could dare to engage in liaisons that were decidedly "*dangereuses*."[11] Most family systems try to manage the conflict between desire and domesticity by sacrificing the yearnings of the former to the demands of the latter, especially when the former belong to women. A hoary host of patriarchal marriage systems rigorously restrict, and at times excise, women's sexual and romantic cravings in order to secure the fruits of their procreative and domestic labors.

Sturdy remnants of many of these traditional kinship regimes, some with boggling permutations of love, sex, marriage, and parenthood, survive in our contemporary world. More marriage systems have been polygamous than monogamous (almost always polygynous—one man with multiple wives—and very rarely polyandrous—one woman with multiple husbands), and arranged marriage systems, like the one that hitched Golde to Tevye, far outnumber free love matches. Casual cross-cultural research can speedily unearth a goody-bag of more exotic sexual, marital, and parental practices as well. Some cultures expect men to kidnap their brides in capture marriages,[12] and others oblige women or men to marry ghosts.[13] Some cultures practice levirate polygamy,[14] which requires a man to wed his deceased brother's widows, while cultures with fraternal polyandry mate women to multiple brothers.[15] The archives of fertility and childrearing customs document not only wet-nursing in France and child-swapping in England but also Sambian boys in New Guinea who must spend years fellating men and ingesting their semen in order to achieve heterosexual potency and Arzawagh Muslim daughters in Niger who are force-fed in order to enhance their sexual appeal, fertility, and marriagability.[16] As for versions of gender and sexuality that extend beyond our understandings of male or female or of GLBT or straight, consider, for example, the sworn female virgins of Albania who live as fierce male heads of their households, the bisexual "mati work" practiced by working-class women in Dutch Suriname, or India's cross-gender, self-castrated hijiras, who must be paid off to bless weddings and births.[17] Etcetera.

And we don't need to trek even a millimeter beyond what are now the borders of the fifty U.S. states to add copious specimens of exotica to our collection of such un-"familiar" practices. American historical archives stock ample supplies of these as well. When the European colonists arrived on these shores, they encountered (and often eradicated) a cornucopia of alien family practices among hundreds of indigenous cultures. For example, there were the unsettling gender norms of the comparatively sexually egalitarian Iroquois, who lived in matrilineal longhouses, not to mention the titillating and shocking Inuit practice of ritual sexual spouse-swapping.[18]

Nor were our American forebears slouches when it came to inventing new forms of intimacy and kinship themselves or imposing "alternative" family lives on the people they enslaved. Through the apprenticeship system, for example, colonial families routinely swapped parental responsibility for vocational and religious training of their adolescent sons, and sometimes their daughters. The sad fate of Hester Prynne in Hawthorne's *The Scarlet Letter* taught generations of schoolgirls like me the severe price colonial women paid for indulging in sex outside the sanctified bonds of matrimony. Yet at the same time, laws denied slaves access to legal marriage, thereby requiring, and sometimes forcing, unmarried slave women to copulate and to breed human property for their owners. Moreover, because owners could disrupt slave unions and families with impunity, slaves had no choice but to create more collective and fluid forms of parenting and kinship.[19] Likewise, from the seventeenth century until the Supreme Court finally overturned anti-miscegenation laws in 1967, American colonies and states passed laws that aimed (unsuccessfully, of course) to prevent interracial intimacy. Closeted plural, and biracial unions and families, like the one Thomas Jefferson created with his slave Sally Hemings, were among the perverse consequences of such laws.[20]

Meanwhile, in the nineteenth century, while white Americans were imposing alternatives to monogamous married family life on black slaves, they were busily inventing a bevy of novel, often exotic, forms of intimacy for themselves. The heyday of radical, utopian communities that rejected marriage, monogamy, and private property and experimented with alternative forms of intimacy in the United States did not take place during the counter-cultural 1960s but a full century earlier. For example, the dissident Protestant Shakers, still famous for their furniture design, rejected sex and baby-making entirely. They established numerous, surprisingly long-lasting, celibate communities whose members lived in sex-segregated "families" that could reproduce only by attracting new recruits or by adopting orphans.[21] In stark contrast, John Humphrey Noyes, the libidinous founder of the Oneida community of upstate New York, invented a system of sexual "stirpiculture" that gave him authority to assign multiple, short-term sexual and procreative matings to his followers.[22] Likewise, in 1831, Joseph Smith, an equally randy contemporary, received the fateful Revelation that emboldened the founder of the Church of Latter-Day Saints to embrace "the principle" of polygyny—a far more traditional domestic accommodation to masculine eros that this book will examine in a variety of shapes and sites.[23]

Somethings Old, Somethings New, Somethings Borrowed . . .

The chapters that follow draw from an eclectic set of research projects on family diversity that I have pursued at home and abroad over the past ten years. I invite readers to explore with me some species of family life that are quite new, some old-fashioned, and one that lies very far from the beaten trail. To gain the most from our family visits, it will help to travel light, leaving as much cultural baggage behind as possible. In particular, I urge readers to set aside expectations about love, marriage, parenthood, and kinship drawn from prevailing Western theories about family, intimacy, and modernity. Our expedition will enable us to consider afresh two bodies of theory that have proven especially influential among scholars as well as citizens.

First, diverse theories of modernization have long predicted that urbanization, economic development, and the global spread of media, markets, and migration would diffuse Western family life throughout the developing world. Cold War optimists anticipated the irrepressible, global triumph of democratic, voluntary, love-match, companionate marriages and egalitarian gender norms over traditional patriarchal marriage regimes.[24]

Some leftist critics, in contrast, feared that individualistic market rationality would wreak havoc on the familial "haven in a heartless world."[25] More recently, theorists of post-modern transformations of intimacy and critics of these changes have faced off over contemporary prospects that eros will utterly vanquish domesticity.[26] A controversial, optimistic account by eminent British sociologist Anthony Giddens theorized that the economic and social conditions of late modernity enable a liberated practice of intimacy that he termed the "pure relationship." He reasoned that with sexuality "severed from its age-old integration with reproduction, kinship and the generations,"[27] equals were becoming free to pursue intimacy purely "for its own sake," and so intimate relationships would endure only so long as they "deliver enough satisfactions for each individual to stay within it."[28]

If Giddens was sanguine about the liberating potential of these developments, they represent the tragic triumph of narcissism over family solidarity of any sort to many critics on both the left and the right of the political spectrum. Yet despite their incompatible values, optimists and pessimists generally share an expectation that globalization will erode traditional family forms. I ask readers to suspend such presumptions as you approach the chapters and families ahead. Collectively, these demonstrate that despite, and at times because of, globalization, there remain more ways of organizing family life in heaven and earth than are dreamt of by those currently engaged in efforts to promote or to prevent marriage—whether straight or gay.

Gay men certainly qualify as among the newest, the most controversial, and in my view, the most creative petitioners for family recognition and rights around the globe today. Their struggles to navigate eros and domesticity are more intense and their strategies necessarily more various and visible than those that heterosexuals or even, as we will see, that most lesbians have to muster. For just these reasons, gay men have much to teach the rest of us. The first two chapters present research on intimacy and kinship among gay men that I conducted in Los Angeles between 1999 and 2003. Chapter 1 focuses on the familial adult bonds that the men I studied forged with lovers, friends, ex-lovers, and others. It includes portraits of sex pigs and celibates; men in monogamous and sexually open relationships; men living alone by choice or by chance; others with mates, whether committed or ambivalent, passionate or platonic, including a long-term exclusive trio. Some of these men sought lives of love and marriage indistinguishable from the 1950s horse-and-carriage trade. Others were bravely redefining fidelity and family life with uneven degrees of success.

Chapter 2 treats parenthood among this first generation of gay men who began openly, often ingeniously, to reconsider and reconfigure it against the odds. Readers will meet gay men bringing up children alone or with male partners, and some with women friends. Many of these men fostered and adopted children of varying ages across all manner of racial, social, religious, national, physical, and emotional boundaries. Some provided sperm to female friends or relatives; others pioneered forms of surrogacy-extended parenthood. You will encounter men who give bold new meaning to the concept "planned parenthood," sometimes forging elaborate agreements to guide relationships among three and four co-parents who span households and cities. Included too are surprisingly rare stories of gay men who steadfastly refused to join the world of diapers and day care, as well as more frequent tales of those whose passion for parenthood simply failed to clear the high bar required of gay men. All of these choices and lives illuminate social forces that underlie the decline of conventional paternity in recent decades but that also allowed new forms to emerge. Lesbian and gay-parent families challenge widely held prejudices about whether children need both a father and a mother and about the ways in which a parent's sexual orientation or marital status does and doesn't matter.

From the novelty of gay L.A., we journey to a tenacious, traditional form of family life on the other side of the globe: polygamy in South Africa. While banned and generally considered depraved in the United States, polygamy is one of the world's oldest and most widely practiced family regimes. Chapters 3 and 4 revisit this stigmatized family system by juxtaposing it with gay intimacy in contemporary South Africa. Drawing from my comparative research on stunningly different family policies and practices in post-apartheid South Africa and the United States, I address divisive questions about family and sexual diversity.

Chapter 3 compares de facto family policy in one of the world's oldest constitutional democracies with de jure family policy in one of the newest. The 1996 South African constitution was the world's first, and is still the only, to ban discrimination on grounds of sexual orientation and marital status. South Africa also is the lone nation in which both polygamy and same-sex marriage are currently legal. This vanguard legal framework, however, far outstrips popular consciousness. Directly opposite, in the United States, recalcitrant family laws, including the Defense of Marriage Act (DOMA) and anti-bigamy statutes, contrast with a colorful history of avant-garde family practices. This includes not only the queer new families of gay "el lay" but also the stubborn persistence of outlawed fundamentalist

Mormon polygamy and the emergence of new, sometimes instrumental versions of plural marriage. Rather than ridicule the popular conservative warning that legalizing same-sex marriage will pave a slippery slope to legal polygamy, chapter 3 takes the argument seriously. By doing so, I identify some unsuspected cross-country trails that traverse the terrain between the two alternatives to heterosexual monogamy.

Chapter 4 ventures more deeply into these brambles. Drawing on field research I conducted in South Africa in 2007, I explore rarely noted paradoxes in the relationship between modernity and polygamy. The chapter suggests that although formal polygamy generally does lose its grip when a society modernizes, as theory and common sense predict, this does not turn out to be an unadulterated victory for monogamy. Instead, I show that informal species of plural marriage survive, and even multiply, not only in South Africa but in the United States as well. What is more, globalization unleashes forces that promote novel, transnational forms of polygamy. The chapter exposes the irrationality, hypocrisy, and the unfortunate, unintended consequences of U.S. policies toward bigamy and adultery that spring from our deep cultural antipathy to polygamy. I join those unpopular figures and rare feminists who argue that laws against bigamy do more to harm women and children than to protect them and that decriminalizing polygamy would be the wiser, less destructive course.

Finally, in chapter 5, readers will encounter one of the most distinctive, enduring family systems ever documented by anthropologists. The Mosuo people of southwest China, as the chapter's title indicates, radically separate erotic horses from domesticating carriages, and without corralling either. Most Mosuo people do not marry their lovers, or anyone else, and couples do not live or raise children together. Men visit their female lovers at night but return to their maternal homes each morning to share daily life and work with their own extended kin and to help raise their sisters' children and grandchildren.

Mosuo family and sexual practices seem as exotic and titillating to mainstream Chinese as they do to Westerners. The remote Mosuo mountain villages have become one of the most popular Chinese destinations for domestic and foreign tourists, including feminist scholars like myself. The normal Mosuo family seems to be the world's lone surviving exception to a family structure based on a conjugal couple that feminist legal theorist Martha Fineman lamented in her book title *The Neutered Mother, the Sexual Family, and Other Twentieth-Century American Tragedies*. It is an exception, however, that may not last.

Readers are about to embark on a family odyssey rife with ironies, para-doxes, and provocations for prejudices and ideologies of all stripes, includ-ing some of my own. This book challenges popular convictions about fam-ily, gender, and sexuality held on the left, right, and center, by feminists and fundamentalists, and especially by marriage-movement advocates and opponents, gay and straight. In writing this book, I seek to bury Tolstoy's dictum, or rather to return it to the fiction shelf. I hope that the sundry conceptions of love, marriage, parenthood, intimacy, and kinship depicted in its pages will encourage readers to make their peace with the fact that family diversity is here to stay. I wish also to persuade you that this is no cause for despair. Rather, the sooner and better our society comes to terms with the inescapable variety of intimacy and kinship in the modern world, the fewer unhappy families it will generate.

1

Love, Sex, and Kinship in Gay El Lay

Who are now the most square people on Earth? Who are the only people
left who want to go into the Army and get married? Homosexuals.
　　　—Fran Lebowitz, quoted in Stuever, "Is Gay Mainstream?" 2000

Promiscuity was rampant because in an all-male subculture there was no
one to say "no"—no moderating role like that a woman plays in the heterosexual milieu.
　　　—Randy Shilts, *And the Band Played On*, 1987

There is room for both monogamous gay couples and sex pigs in the same
big tent of gay community.
　　　—Eric Rofes, *Dry Bones Breathe*, 1998

NOT SO LONG ago, the notion of a gay or lesbian wedding or family
seemed oxymoronic to most people, including many lesbians and gay
men themselves. The 1970s-era gay liberation movement, like the 1960s
counter-culture and the women's liberation movement that inspired its
birth, rebelled against the gender and sexual constraints of marriage and
the nuclear family. "Smash Monogamy," "Make Love Not War," "Let It All
Hang Out" were popular banners waved by political youth in that innocent
pre-AIDS era. "We expose the institution of marriage as one of the most
insidious and basic sustainers [sic] of the system," proclaimed the Gay Liberation Front in 1969.[1]
　　Militant feminists and gays and lesbians blithely garnered reputations
as anti-marriage and anti-family, and many gay men embraced their image
as sex pigs with pride rather than shame. Often outcasts and exiles from
their families of birth, numerous gays and lesbians adopted utopian visions
of intimacy and kinship. Instead of matrimony and parenthood, they han-
kered for sexual freedom and unconventional "families we choose."[2] Yet by

the 1980s, a lesbian gayby boom was under way, and by the 1990s the gay rush to the altar and the nursery had become a stampede. Increasingly the families that lesbians and gay men seemed to be choosing looked an awful lot like the love, marriage, and baby carriage ideal of my youth. As one daughter in a study of children with lesbian parents described her family, "aside from one little, tiny detail, we are so incredibly normal."[3]

Of course, the sexual orientation of spouses and parents doesn't seem such a little, tiny detail to millions of religious and social conservatives. When the Hawaiian Supreme Court appeared poised to recognize gay marriage in the mid-1990s, the mere prospect incited such a powerful backlash that same-sex marriage began to supplant abortion as the most popular right-wing political wedge issue in U.S. electoral politics. Historic court rulings for gay unions and marriage rights in Vermont, Massachusetts, and Canada in the next decade ignited a potent blowback effect. Campaigns against gay family rights began to score disproportionate victories—from the federal Defense of Marriage Act (DOMA) in 1996 to dozens of state initiatives and constitutional amendments to prohibit gay marriage and adoption rights. In fact, in the United States every state ballot initiative against these rights but one has passed ever since, including Proposition 8 in California and three other state initiatives in November 2008 and a referendum in 2009 that overturned the newly won right to same-sex marriage in Maine.[4]

Judicial and electoral contests over gay marriage, adoption, and child-custody rights often draw on social science research that compares couples and parents who are gay or straight. Popular questions include the following: Are lesbian and gay couples and parenting more like or different from straight family relationships? If same-sex couples win the right to marriage, will marriage change them, or will they change marriage, and for better or worse? How do children raised by lesbian or gay parents turn out? Are they more likely to be gay? Gender-confused? Do children need both a mother and a father? Such questions are important, and I've contributed to social science literature and to public conversations about the research evidence myself.[5] However, because we too often take straight couples, parents, and families as the gold standard and compare gay relationships to them, we miss the opportunity to explore some of the innovative practices of eros and domesticity that many gays and lesbians have been pioneering, and from which everyone can learn a great deal.

In this chapter and the next, I resist the dominant approach and adopt a more capacious view of intimacy and family. Moving beyond a focus on marriage, couples, and nuclear families, I examine much wider definitions of intimacy, fidelity, parenthood, and family. This chapter focuses primarily on adult love, sex, and family ties; the next, on parenting and other inter-generational bonds.

Gay "El Lay"

Gay men would seem to make unpromising subjects for a study of family life. They lack the biological equipment, the social training, and the con-ventional institutional and legal resources for forging families. As males, gay men do not receive formal socialization in the feminine labors of "love and ritual"—kin work, emotion work, domestic labor, child care, nurtur-ing.[6] Because they are gay, they cannot rely on women to perform these services for them. Not only do gay men, like lesbians, still lack the right to marry in most of the United States and the rest of the world, they can-not expect women to furnish them ready access to parenthood. Because women are not the primary objects of their affections, gay men can pur-sue masculine erotic desires unconstrained by women's wishes or con-cerns and without any fear or hope that a baby might appear. Doing so, gay men more frequently than others pursue sex across social boundaries of race, age, education, income, nationality, language, and religion.[7] And, of course, the HIV/AIDS epidemic decimated the first generation of unclos-eted gay men, thwarting the prospect of paternity and picket fences even among those who may have yearned for these. Yet despite daunting barri-ers and tribulations, gay men have been redesigning kinship with creativity and verve.

Counter-intuitively, Los Angeles, a city often caricatured as La-La-Land or Tinseltown, proved an ideal site for my field research on diverse "families of man." A vanguard global mecca for sexual migrants among its throngs of dream seekers, Los Angeles is home to the second-largest, and likely the most socially diverse, yet comparatively understudied population of gay men on the planet. It is the birthplace, among numerous gay institutions, of West Hollywood—the first gay-governed municipality in the world; the Mattachine Society, a national gay rights organization formed in 1951; the One Institute, a homosexual rights organization founded in 1952 that is now the world's largest archive of gay, lesbian, bisexual, and transgen-der history; the primarily white, but now international, gay Metropolitan Community Church; the primarily black gay Unity Fellowship Church;

the gay Catholic group Dignity; and AIDS Project Los Angeles, one of the oldest, largest, and most effective AIDS prevention, advocacy, and service organizations in the world.

At the same time, arguably few cities in the world better symbolize sexual excess, narcissism, or a rejection of family values. And perhaps no population seems to threaten family values much more than the gay male denizens who crowd the bars, beats, and boutiques of West Hollywood. To many observers, and plenty of gay men among them, "Weho" culture signifies gay male decadence in situ. It epitomizes the sexual culture that both conservative gay intellectuals like Andrew Sullivan and anti-gay conservatives, like founder of the Family Research Council Paul Cameron, frequently denounce.[8] Cursory contact with gay culture in Los Angeles could readily reinforce stereotypes about gay men's narcissistic preoccupation with erotic allure. Advertisements for corporeal beautification and modification flood the pages, airwaves, and websites of the local gay male press: familiar and exotic cosmetic surgery and body sculpture procedures, including penile, buttock, and pec implants; liposuction; laser resurfacing; hair removal or extensions; cosmetic dentistry; personal trainers and gym-rat regimens; tattooing and tattoo removal; body piercing; hair coloring, growing, and styling; tinted contact lenses; manicures, pedicures and body waxing; as well as color, style, and fashion consultants and the commodified universe of couture, cosmetics, and personal grooming implements that they service.

Nonetheless, when I conducted local field research on gay men's intimate affiliations, I immediately encountered Tinkertoys as often as tinsel. Los Angeles might well be the cosmetic surgery capital of "planet out," but much less predictably, the celluloid metropolis was also at the vanguard of gay fatherhood. Organized groups of "Gay Fathers" and of "Gay Parents" formed in the city as early as the mid-1970s and contributed to the genesis of the Family Equality Council (formerly Family Pride, Inc.), which is among the leading national grassroots organizations of its kind anywhere.[9] Los Angeles also gave birth to Growing Generations, the world's first gay-owned assisted-reproduction agency, founded to serve an international gay clientele. Several of its first clients were among nine families who in 1998 organized the Pop Luck Club (PLC), a pioneering local support group for gay fathers and their children which rapidly became the largest organization of gay-father families in the world. Despite the city's historical significance and the fact that, as geographer Moira Kenney has observed, "Gay L.A. is more representative of the full spectrum of gay life than are San

Francisco and New York," it remains "the greatest hidden chapter in American gay and lesbian history."[10]

Between June 1999 and June 2003, I conducted field research on gay men's intimate relationships in the greater Los Angeles area. My research included lengthy, multi-session, family life history interviews with fifty self-identified gay men who were born between 1958 and 1973 and with members of their designated kin. I did field research also within their community groups, social and political events, religious institutions, and organizations, like the PLC. Most of the men I studied came of age and came out after the Stonewall era of gay liberation and after the AIDS crisis was widely recognized. Popular discourses about safe and safer sex, the gayby boom, gay marriage, domestic partnerships, and "families we choose" informed their sense of familial prospects. This was the first cohort of gay men in the world who were young enough to be able to imagine becoming parents outside of heterosexuality and mature enough to be in a position to choose or reject it. The men and their families came from varied racial, ethnic, geographic, religious, and social-class backgrounds. They also practiced many different relational and residential options. My research sample included sixteen gay men who were single at the time of my study; thirty-one who were coupled, some in open relationships, others monogamous, most of whom cohabited but several who did not; and a committed, sexually exclusive trio. It included men who lived or parented alone, with friends, lovers, former lovers, biological or legal and adopted kin, and children of every "conceivable" origin.

I attempted to contact the men and a few of their women kin again when I began to write these chapters in the fall of 2008. That was several months after the historic California Supreme Court decision in favor of same-sex marriage and in the midst of the pitched electoral-season battle over Proposition 8, which proposed to amend the state constitution to ban such marriages. I was able to locate and update the personal and family histories of twenty-nine of the fifty men from my study. Fearing that Proposition 8 would pass, seven of the eleven couples I located had hastened to marry during what did indeed prove to be a brief historic opportunity. I learned of only two couples who had broken up in the intervening years. I was unable to locate anyone from one complex household that I presume must have dissolved after the death of its central figure. Several of the men I contacted had new lovers, of course, and several men had become fathers or added more children to their families over the years.

The personal histories and lives of the men I studied challenge widely

gay
eri *henoy* *antogest*
advent *pitfalls*

Findings

held beliefs, including a few I once shared, about masculine eros and domesticity. They suggest that gay men enjoy some unexpected advantages
at the same time that they confront paradoxical pitfalls when they pursue
intimacy and kinship outside the heterosexual conventions of gender, sexuality, and family. The stories that follow offer models, as well as muddles,
from their efforts to redefine desire, domesticity, fidelity, and kinship.

Four Fellow Families

A Monogamous Gay Couple

Sharcerio
Trelear

Jace
Black Am

Shawn O'Conner and Jake Garner were an interracial, binational couple, both in their late thirties when I met them in 1999. They had been living together for five years in Silverlake, an ethnically and socially mixed
Los Angeles community popular with artists, students, activists, and gays.
Shawn, a creative landscape and garden designer, was a sexual immigrant
who, after a suicide attempt at the age of nineteen, had fled his homophobic, abusive, working-class family and life in Belfast, Northern Ireland, and
migrated first to London and then to San Francisco before he settled in
Los Angeles. Strongly attracted to black men, Shawn had joined the Los
Angeles chapter of Black and White Men Together, a gay multi-racial organization, where he met Jake at a picnic in 1993. The attraction, however,
was not immediately mutual. Jake is the son of an educated, happily married, middle-class African American couple who were civil rights activists.
Jake's parents had integrated the white suburban neighborhood where he
and his siblings grew up and where he developed enduring misgivings
about white guys who had a special taste for "hot coffee." Moreover, Jake
recalled, "I wasn't attracted to blond white men." However, Shawn's lively,
funny, smart, engaging, and persistent personality overcame Jake's reservations, and before long these "black and white men together" found themselves sharing a home and building a life.

It had taken Jake's generally progressive parents several years to come
to terms with his homosexuality, but after doing so they had welcomed
Shawn like a son-in-law into their strong, supportive family circle. Shawn,
on the other hand, was totally estranged from his Irish-Catholic family of
origin. Instead, he had self-consciously crafted an intentional family from
a multi-cultural and socially varied array of men and women, gay and
straight, in Los Angeles: "Being my mother doesn't automatically qualify

you as part of a circle of my friends and who I consider family. And there's a lot of, 'Your sisters above all,' and, like, 'No, they mean nothing to me.' They have to prove themselves that they are my friends. The mere fact that we have the same bloodline doesn't automatically, you know, get 'em into that circle." For his chosen family circle, Shawn had supplanted his "bloodline" mother with an adoptive maternal older sister—a sixty-something divorced, Jewish, heterosexual woman who served as his accountant, had invested in his business, and shared his love for frequent excursions to Tijuana. Among Shawn's chosen brothers was Agostín, a close friend and former lover. A highly educated Asian-Latino sexual immigrant from Mexico, Agostín lived alone nearby and taught Spanish, Portuguese, French, and Italian to international business personnel. Agostín and Shawn spoke almost daily and visited weekly, and Agostín often shared vacations and holidays with the couple and other friends.

Both Shawn and Jake depicted themselves as a monogamous couple who struggled with differences over love, sexuality, and commitment. They also had difficulties over finances. Jake, who was much more reserved than his flamboyant Irish mate and more ambivalent about his gay identity, held the upper hand and occupied conventionally masculine terrain in the couple's balance of emotional power. Although both men practiced monogamy, this mattered much more to Shawn than to Jake. Sexual exclusivity, in Shawn's more "feminine" view, is all about love and commitment: "Monogamy means you're saying to your lover, 'It is only you that I will allow myself to be shared with. I am choosing you to be that person.' Sex in itself isn't so important, and it alone doesn't make a relationship. It [a relationship] is so much more than that." Jake's commitment to monogamy, in contrast, was much less considered, emotional, or symbolic. His relationships, he reported, had been implicitly monogamous. "It's not that I'm ironclad opposed to non-monogamy," Jake explained, but "when I'm in a relationship, I just kind of assume" that it will be exclusive. Jake's greater, and more stereotypically masculine, capacity to separate sex from love and his interest in cyberporn often left Shawn feeling "shitty," as he put it.

What was even more upsetting to Shawn, though, was that Jake had resisted the public commitment ceremony that Shawn so dearly wanted: "A sore subject. I want one. Jake doesn't. A commitment ceremony is very important to me. I want the whole thing: the toaster, the rings, I want to register at the Pottery Barn—hell, I even want the ice sculpture for Chrissakes [laughs], the whole nine yards! . . . There's no real acknowledgment of our relationship, there's no recognition of gay relationships. I want the actual acknowledgment of family and friends that this is for real; this is not temporary. I want it to be for ever and ever." Jake, however, was less certain of his love for Shawn or of his commitment to their relationship. Shawn recognized that his emotional neediness and assertive style often overwhelmed Jake: "I'm needy, you know, I need affection, I need to be told I'm loved, and when I don't feel that, I become, you know, more like Velcro. And that's something that Jake has a hard time with." Jake, in turn, recognized that he resorted to the conventional "masculine" response of withdrawing emotionally when he felt overwhelmed by Shawn's demands, thereby allowing his anger to fester: "I need a lot more space than Shawn does. . . . My pattern is to withdraw and simmer. I build up resentment, and then there will be an explosion."

The couple's economic conflicts, however, ran counter to their emotional gender patterns and class origins. Despite the much higher social class in which Jake was raised and the college degree in computer engineering he earned at a research university, he had become uncomfortably financially dependent on and subordinate to Shawn. Jake had quit his last high-powered engineering job in 1999, because he found it too stressful. Instead of seeking a new top-level, well-paying position, he began managing Shawn's financially precarious landscape design and gardening business. Both agreed that working and living together 24/7 over the next three years had taken a heavy toll on their relationship. If Shawn displayed conventionally feminine emotional vulnerability to Jake's masculine withholding behavior in the sphere of love and intimacy, their career ambition ledger was quite another story. Shawn conceded that he is a stereotypical masculine, Type A, ambitious workaholic and a controlling, demanding boss: "It's important for me to be successful. I always need more." He felt determined to expand his landscaping business and to make more money. "I mean, money is important to me. Success is important to me." It troubled him that, in contrast, Jake, in his view, "has zero drive" and walked away from a high-powered job because he felt miserable doing it. Jake, in turn, resented Shawn's intrusive, controlling, micro-managing style: "I need a lot more space than Shawn does. We were always together, and he was my boss. I kinda like to do what I like to do, and he likes to tell people what to do. So it led to a lot of head butting."

Serving as Shawn's nonjudgmental sounding board and observer, Agostín gave the couple's prospects a pessimistic prognosis. In his view, Shawn was on the verge of losing hope. "Shawn calls a spade a spade," Agostín explained. "Even though he has been trying very hard to keep the relations going, if Jake is in his shell and doesn't come out of it, I don't feel there is a two-way communication there. I imagine that when they have their discussions, the only one who is talking is Shawn [*laughs*]. And I think he's going to give up."

A stroke of occupational fortune along with some couples therapy deferred Agostín's prophesy of impending doom. Just when Shawn's business had been teetering on the brink of bankruptcy, a local private college recruited him to take over landscape design and maintenance of its lavishly planted campus. Lured by a generous salary with benefits, Shawn promptly liquidated his business, thereby throwing Jake into the ranks of the unemployed. Jake floundered around for a while, coaching a few high school gymnasts here, doing a bit of freelance computer-tech support there, and surfing the Internet for hours on end, but Shawn was too preoccupied with his own new job to react with his customary impatience and disapproval. Eventually, a friend helped Jake secure a relatively undemanding administrative post at a local community college. Having access to separate and more stable employment and income removed one major source of the couple's chronic conflicts and curtailed some of their abundant opportunities to butt heads. They were about to celebrate their tenth anniversary the last time I visited them before I moved to New York in 2003, and all bets were off as to whether Shawn had an ice sculpture in his future.

I was by no means shocked in 2008, however, to learn that Agostín's prognosis had proven correct. Only two of the eleven couples from my original study whom I located again had not survived the intervening years. Jake and Shawn were one of these. Shawn wrote to say that they had broken up about a year earlier, after he had caught Jake "cheating":

> Infidelity is a hard thing to get over, and I never could regain the trust. In hindsight I think he did it to break up as he could not do it any other way. We remain very good friends and actually should teach people the right way to break up. We both kept our ego in check knowing we did not want to throw away 14 years of our lives, and while we both loved each other, we were no longer in love with each other. In honesty, Jake wanted to be in love with me but could never quite get there. I think the break up is good for us both, specially him. So to answer your question, we went from monogamous, to open, to break-up, and I am now in another monogamous relationship.

If the demise of Shawn's relationship with Jake was far from startling, the location of Shawn's new monogamous relationship and email address caught me up short. It turned out that, once again, his desires had inspired an international migration. While on a business trip to Mumbai in 2007, he had met and fallen in love with Akroor, a beautiful, much younger, closeted gay Indian man. Ever the passionate romantic, Shawn six months later had secured a work visa and moved with his landscape and floral design business to the teeming South Asian metropolis. I was fortunate enough to be able to make a site visit to the besotted, blissful couple when I made my own first visit to India in January 2009—in order to attend a wedding, of course!

A Sex Pig and His Celibate Mate

Matthew Laforte and Robert Cavendish, a white, affluent couple, both from upper-class Angeleno families, had successfully navigated their way through quite a different dyadic dilemma from that of Shawn and Jake. When I first met Matthew in 1999, he was a deeply intellectual forty-two-year-old philosophy doctoral candidate with avid interests in queer theory and practice. Robert, in contrast, twenty years his senior, had been a successful but completely closeted corporate financial manager who took early retirement at fifty-six before he dared to openly identify as gay. They had met at a suburban gay bar in 1988, gone home together the first night, and soon began to join their lives. Sharing a cultivated class background as well as a love of camping, opera, chess, cooking, and each other, they fell seamlessly into compatible, committed domesticity, embraced by each other's Republican but inclusive and socially tolerant families.

During the time of my study, the couple and their pampered schnauzer lived in a meticulously appointed, though unostentatious, traditional two-bedroom house that Robert owned in the sedate, affluent suburb of Los Angeles in which he had grown up. Matthew did the cooking, but in addition to providing most of the financial support, Robert did the dishes, the shopping, the laundry, the gardening, and most of the housework as well. Having already achieved a successful career, Robert believed it was Matthew's turn for worldly accomplishment. "I'm thrilled," he declared with pride, "to be the one to get the pompoms out to be a cheerleader for Matthew's career." In fact, Robert took early retirement in part to devote himself to supporting Matthew's budding academic career, which he accurately anticipated was likely to demand relocating within a few years. Soon after Vermont became the first state to offer civil unions to same-sex

couples in 2000, Robert and Matt made a beeline to the Green Mountains
to exchange rings and vows.

Although Matt described himself unapologetically as a "sex pig," his by
then fourteen-year-long loving, committed union with Robert was no longer sexual. Monogamy had been presumed but not stated at the passionate
outset of their romance, as is common in many gay as well as most straight
relationships. Four or five years later, however, Robert's interest in sex began to wane, and so conflicts between the couple waxed. As Matt became
increasingly frustrated, he resorted to furtive cruising excursions and began to explore interests in erotic fetishism. "I'm Mr. Sex," Matt exclaimed,
itemizing a broad range of fantasy and sexual interests. "It is a question
of, 'What role do I want to put on today?' Maybe it's a biorhythm thing
—every two weeks I want something new."

Matt acknowledged that after a while he "got kinda reckless" and gave
his address to a fetish group that sent him mail at home. Robert interro-
gated him about a letter that arrived, and this precipitated a painful but
frank and ultimately constructive discussion about their sexual differences.
They had directly confronted the fact of their increasingly incompatible
erotic desires, committed themselves to preserving their primary spousal
bond, and negotiated terms that allowed Matthew to satisfy his heartier,
more adventurous sexual appetites outside their relationship. Robert had
granted Matt permission to openly and honestly explore his fetish interests
and to engage in episodes of sexual cruising, so long as each instance was
an isolated encounter with a different sexual partner. Matt, in turn, released
Robert from the burden of declining his sexual overtures: "I'll assume you
don't want it," he had proposed, so that Robert could feel freer to "spoon in
bed together" and to touch him without having to worry that Matt might
misinterpret affection for sexual desire.

This arrangement had worked well for both of them for several years,
until, as mainstream personal-advice columnists like Ann Landers would
have predicted, Matt developed a potent, reciprocal, romantic crush on a
sexual partner. Believing dishonesty and denial would be greater threats to
his union with Robert than the obvious risk of openly pursuing the outside romance, Matt had broken the unwelcome news. Once again, the couple renegotiated the sexual terms of their relationship. Once again, Robert
generously granted his beloved the right to openly pursue his outside passions. Again Matt vowed to maintain his bond with Robert as primary. "I
couldn't live with myself if I left Robert, even if I was physically present but
left mentally," Matt volunteered. "Our household is my first concern. Our

gold standard is trust." Accordingly, he had promised to keep no secrets from Robert, to return home every night to sleep with him, and to take every measure possible to prevent his outside affair from destroying their relationship.

On the other hand, although Matt presumed that Robert occasionally indulged in sexual encounters of his own, he did not actually know or ask. "We have another rule," Matt explained. "I tell, but he doesn't. He doesn't like to talk about what he does. I've precipitated all of the sex arrangements and discussions. I play a much more dangerous game, so I want to be open about what I do."

Robert and Matt's game had survived two major moves to launch Matt's academic career, including transnational migration to western Australia, and they had passed the silver anniversary mark when I caught up with them again in 2008. Fortunately for them, Australia granted visas to same-sex partners, and they had registered as domestic partners in California as soon as it had been possible. Unlike most of the committed pairs in my study, however, Matt and Robert had never bothered to wed. In response to my question about it, Matt wrote,

> I was interested in getting married, when we were living in New Hamp-shire (heading over to MA), but he [Robert] did not want to. I am oddly hurt a little and oddly don't care that much at the same time. I guess it does not seem like a big deal. Weird. But maybe not so weird as we have negotiated and made our own agreements about how we are going to live. An actual marriage, to me at least, seems like it could not have the reality of the forged understandings we have come to.

Those forged understandings had survived the silver anniversary as well: "The terms remain the same, though given the size of the city in which we live discretion becomes something of an issue. My career, also, is demand-ing, and I am not on the prowl nearly as much. But that is ok—the cruel master eros seems less demanding these days. So I play a little, and it's to-tally cool."

Three Polyamorous Brothers-in-Law

Matt and Robert enjoyed close relationships with most of their siblings, nieces and nephews, and extended kin. Particularly titillating to Matt, Robert, and most of their relatives was the household in which Matt's gay brother-in-law Kevin Engelhard lived. In 1997 Matt's younger sister, Sophia, had married Kevin's older brother. When I interviewed Sophia in 2001, she reported that their three-year-old daughter was basking in the adoration of five gay uncles. Sophia chortled, "I get a giggle out of it." Evincing admiration and perhaps a bit of envy, Matt described a successful, if improbable, domestic-sexual trio that Kevin and his committed life companion, Tom Leske, had formed. The thirty-something couple had invited Scott Jones, a "gorgeous boy toy" twelve years younger than they, to join their bed, household, and marriage.

Kevin and Tom had exchanged rings, fused their finances, and lived together in wedded harmony for eight years before they added Scott to their family. Their sexual relationship, like Matt and Robert's, had evolved from early years of tacit monogamy into a negotiated form of open relationship. In this case, Kevin and Tom had agreed to permit each other "occasional serendipitous" recreational sexual encounters and also to occasionally go cruising jointly for a sexual threesome. They were not seeking a permanent threesome, however, the first night they invited Scott to share their bed with them, nor even when they offered him temporary lodging after Scott's landlord had suddenly sold the apartment building where he had been living. However, all three men soon fell in love with one another, and Scott never moved out of their bed or lives. Instead, one year later, Kevin and Tom placed a ring on Scott's finger as well.

Over the first five years of this three-way marriage, the men had negotiated a creative set of principles and practices to sustain what they described as a genuinely harmonious ménage à trois. Kevin and Tom jointly owned their small home in the city and a rustic mountain cabin retreat. On each anniversary of Scott's incorporation into their marriage, they transferred 5 percent ownership of their shared real estate to him, gradually vesting him as an equal partner. What's more, although Kevin and Tom had an open relationship when they met and jointly courted Scott, the trio decided to be sexually exclusive among themselves, "duogamous," one might say. Each claimed to feel secure in his love and place in the family, accepting the ebbs and flows of their affinities, libidos, and attractions. "We're all very versatile sexually," Scott explained, "and none of the three of us have any jealousy issues."

In fact, the trio had devised careful house rules to keep the green demon under control. No two were allowed to exclude the third from any activity, occasion, space, or interaction—sexual or otherwise. On the other hand, no one was obliged to join the other two in anything that did not appeal to him. This allowed everyone far greater flexibility than couples possess to enjoy as much time alone or together as he preferred. No one ever needed to be alone unless he wished, and yet togetherness was never imposed on anyone who was feeling an urge for separate time or space. The trio's sexual opportunities expanded as well. "If straight men knew how much more sex gay men have," Scott observed mischievously, "more of them would be gay." If two of the men engaged in sex before the third arrived home, their rules prevented them from refusing his sexual overtures "just because they got off without him." Nor could two who were sexually aroused eject the third from the bed, if he was already there but not in the mood.

Working all of this out required trust and "a lot of communication," they agreed, and so they scheduled periodic "family chats" to discuss issues and conflicts that emerged. "We say," Kevin summed up, "that being a trio is twice as much fun but twice as much work." Defying all odds, the happy trio still seemed to be having double the work and fun when I contacted them again in October 2008. They had moved to another state, where they were about to celebrate their tenth triadic anniversary.

Black, Gay, Proud, Single, and Seeking

Michael David, a single, African American, gay man who was thirty-two years old in 1999, had likely done more than twice as much work as any of the family fellows I have described so far, but he had not yet been rewarded with even half the fun—not that Michael, a social studies teacher in an inner-city high school who was renting a comfortable apartment in a stable working-class black neighborhood, sought or merited pity. On the contrary, he recounted with justifiable pride an inspirational Horatio Alger life history, narrating a heroic tale of a self-made man who triumphed over insuperable odds.

Michael had been born in Baltimore into a complex, unstable, blended family. Both of his working-class parents had struggled with drug and alcohol dependency. When Michael was six, his parents divorced, his father remarried and started his third family, and Michael's mother took him and his older brother first to Los Angeles and then to Dallas, trying to rebuild her life. Michael had been semi-orphaned during much of his adolescence, because his mother was imprisoned for cashing bad checks to support her drug habit. "I pretty much raised myself," he reported. Michael spent most of his teen years crashing in the homes of friends, punctuated with survivalist episodes of homelessness on the streets of Dallas.

Fortunately, Michael had always done well in school. School offered him a source of validation and refuge from the chaos and disarray of his family life. He had kept his mother's incarceration a secret from his father and his extended family back east because he feared they might make him return to Baltimore, where he would have to enroll in a school vastly inferior to the one he was attending in Dallas. Blessed with a sunny disposition and with an aptitude and appetite for learning and for friendship, Michael repeatedly attracted surrogates to provide parental support from among his teachers, his friends' parents, and local youth group leaders. When the mother of his brother's girlfriend met Michael, she perceived his academic potential and took him "under her wing." She helped him to apply for a full scholarship to a private university in Texas that proved his ladder to the middle class. After Michael graduated with a bachelor's degree in history in 1994, he moved back to Los Angeles, where he earned a master's degree and began his teaching career hoping to inspire other ghetto youth to emulate his trajectory.

In Los Angeles, Michael also had begun a gradual process of coming out as gay. Initially, he explored his long-suppressed homoerotic desires by hiring white male prostitutes, with whom he spent as much time discussing the meaning as engaging in the sexual behaviors of the gay identity he was struggling to accept. As Michael became more comfortable with his sexuality, however, he began to fear that as he "became" gay, he might "grow away from being black." He regarded conflicts between his black and gay identities as the greatest struggle he had faced since coming out. Michael found it harder to come out to black friends than to white ones, not because the former actually had been less supportive of him when he did but because he felt more vulnerable to the prospect that they might reject him. Accordingly, he had begun to take active measures to deepen his racial identity and strengthen his ties to black culture and community. During his closeted college years, most of Michael's friends had been white, but after he came out as gay, he consciously sought to develop a circle of black friends, gay and straight. "Although it hasn't been easy," he told me that he had gradually succeeded in integrating the two into "one big, happy family."

Although Michael first explored his gay sexuality with white sex workers, he later made a conscious decision to restrict his sexual/romantic partners to members of his own race. "I just love black people," he exclaimed, emphasizing the importance he attached to sharing racial consciousness with a black gay lover. In part because of his restrictive criteria, Michael had been less lucky in love than he had been in friendship, education, and work. Seeking a partner who was not only black and gay but also college educated severely limited his pool of possible mates. An

factors
making
it
difficult
to find
partners

even greater handicap, however, was Michael's discomfort with gay cruising culture. "I don't date guys I meet in bars," he explained. He had "this
fantasy of meeting a boyfriend in a non-bar environment," because the gay
bar pickup scene is "based on just sex, and that's not long-lasting," he said:
"at least not for me. . . . I found that sex without romance is lacking." In addition, Michael didn't fare well in gay cruising culture, because, despite his
charm and warmth, his large, unsculpted body did not meet the community's dominant aesthetic standards. And if all of these were not challenges
enough, Michael's feminist gender ideology may have been the coup de
grâce. He desired an egalitarian relationship that rejected heterosexual gender conventions, but he claimed that he had trouble finding a like-minded
boyfriend: "The main problem I've had with men is that a lot of men want
to have gender roles."

Throughout the four years of my fieldwork, Michael remained single
and was actively seeking a boyfriend with whom to create the family he
dearly hoped to build. Very much a "family fellow," Michael stayed emotionally attached to both of his parents, despite the serious limitations and
lapses in their parental histories, and despite his father's homophobic reac-
tion when he learned that his son was gay. Michael was deeply embedded
in his geographically dispersed extended family and maintained a devoted,
active presence in the lives of his then eight nephews and nieces, his numerous half- and step-siblings, and his cousins. Rare was the month when
Michael's couch was free of visiting kin, or the week when he was not send-
ing a birthday gift to a cherished young relative.

Michael claimed that he was determined to become a father himself
within the next few years, whether or not he realized his deep desire to find
that elusive educated, egalitarian, politically progressive, attractive, monogamous, gay, black "soul" mate, life partner, and co-parent of his dreams.
Indeed, Michael's desire for intimacy was so strong that he believed he was
even more certain to become a father if he remained single than if Cupid
were to answer his romantic prayers. As we will see in the next chapter,
Cupid would live up to his reputation for capriciousness.

Learning from the Families of Man

Judged by the prevailing community standards of social and sexual mores, many of the practices of intimacy and kinship that I have described
qualify as unconventional, if not exotic. The duogamous ménage à trois

who combined corporate vesting and "family chats" and evolving guidelines for sexuality and sociability are perhaps the most unusual, and the most difficult to emulate. Less unique, but still quite unlike most sexually frustrated, heterosexual married couples, Matthew and Robert honestly faced their incompatible sexual desires and openly negotiated the turn to an asexual but committed loving civil union that accommodates their unequal desires for sexual encounters outside of their relationship. Challenging heterosexual conventions and feminist prejudices alike, Robert also uncomplainingly served as both primary homemaker and breadwinner for his younger mate. Shawn and Jake blended biological and chosen kin, including former lovers, who traversed a striking range of demographic boundaries—race, nation, social class, education, age, gender, sexual identity, marital status, religion. Michael anticipated becoming an unwed adoptive black gay dad.

At the same time, I also have sketched a host of familial desires, behaviors, patterns, and conflicts that should seem painfully familiar to many heterosexual women, such as Shawn's ultimately unsuccessful struggle for commitment, affection, and greater economic responsibility from Jake, or Michael's challenging search for a man who cares more about personality, character, and convictions than about his biceps and body mass. Although these issues echo familiar pitfalls in heterosexual relationships, the gender difference (or similarity) of the usual suspects helps to illuminate, and sometimes to challenge, many otherwise clichéd conventions of gender and sexual practice.

Men Are Pigs

A decade ago, I created a file with the tongue-in-cheek, feminazi title, "Men Are Pigs," in which I recorded stereotypical, indeed hackneyed, complaints about lust, love, and loyalty that straight women routinely swap about the men in (and out of) our lives. The following selection of sentiments from that archive is as representative as it is familiar:

"It was a nice distraction from having just been dumped by my boyfriend. Men are pigs, even the nice ones!"

"Lance can't get turned on by someone he respects and loves; he can only have sex with someone he's not emotionally committed to, or if he's drunk. I couldn't tolerate it, so I had to move out."

"When I got home from work the other night, Jake had been surfing the net for so long that he was like totally in heat. And we had sex. We didn't make love; we fucked! And it's like I woke up the next morning, and it's like, 'I just feel so fuckin' shitty. Why did I do that?' I said, 'It was great, I got off, but I feel rotten.' I have felt rotten the last two days."

"I would date men, and it would start out wonderful, but it was all about sex. And to me that's something really sacred and really special. . . . If you didn't sleep with them by the third date, you never heard from them again. I just couldn't do that."

"Let's face it, when you reach a certain age, men are either already taken or they're looking for someone younger and more beautiful. We all know how men are — dogs. Absolute dogs."

The twist, as readers probably have guessed, is that women did not utter these complaints about men. Gay men did. The same is true of numerous flip-side romantic narratives I recorded, such as this one: "I went out to a street fair with my neighbor and met a man called Rob and just fell like I don't know that I've fallen before. He knocks my socks off and is damn near everything I want in a man; he's kind, loving, compassionate, gives of himself to others and his community, and treats me like the princess that we all know I am." Apart from the gender of the plaintiffs and the princess, little here would surprise most straight women. Nonetheless, the gender of the parties is no small or simple matter. In a gendered world, which is to say the world as we know it, gender can transmute apparently similar desires, utterances, and behaviors into strikingly different matters and meanings.

Perils and Pleasures of the Male Gaze

It is not merely a cultural stereotype, for example, to observe that many gay men tend to be even more preoccupied than most straight women with their bodies and with beauty, attire, adornment, and self-presentation. No doubt the Tinseltown culture of Los Angeles is unusually extreme in this regard, but I doubt that most of my research subjects or viewers of *Queer Eye for the Straight Guy*[11] would disagree with my observation. Arguably, gay men are even more harmed than heterosexual women by injurious effects of what feminists once termed "sexual objectification" and of the age bias that accompanies an emphasis on visual criteria for intimacy.

Why, a feminist might wonder, would men impose this merciless regime on other men? Why would men put up with it? And what does this imply about the power dynamics of gender and eros? As the caricatured complaints about male piggery suggest, because gay men operate in a male sexual economy that grants them greater license to pursue erotic passions, they subject one another to heightened levels of the tyranny (as well as the titillating and serendipitous pleasures) of the male gaze. In cruising culture

—the gay male sexual sport arena—it's all in the gaze. Erotic attraction and connection can occur (or fail) in the blink of an eye. Paradoxically, as a result, gay male access to the untrammeled field of masculine sexual pursuit that the late gay sociologist Martin Levine depicted as "hyper-masculinity" converts male sexual subjects into the feminine position of hyper-sexualized objects. Participants are predators and prey at once, and this dual status encourages gay men to internalize the harsh discriminatory judgments of the masculine gaze, with intensified effects. The exaggerated emphasis on appearance at the core of this dynamic imposes challenges for gay men who seek eros and intimacy but fall outside desirable standards of beauty and youth that are every bit as painful as those feminists describe for women. Michael David, as we saw, is not single by choice. To some extent a victim of the male gaze, Michael reported that women were much more likely to pursue him than men: "Women seem to see me as open, friendly, and sensitive. I don't do too well in the gay bar scene."

On the other hand, cruising culture also enables some creative, expansive approaches to intimacy that few women (or straight men) enjoy. Because many more men than women can separate physical sex from romantic and domestic commitments, gay men often find it easier to negotiate and renegotiate a variety of terms for meeting their changing sexual needs. Not only are gay men freer to practice polyamory, like the successful ménage á trois I described, but a significant number of committed gay couples allow themselves to indulge in extracurricular cruising or "fuck-buddy" liaisons, subject to a variety of rules.[12] Recall the generous, asymmetrical form of open relationship that Robert negotiated with his younger lifetime companion, Matthew, after his own sexual desires waned, as well as the joint cruising in which Kevin and Tom indulged before they jointly married Scott.

Likewise, gay male culture rightfully prides itself on greater comfort with fluid boundaries between lover and friend. Former lovers can become integrated into chosen kin ties more readily than among heterosexuals, as happened with Shawn's Latino-Asian ex-lover, Agostín, and ultimately with Shawn and Jake themselves. Other times, friends become lovers or sexual playmates for a while. If the greater license that many gay men enjoy to separate physical from emotional forms of intimacy has obvious risks, it also allows successful departures from prescriptive conjugal monogamy.[13] Some of these innovations mitigate the stereotypical snares of loneliness, sexual frustration, or incompatibility that many heterosexual singles and couples suffer.

Cruising to Familyland

So, many men and women, whether straight or gay, agree that men are pigs. A popular belief is that without the sobering influence of women, masculine sexuality threatens family and social bonds. Religious and social conservatives typically portray gay male sexual culture as masculine libido incarnate, the dangerous antithesis of family and community. "Untrammeled homosexuality can take over and destroy a social system," warns anti-gay psychologist Paul Cameron, sounding rather envious: "Marital sex tends toward the boring end. Generally, it doesn't deliver the kind of sheer sexual pleasure that homosexual sex does. The evidence is that men do a better job on men, and women on women, if all you are looking for is orgasm."[14] Quite a few mainstream gay male authors agree that gay recreational sex with an unlimited number of partners represents the dangerous excesses of *masculine* sexuality. The late gay journalist and AIDS victim Randy Shilts charged unfettered masculine sexuality with escalating the epidemic spread of AIDS. In his view, gay baths, bars, and cruising sites served masculine, rather than specifically homoerotic, male desires: "Some heterosexual males confided that they were enthralled with the idea of the immediate, available, even anonymous sex a bathhouse offered, if they could only find women who would agree. Gay men, of course, agreed quite frequently."[15] Likewise, Levine interpreted gay male cruising culture as an arena of hyper-masculinity, where, without the "constraining effects of feminine erotic standards, gay men were able to focus more overtly and obviously on the sexual activities in finding sexual partners. . . . Cruising, in this sense, is a most masculine of pastimes. Gay men were simply more honest—and certainly more obvious—about it."[16]

Conservative arguments for gay marriage often rest on a similar view of male sexuality. Andrew Sullivan, for example, pleaded "The Conservative Case for Gay Marriage" on the grounds that "the discipline of domesticity, of shared duties and lives, of the inevitable give-and-take of cohabitation and love with anyone, even of the same sex, tends to benefit men more than the option of constant, free-wheeling, etiolating bachelorhood." *New York Times* columnist David Brooks was more vehement about why conservatives should support gay access to "The Power of Marriage": "The conservative course is not to banish gay people from making such commitments. It is to expect that they make such commitments. We shouldn't just allow gay marriage. We should insist on gay marriage. We should regard it as scandalous that two people could claim to love each other and not want to sanctify their love with marriage and fidelity."

On the opposite ideological bank, queer theorists, such as Michael Warner, share Sullivan's view (or, in Warner's case, a fear) that the contemporary gay race to the chapel and the tot lot will erode the utopian, transgressive character of queer sexual culture. Gays who have succumbed to what lesbian comedian Kate Clinton termed "mad vow disease," Warner charges, fail to recognize that "marriage has become the central legitimating institution by which the state penetrates the sexuality of its subjects; it is the 'zone of privacy' outside which sex is unprotected."[17]

Most straight conservatives, however, oppose same-sex marriage. Although they endorse the diagnosis that masculine eros is anti-social, they consider the remedy that commentators like Sullivan and Brooks propose to be insufficient and naive. Conservative British *Daily Mail* columnist Melanie Phillips insists that, "because men are naturally promiscuous, two men will stick together as naturally as the two north poles of a magnet. It is not marriage which domesticates men—it is women."[18] In short, sexual radicals and conservatives converge in viewing gay male sexuality as a realm of masculine desire that subverts domesticity and committed family ties. "If you isolate sexuality as something solely for one's own personal amusement," Paul Cameron warns, once again betraying a curious aura of envy, "and all you want is the most satisfying orgasm you can get—and that is what homosexuality seems to be—then homosexuality seems too powerful to resist."[19]

Yet, *is* orgasm, or even carnal pleasure, all that gay men are looking for when they cruise? And, more to the point, is that all they find? My research indicates that cruising yields more complex and contradictory family consequences than most people imagine. Unencumbered, recreational sex certainly does violate conventional family values and carries a range of risks. Counter-intuitively, however, it can also generate impressive bonds of kinship and domesticity, as two more stories from my research in gay L.A. illustrate.

Ossie and Harry—A Gay Pygmalion Fable

Ossie, Harry, and their two young children, a picture-perfect, affluent, adoring nuclear family in an elegant, spacious Spanish home, represent an utterly improbable, gay fairy-tale romance of love, marriage, and the baby carriage. A transracial, transnational, cross-class, interfaith couple who had been together eight years when I first interviewed them in 1999, Ossie and Harry claimed to have fallen in love at first sight on a "Roman Holiday" in 1995. Harry, a prosperous, white, Jewish, Ivy League–educated, successful literary agent, was thirty-one years old and vacationing in Italy when he spotted twenty-four-year-old Ossie on a crowded street. Talented but undereducated, a Catholic Afro-Brazilian raised in an impoverished single-mother family, Ossie had migrated to Italy several years earlier as a guest worker. Keeping a discreet distance, on that fateful day in 1995, Harry followed the strikingly attractive object of his gaze until, as felicitous fate would have it, Ossie entered a gay bar. The rest is a Hollywood history.

Although the lovers met by cruising, they both claimed to have fallen in love instantly. Ossie said he told Harry that he loved him that very first night: "I just knew. I just told him what I felt." They reported sharing all of their "hopes and dreams" from the moment they met, and preeminent among these was the desire to have children: "When we first met we talked about everything," Harry recalled: "and all of our dreams, and one of them was to have a family and what it meant to be gay, you know, if we were together, and what we would be giving up potentially, what the sacrifices might be; and so that was one of the things that was going to be a potential sacrifice was not being able to have children." "Me too," Ossie interjected. "I always knew I wanted to have children." "But we talked about how we didn't think it was possible to have them together," Harry continued. "We both talked about how it was a dream that we both had and that it was kind of something that we thought we might have to forsake together."

The new lovers plunged headlong into a deeply romantic, intense, committed, monogamous love affair that seemed only to have deepened after nearly a decade of bourgeois domesticity. After a year of transatlantic, bilingual courtship, Harry sponsored his beloved's immigration to the United States, financed Ossie's education in occupational therapy and vocal music, and assisted his rapid acquisition of fluency in English and of bourgeois cultural habits, all domains in which Ossie proved to be gifted. After the couple had celebrated their union with an interfaith commitment ceremony in 1998, they had dinner with a gay couple who had recently become fathers through surrogacy. "It was all kind of Kismet," Harry recalled. "They told us about their two sons, and we kind of admitted that it was something we fantasized about." Inspired by this example, Ossie and Harry contacted Growing Generations and decided immediately to engage a "traditional" surrogate in order to realize the dream of fatherhood that they had feared they would have to sacrifice on the altar of gay love. The agency successfully matched them with a white woman who has since borne them two babies—first a white daughter conceived with Harry's sperm, and three years later, a biracial genetic half-sister, conceived with Ossie's.

No gay union in my study encapsulates a more dramatic example of successful romance across a wider array of social inequalities and cultural differences than the bond between Ossie and Harry. Formally, Harry enjoyed a staggering number of social and cultural advantages over the younger, buff and beautiful Ossie—including those involving income, wealth, education, occupation, race, nation, language, and citizenship, not to mention access to the ongoing support of his native world of supportive kin, long-term friendship, community, and culture. Moreover, because the co-parents shared a strong prejudice against hiring child care, Ossie had become a full-time, at-home parent and was economically dependent on Harry, to boot. "We don't use babysitters at all," Harry boasted, as he burped their first infant daughter during my initial visit. "We don't want any nannies, babysitters, nothing," he emphasized, espousing a childrearing credo that few contemporary mothers in the West could contemplate affording, even were they to desire it. Initially, Harry had stayed home for several months blissfully caring for their first newborn while Ossie was employed. However, because Harry commanded far greater earning power, he decided that it was in his family's interest that he resume the breadwinner role. He had been supporting Ossie as full-time, at-home parent since then.

Nonetheless, despite forms of structural inequity glaring enough to make Betty Friedan's historic critique of the feminine mystique seem tepid, this was no transvestite version of the male-dominant, female-dependent, breadwinner-homemaker patriarchal bargain of the 1950s modern family. Defying all sociological odds, Ossie seemed to enjoy full emotional and decision-making parity with Harry both as partner and parent. In deference to Ossie's jealous, possessive wishes, Harry had let go of friendships with his former lovers. Harry regarded his breadwinner role to be a sacrificial burden rather than a creative outlet or a source of status and power: "I hate work," Harry maintained. "It's a necessary evil." He had begun conducting as much of his professional work from home as possible so that he could participate fully in the hands-on burdens and blessings of early parenting—diapering, feeding, dressing, toilet training, and bathing, along with playing, reading, cuddling, educating, cajoling, consoling, disciplining, and chauffeuring. Indeed, not only did Harry dread the unavoidable business trips that periodically separated him from his children and spouse, but he seemed genuinely to envy Ossie's uninterrupted quotidian contact with the children. "I don't need to make my mark," Harry claimed. "There's nothing else I need to accomplish. So that's the most important job I have [being a parent and mate], which is why it's a real conflict." What's more, Harry voluntarily had relinquished the weighty patriarchal power of the purse by taking legal measures to fully share all property with Ossie, as well as child custody of both daughters. Few heterosexual marriages share resources, responsibilities, or romance so fully or harmoniously as these two seemed to do.

No evil demon had disrupted the romantic fairy tale when I contacted Harry again in October 2008. "We're doing great," he wrote. "The kids are now 8 and 6, and Ossie and I are still very much in love—coming up on 17 years! . . . We are still monogamous and will, I imagine, always remain as such. We are very fortunate to have found each other and to be so aligned in many ways—including our monogamy." Of course, a good fairy tale requires obstacles to surmount. In this case, one of the children had been "diagnosed with some pretty significant developmental delays," and so Harry had reduced his work and devoted himself to her special needs. Now, she had almost caught up to her peers, which Harry viewed as "truly miraculous." What's more, the year before, the couple had reversed breadwinner-homemaker roles, and Harry assumed the full-time mate and parent job that he valued most. "Ossie's working full-time now and really enjoying that," Harry reported. "But he's doing that for self-fulfillment more than anything. It's not about covering the bills. . . . I have become the full-time dad and I'm really enjoying that role although it's a lot of driving!"

Mother Randolph and His Foundling Boys

Dino, an eighteen-year-old, fresh "wetback," Salvadoran immigrant, described how he had been waiting at a bus stop in 1984 when a forty-five-year-old Anglo entertainment lawyer with a taste for young Latino men cruised by and picked him up. When the lawyer discovered that his gregarious, sexy, young trick was homeless and unemployed, he brought Dino home to live and keep house for him for several weeks. There the eager youth began to acquire the mores and mentors, along with the mistakes, from which he had since built his life as an undocumented immigrant among chosen kin in gay L.A.

Randolph proved to be the most significant of these mentors. When I first met Randolph, he was in his mid-sixties and had recently become disabled with severe Parkinson's disease. A cultivated, but bawdy, financially secure and generous former interior designer, Randolph told me the story of how he had met Dino and had come to live with his "Foundling Boys" and about a circuitous journey with his deceased life partner of seventeen years who he had met while cruising in a "stand-up sex club." Ten years into what had become a committed, but sexually open, relationship between the couple, Randolph's lover had shocked him by deciding to undergo male-to-female sex-reassignment surgery. Randolph reported feeling traumatized by this turn of events and that the couple's relationship had foundered. They separated for more than a year while his lover was transitioning from male to female. After the transition, however, Randolph had recognized that his love for the person transcended the discomfort he felt over the gender switch and the impact it had on his own strong homoerotic sexual preference. And so the couple had reunited.

Paradoxically, this gender upheaval had propelled Randolph back into a facsimile of living as a heterosexual man, even though he had renounced this identity as inauthentic, at considerable risk, a full decade before the 1969 Stonewall rebellion. Sadly, several years after her surgical transformation, Randolph's lover was diagnosed with AIDS, a cruel legacy of her prior life as a sexually active gay man in the pre-AIDS era. By then too, Randolph's Parkinson's symptoms had begun to emerge and made it impossible for him to take care of his lover, or of himself. Blessed with ample financial, social, and spiritual resources, Randolph had gradually assembled a rainbow household staff of five gay men to care for him and his lover, and they had gradually developed into a kind of a family.

Chance encounters through sexual cruising were responsible for most of the relationships in this rainbow household family, as had been the case for the lasting union between Randolph and his lover. A former employee of Randolph's had met Dino at a gay bar in 1993 and introduced him to his benefactor. By then Dino had been diagnosed as HIV-positive, and he was drinking heavily. Randolph had a long history and penchant for rescuing gay "lost boys," and he had hired Dino to serve as his primary live-in cook and household manager. By the time I met Dino, he had become asymptomatic thanks to the health care that Randolph purchased for him, and he was sober, grateful, and devoted to Randolph. Dino resided at Randolph's Mondays through Fridays and spent his weekends with his lover of five years, a fifty-something, Anglo dental hygienist who had cruised him at a Gay Pride parade. Each Wednesday night, Dino's lover made an overnight conjugal visit to Randolph's household, and he also participated in the holiday feasts that Dino would prepare for Randolph's expansive, extended, hired and chosen family.

Randolph employed three additional men who worked staggered shifts as his physical attendant, practical nurse, and chauffeur, as well as a fourth who worked as part-time gardener and general handyman. The day nurses were Mikey, a twenty-three-year-old, white former street hustler and drug abuser, and Ricardo, the newest of Mikey's three roommates in another multi-cultural, intergenerational, gay male household. The devoutly Catholic Ricardo, who was also twenty-something, was a recent illegal Mexican immigrant who still was struggling with religious guilt over his homosexual desires. Randolph's night nurse, Bernard, was a married, bisexual African American man in his fifties who used to enjoy casual sex with Randolph on the down-low. Finally, Randolph employed his dear friend Lawrence as his gardener, a white gay man in his late forties, also HIV-positive, with whom Randolph had been close ever since they had hooked up in a San Diego tea room more than three decades earlier.

Randolph referred to Dino and his day nurses parentally as his "boys." "Well, I'm their father and their mother," he explained. Randolph's lover had died in 1999, and so, he said, "these boys are certainly the most important family that I have these days. They mean more to me, and *for* me, than anyone else." From his wheelchair-throne, "Mother Randolph," as he enjoyed calling himself, presided with love, wit, wisdom, and, it must be acknowledged, financial power, as well as responsibility, over a multi-cultural, mutually dependent, elastically extended, chosen family that reminded me a bit of the black drag houses immortalized in the documentary *Paris Is Burning*.[20] Few of these intimate attachments had remained erotic. However, a serendipitous series of sexual encounters had initiated most of the creative kin ties in this expansive rainbow "family of man."

I was deeply disappointed that my concerted efforts to locate anyone from this family again in 2008 proved fruitless. The former telephone numbers I had for Randolph, Dino, and Mikey were no longer in service, and my dogged Internet search hit a cold trail. I sadly presume that Randolph had died in the intervening years, and with him his rainbow household. Whether or not he had bequeathed any of his estate to Dino, Mikey, and his other boys, or how they have fared without him, I was unable to learn.

The Gay Family Cruise

Gay male sexual cruising directly violates mainstream norms of monogamy and marriage. A sizable constituency of gay men finds the culture of sexual adventuring to be as disturbing and threatening as mainstream heterosexual society does. Although Ossie and Harry met by cruising, they, along with many other gay men, practice sexual exclusivity and strongly disapprove of polyamory and casual sex. These more sexually conservative family values appear to be particularly prevalent among gay men who are fathers, among the religiously observant, and among the generation of gay men who came of age in the period immediately following discovery of the AIDS virus.

However, as many of the stories in this chapter illustrate, the gay male arena of sexual sport also spawns less obvious, more creative and capacious effects on intimacy. Sexual cruising, as we have seen, can initiate lasting familial ties more often than is commonly recognized. Anonymous erotic encounters sometimes yield fairly conventional forms of love and "marriage." "Sexual encounters are often pursued as a route to more long-term, committed, emotional relationships," as the co-authors of a British study of same-sex intimacies observe. "Particularly for some men who are not in a couple relationship, casual sexual relationships can offer the potential for meeting the 'right' person."[21] Or, as a gay friend of mine puts it more humorously, "Sex can be a great icebreaker."

Randolph, as we have seen, cruised his deceased mate, Dino met his lover, and even the implausibly idyllic, romantic, monogamous union and nuclear family formed by Harry and Ossie commenced on a sexual cruise. Many other interviewees, including several whose stories appear in the next chapter, also reported histories of long-term relationships that began with anonymous sexual encounters. Syndicated gay sex-advice columnist-provocateur Dan Savage endorses this comparatively mainstream family cruise route with uncharacteristic sentimentality: "Desire brought my boyfriend and me together. And it's simple desire that brings most couples, gay or straight, together. Responsibly acted on, this desire is a good thing in and of itself, and it can often lead to other good things. Like strong, healthy families."[22]

Although anonymous gay sexual encounters do not ordinarily lead to conjugal coupling, they sometimes spark "strong healthy" friendships that evolve into kin-like ties. Through such side effects of casual sex, Randolph had met his close friend and gardener, "Mr. Baldwin"; Dino had acquired, at first temporary and later his long-term lodging, employment, and familial support; and Mikey had repeatedly found refuge from Hollywood's mean streets. Thus, even when a gay man ostensibly is "only looking for the most satisfying orgasm" he can get, sexual cruising allows him to find a whole lot more. "Some people like the sport of chasing somebody and seeing if they can get them," Mother Randolph observed. "For some people the game is worth more than the candle. My interest is specifically in the candle." When I asked Randolph, however, whether an orgasm constituted the candle, he quickly identified more enduring embers: "Yes, and also the love-making, if it was that sort of situation. If I had a guy home in bed, I was big on foreplay and all of that. In fact, often I didn't want my partner to go home after fucking. I often liked them to stay over. And a lot of my sexual partners became eventual friends—Mr. Baldwin [the gardener] over there at the sink being one of them."

A venerable gay history of cruising to kinship and community predates the contemporary popularity of gay family discourse. Even in the first two decades of the twentieth century, as George Chauncey's prize-winning historical study, *Gay New York,* copiously documents, gay men frequented bars and bathhouses not only to seek quick sexual encounters but also because they "formed more elaborate social relationships with the men they met there, and came to depend on them in a variety of ways." Chauncey draws on the extensive diaries of Charles Tomlinson Griffes, a successful early-twentieth-century composer who "was drawn into the gay world by the baths not just because he had sex there, but because he met men there who helped him find apartments and otherwise make his way through the city, who appreciated his music, who gave him new insights into his character, and who became his good friends."[23]

Socially transgressive, intimate bonds (whether long-term or more ephemeral) are one of the underappreciated by-products of gay cruising. Thanks in part to this arena of sexual sport, interracial intimacy occurs far more frequently in the gay world, and particularly among gay men, than in heterosexual society. Partly because I intentionally recruited participants across racial and class borders, of thirty-one men in my study who identified themselves as coupled at the time I interviewed them, fourteen were paired with someone of a different race. This was substantially higher than the 15.3 percent of gay interracial couples in the 2000 U.S. Census data.[24] However the 2000 Census vastly understated the degree of both gay and interracial intimacy, because it only counted co-residential couples who elected to identify themselves as same-sex partners.

One provocative by-product of sexual cruising culture is that it offers gay boys from subordinate social classes, races, and cultural milieus a better shot at climbing up the social ladder than their straight siblings and peers enjoy. In the unvarnished prose of gay author William J. Mann, "the dick dock in Provincetown is a great equalizer. I've watched my share of condo owners suck off their share of houseboys."[25] Although only a small percentage of those "houseboys" garner more than a quickly lit "candle" from these furtive encounters, these nonetheless provide opportunities for social mobility that their non-gay peers rarely encounter. Mann, marveling over his personal meteoric rise from working-class origins in a small factory town, reflects, "'How the hell did you ever wind up here, kid?' I've asked myself time and again. . . . How did I end up sharing a house in the tony west end of Provincetown every summer for the entire summer, year after year? It's simple: I'm gay. Had I not been gay—had I been my brother, for example—I would never have discovered the access that led me to a different place."[26] Both Mann and his brother had attended the same state university near their hometown. "But only I ventured into a world my parents had never known. Had I not been a gay kid," Mann recognizes, "I would never have been invited into that world." A visiting gay lecturer, for example, took the youthful Mann to dinner and later introduced him to prominent writers, and to a gay world: "I met people, I read books, I listened to speeches."[27]

Gay males also derive some benefits from male privilege if they wish to cruise their way to greater cultural capital. They avoid many of the social constraints and risks that confront their sisters, whether straight, lesbian, or in-between. Sons typically shoulder fewer domestic responsibilities than daughters and enjoy more personal autonomy, physical mobility, and sexual freedom (not to mention without the risk of pregnancy). In addition, males who escape the snares of underclass masculinity enjoy greater career and earnings opportunities than comparable females.[28] In short, in this situation, mixing a subordinate sexual identity with gender privilege can lead gay boys to move both out and up—away from their families and communities and up the social ladder.

Gay Hypergamy and Rainbow Kinship

In fact, some gay men benefit from variations on a rather old-fashioned feminine strategy for upward mobility. Ossie, Shawn, Dino, Mikey, and Ricardo were among ten of the fifty gay men in my study who traversed even greater social, geographic, economic, and cultural distances than William Mann described. All were beneficiaries of what I like to call gay hypergamy. In anthropological vocabulary, hypergamy designates marriages in which women "marry up" the social-status ladder. In the classic situation, lower-ranking kin groups trade on their daughters' youth, beauty, and fertility to marry them (and thereby the fortunes of their natal families) to older, wealthier, often less attractive men from higher-ranking families. Modern traces of this pre-industrial, patriarchal pattern persist today, of course. The fact that there is a dictionary entry for *trophy wife*—"an attractive, young wife married to a usually older, affluent man"[29]—but none for *trophy husband,* underscores this asymmetry. As an extreme example, sex symbol and celebrity Anna Nicole Smith married the late billionaire octogenarian J. Howard Smith, sixty-three years older than she. The more pejorative and rather sexist dictionary definition for *gold-digger*—"a woman who seeks money and expensive gifts from men"[30]—reveals the cultural assumption that heterosexual women still can barter youth, beauty, and erotic appeal (and sometimes even fertility) for lavish material rewards from older, unattractive, wealthier, more powerful men.

And so can some gay men. Cruising culture, combined with more flexible mating norms, allows gay men to cross conventional social borders in their intimate encounters more frequently than straight men do. While the majority of these may be fleeting and anonymous episodes, the sheer volume of gay erotic exchanges outside the customary bounds of public scrutiny and social segregation multiplies chances to form more enduring attachments across social divides. But for its gender composition, the Cinderella-fairy-tale character of Ossie's marriage to Harry represents hypergamy in nearly the classic anthropological sense of marrying up by exchanging beauty, youth, and charisma for higher cultural status and material resources. In fact, this is a familiar enough gay scenario that a gay friend of mine labels it "Cinderfella." In saying this, I do not mean to insinuate that Ossie or Harry intentionally used strategic or manipulative bartering tactics in their courtship transactions. For that matter, I do not believe that most heterosexual marriages between wealthy, powerful older men and younger, beautiful women spring mainly from the cynical motives that terms like *gold-digger* or *trophy wife* connote. Rather, contemporary exchanges of sex appeal for wealth and status represent psychic and cultural residues of an earlier era of patriarchal hypergamy that still resonate in the dating and mating marketplace today. Interestingly, gay men seem able to hitch up in this way, even more often than straight couples do.

Learning Not to Labor

Gay men, in fact, are more likely than heterosexual women to benefit from hypergamy today, precisely because gay male intimacy more often crosses race, sex, and age differences. Gay sexual culture offers surprising social-mobility opportunities to some underprivileged youth. Understandably, research and writing about gay youth concentrates primarily on the heightened social hazards they confront—hazing, bashing, isolation, substance abuse, sexual exploitation, HIV/AIDS and less lethal sexually transmitted diseases, depression, rejection by family and community, as well as suicide and homicide.[31] Also understandably, the predominant view portrays these risks as particularly high for youth who must contend with the hypermasculine cultures that dominate most subordinate racial-ethnic, underclass, working-class, and rural communities.[32] Undoubtedly, gay ghetto youth confront a form of what feminists of color have labeled the "triple jeopardy" of race, class, and gender subordination.[33] Without minimizing these hazards and burdens, however, my field research reveals that male youth from these environments who experience homoerotic desires also can gain indirect social advantages from their sexual marginality.

I first arrived at this notion while viewing *Nuyorican Dream* with one of my research subjects at the 2001 annual gay Outfest film festival in Los Angeles.[34] This superb documentary portrays the familial bonds and troubled lives of three generations of an underclass Puerto Rican family in Brooklyn, New York. Robert Torres, a thirty-year-old gay high school teacher, is the film's protagonist and narrator. He is the only one of five siblings who escapes their family's impoverished, dangerous ghetto environment and achieves educational and social success. Devoted to his single mother and family, Robert struggles, with scant progress, to rescue his siblings from the ubiquitous pitfalls of poverty and racism that engulf them—the lure of drugs, crime, violence, truancy, and teen pregnancy. His strong familial commitment and unlikely social mobility reminded me instantly of Michael David, the black "Horatio Alger" I described earlier.

Ruminating later, I realized that variations on this theme applied to the family histories of a striking number of my gay interviewees, including Ossie, Northern Irish immigrant Shawn, illegal immigrants Dino and Ricardo, as well as my movie-viewing companion at the time, a thirty-year-old white doctoral student and AIDS-prevention worker from a midwestern, working-class family whose older brother had served time in prison. Each had achieved social mobility against the odds and in contrast to the troubled trails that most of their heterosexual siblings trekked.

Homoerotic desire and male gender interact with paradoxical effects on social prospects. Youthful awareness of homoerotic desire unleashes push and pull factors that can draw adolescent boys out of dangerous, lowerclass environments. This contrasts directly with the fate of the working-class British "lads" in a classic study by Paul Willis who were unwittingly "learning to labor" in subordinated, dead-end, working-class jobs by living up to rebellious, adolescent heterosexual, working-class norms of masculinity.[35] Boys growing up in the same sort of milieu who experience homoerotic desires are apt to fail at the harsh macho gender curriculum. Those who survive the potentially lethal dangers of this failure less frequently "learn to labor."

Gay-oriented youth have good cause to seek alternative routes to self-esteem and to try to escape from the self-destructive, dangerous, "live fast and die young" culture of what Australian sociologist R. W. Connell has called "protest masculinity, . . . a marginalized masculinity which picks up themes of hegemonic masculinity in the society at large but reworks them in a context of poverty."[36] Rather than learn to labor, gay youth are apt to feel more compelled than their brothers to pursue "feminine" strategies for winning cultural approval and social success. As feminist scholars have argued, working-class and middle-class identities are strongly gender coded. Images of blue-collar workers are decidedly masculine, but femininity signals middle-class conformity and propriety.[37] Like Robert Torres, Michael David, Shawn O'Conner, Dino, Derek, Ossie, and Randolph, gay-inclined male youth are more likely than their more conventionally masculine brothers to pursue educational, creative, or aesthetic sources of gratification. They also are more likely to flee their homophobic natal communities and countries and to migrate in search of more gay-tolerant metropolitan or other progressive milieus.[38] Ossie represents the most extreme example of a Pygmalion, but a myriad of gay Horatio Alger tales peppered my research. Shawn, as we saw, became a landscape and floral designer and fled his repressive, hostile, working-class Belfast origins. Michael pursued academic success, won a college scholarship, escaped semi-homelessness, and traded Texas for California. Dino, an undocumented immigrant who learned to cook gourmet meals and to run Mother Randolph's gracious Hollywood Hills household, was one of eight children born in a Catholic peasant family who lived and worked on a coffee finca in war-torn El Salvador.

Elements of hypergamy were common among even relatively privileged gay matings, such as in upper-class Matthew's union with even wealthier, older Robert, as well as within Tom and Kevin's joint marriage to their more youthful, less affluent, newer mate. Gay fiction, memoirs, and histories also demonstrate that this is a familiar feature of gay life that helps to account for why gay identity appears to be normatively middle class. By

expanding the concept of gay hypergamy somewhat, we can use it to designate even relatively brief and informal intimate liaisons between exotic,
erotic youth and older, more affluent and sophisticated men. Cruising on
the "dick dock" in Provincetown, in the baths of old New York, at a bus
stop in Los Angeles, and at beats, cottages, tea rooms, and ports of call
around the world allows for more democratic social mixing and matching
and greater opportunities for upward mobility than heterosexual society
generally offers.[39] Whether or not these "candles" ignite a satisfying orgasm, they can melt social barriers—as icebreakers are meant to do—and
thereby expand the bonds of kinship, as in the rainbow family ties between
Mother Randolph and his adopted, and hired, "foundling boys."

It turns out that gay male "promiscuity" is not as antithetical to supportive and committed, or even to comparatively conventional, family
values as its critics and some of its champions imagine. As we have seen,
some gay men cruise their way to intimate attachments and a social rainbow of kinship bonds. The culture of unbridled masculine sexuality is no
idyllic arena of egalitarian, liberated intimacy. Erotic exchanges among gay
men that cross racial, generational, and social-class boundaries can visit
the same sort of exploitative, abusive, humiliating, and destructive effects
on the more vulnerable parties that women too often suffer in asymmetrical heterosexual relations. Gender does introduce a crucial difference,
however, in the social geometry of heterosexual and gay hypergamy. The
exclusively masculine arena of gay hypergamy opens up a possibility for
greater reciprocity over the life cycle than women can typically attain. The
extreme double standard of heterosexual beauty and aging inflicts severe
erotic and romantic constraints on even very prosperous and high-status,
aging former "gold-diggers" or "trophy" widows.

Aging gay men also suffer notable declines in their erotic appeal compared with when they were in their physical prime, but they operate on a
wider playing field than most aging straight women. Gay men who cruise
to higher status, like Ossie and Dino, can more plausibly anticipate the
prospect of switching places in hypergamy someday. In the likely event that
they survive their older mates, they enjoy greater odds than aging former
trophy wives of exchanging their acquired cultural and material capital for
romance with less socially privileged, younger, attractive men. Of course,
in order to secure a financial inheritance, they would have had to have negotiated a legal agreement or lived in one of the few states or nations that
allow same-sex marriage or civil unions.

Gay men aboard the family cruise ship have been reconfiguring eros, domesticity, and kinship in ways that both reinforce and challenge conventional gender and family practices and values. By no means is gay cruising a utopian arena of race and class harmony, but it does facilitate more democratic forms of intimate social (as well as sexual) intercourse across more boundaries (including race, age, class, religion, nation, education, ideology, and even sexual orientation) than occur almost anywhere else.[40] Enduring bonds of chosen family and kinship sometimes sprout from these transgressive trysts. Whether or not conservative British columnist Melanie Phillips is correct in her view that men are "naturally promiscuous," she is plain wrong that masculine erotic impulses preclude two men from forming lasting love. For monogamous gay couples like Ossie and Harry and for unapologetic sex pigs like Matthew, Mother Randolph, and some of his foundlings, it turns out that sexual cruising can be a creative mode of family travel.

Redefining Family and Fidelity

I don't expect that these stories will inspire many readers to try to emulate the gay male model of a family cruise or hypergamy. In fact, although I personally appreciate, and can even envy, the unconventional emotional and erotic make-up of the harmonious ménage à trois and the impressive capacity to manage sexual jealousy that both Randolph and Robert displayed, this is not the sort of thing that one can will oneself to possess. I present these stories, instead, because I believe they offer broad lessons about contemporary intimacy and kinship that deserve serious consideration and respect. Many gay men negotiate the basic tension between desire and domesticity more creatively and honestly than mainstream heterosexual culture encourages people to do. In part because the AIDS epidemic subjected gay men's sexuality to extraordinary levels of collective scrutiny and debate, it incited them and their loved ones to perform Herculean levels of caretaking outside default-mode family forms. Vast numbers of gay men rose to this challenge without access to marriage, partner benefits, or public acknowledgment of their relationships. Because gay men have been compelled to create their relationships outside the prescribed template of "the sexual family," they have devised ways to unhitch and recombine love, lust, commitment, nurturance, residence, and, as we'll see in the next chapter, parenthood.

Partly due to necessity and perhaps partly due to gender, gay men do seem to manage sexual jealousy and to turn former lovers into friends and kin more easily than most heterosexuals tend to do. These are useful skills in a divorce-prone culture. As we have seen, and as the trio quipped, pursuing eros exclusively among men offers gay men more opportunities for sex, if they so desire. Better yet, in my view, accepting a stigmatized sexual identity seems to allow gay men to be more forthright and less defensive about acknowledging whatever their erotic desires may be. Whether or not the rest of us want more sex in our lives, we and our societies could certainly benefit from more forthrightness and less shame or hypocrisy about our sexual yearnings. Gay men could inspire us to redefine fidelity and sexual ethics in ways more compatible with liberal democracy.

Gathering these stories of love, sex, and family led me to wonder how and why the concept of "infidelity" ever came to acquire its contemporary reference to sexual adultery. When the concept arose in the fifteenth century, an infidel was a religious rather than a sexual sinner, someone who was living outside the (Christian) faith. I first wrote this chapter in the summer of 2008 in the wake of what seemed like a record-breaking season of political sex scandals and exposés in the United States—most prominently those involving presidential candidate John Edwards and, in my own state of New York, Governor Elliott Spitzer and then capped off by the unwed teen pregnancy of Bristol Palin, the daughter of the 2008 Republican vice presidential nominee, Sarah Palin.[41] The sexual escapades of staunch right-wing, family-values warriors South Carolina governor Mark Sanford and Nevada senator John Ensign, a Capitol Hill Christian Fellowship resident, had usurped the media limelight when I returned to revise this chapter during the summer of 2009. It seems increasingly difficult to fathom how these perennial breaches of private marital vows can remain matters of great public import, or why a sexual ethics for the twenty-first century should remain wedded to a monolithic erotic standard, particularly one that is so regularly honored in the breach.

The stories of gay intimacy in this chapter suggest to me the superiority of an ethic of sexual integrity, responsibility, and respect over a uniform insistence on sexual exclusivity. The best of these stories model a mature willingness to acknowledge the variety, complexity, fluidity, and sheer mystery of individual sexual longings, limits, aesthetics, and meanings. Inspired by their examples, we might cease promoting monogamy for all and castigating those who lapse. Instead we might redefine fidelity to signify faithfulness to the particular sexual, emotional, and social commitments that intimates mutually arrive at through honest negotiation and renegotiation. In this way, Ossie and Harry unequivocally embraced monogamy. In this way, Matt and Robert, Randolph and his transgendered mate, and the harmonious trio did not. All were faithful to their beloveds, and all of their relationships endured (in Randolph's case, 'til death did part them). Jake, on the other hand, was unfaithful to Shawn, and this severed their union. His infidelity was not a sexual but an ethical breach of trust. Sexual integrity should trump exclusivity.

The gender twist involved is that it was men who complained of male piggery, traded sexual for cultural capital, and struggled over the domestic division of labor. The terms of intimate fidelity that most of them practiced raise cultural curtains that allow us to inspect some of the backstage props and the stage sets in which most of us enact our particular gender, sexual, and familial scripts. These family fellows complicate and challenge popular understandings of masculinity, femininity, and sexuality and raise anew ancient questions about the sources, meanings, and possibilities of diverse human desires and attachments.

2

Gay Parenthood and the End of Paternity as We Knew It

Because let's face it, if men weren't always hungry for it, nothing would ever happen. There would be no sex, and our species would perish.
—Sean Elder, "Why My Wife Won't Sleep With Me," 2004

Because homosexuals are rarely monogamous, often having as many as three hundred or more partners in a lifetime—some studies say it is typically more than one thousand—children in those polyamorous situations are caught in a perpetual coming and going. It is devastating to kids, who by their nature are enormously conservative creatures.
—James Dobson, "Same-Sex Marriage Talking Points"

Unlucky in love and ready for a family, [Christie] Malcomson tried for 4½ years to get pregnant, eventually giving birth to the twins when she was 38. Four years later, again without a mate, she had Sarah. "I've always known that I was meant to be a mother," Malcomson, 44, said. "I tell people, 'I didn't choose to be a single parent. I choose to be a parent.'"
—Lornet Turnbull, "Family Is . . . Being Redefined All the Time," 2004

GAY FATHERS WERE once as unthinkable as they were invisible. Now they are an undeniable part of the contemporary family landscape. During the same time that the marriage promotion campaign in the United States was busy convincing politicians and the public to regard rising rates of fatherlessness as a national emergency,[1] growing numbers of gay men were embracing fatherhood. Over the past two decades, they have built a cornucopia of family forms and supportive communities where they are raising children outside of the conventional family. Examining the experiences of gay men who have openly pursued parenthood against the odds can help

us to understand forces that underlie the decline of paternity as we knew
it. Contrary to the fears of many in the marriage-promotion movement,
however, gay parenting is not a new symptom of the demise of fatherhood,
but of its creative, if controversial, reinvention. When I paid close attention
to gay men's parenting desires, efforts, challenges, and achievements, I un-
earthed crucial features of contemporary paternity and parenthood more
generally. I also came upon some inspirational models of family that challenge widely held beliefs about parenthood and child welfare.

The Uncertainty of Paternity

Access to effective contraception, safe abortions, and assisted reproductive
technologies (ART) unhitches traditional links between heterosexual love,
marriage, and baby carriages. Parenthood, like intimacy more generally, is
now contingent. Paths to parenthood no longer appear so natural, obligatory, or uniform as they used to but have become voluntary, plural, and
politically embattled. Now that children impose immense economic and
social responsibilities on their parents, rather than promising to become a
reliable source of family labor or social security, the pursuit of parenthood
depends on an emotional rather than an economic calculus. "The men and
women who decide to have children today," German sociologists Ulrich
Beck and Elisabeth Beck-Gernsheim correctly point out, "certainly do not
do so because they expect any material advantages. Other motives closely
linked with the emotional needs of the parents play a significant role; our
children mainly have 'a psychological utility.'"[2] Amid the threatening upheavals, insecurities, and dislocations of life under global market and military forces, children can rekindle opportunities for hope, meaning, and
connection. Adults who wish to become parents today typically seek the
intimate bonds that children seem to promise. More reliably than a lover
or spouse, parenthood beckons to many (like Christie Malcomson in the
third epigraph to this chapter) who hunger for lasting love, intimacy, and
kinship—for that elusive "haven in a heartless world."[3]

   Gay men confront these features of post-modern parenthood in a magnified mode. They operate from cultural premises antithetical to what U.S.
historian Nicholas Townsend termed "the package deal" of (now eroding)
modern masculinity—marriage, work, and fatherhood.[4] Gay men who
choose to become primary parents challenge conventional definitions of
masculinity and paternity and even dominant sexual norms of gay culture

itself. Gay sex columnist Dan Savage mocked the cultural stakes involved when he and his partner were deciding to adopt a child: "Terry and I would be giving up certain things that, for better or worse, define what it means to be gay. Good things, things we enjoyed and that had value and meaning for us. Like promiscuity."[5]

Gay fatherhood represents "planned parenthood" in extremis. Always deliberate and often difficult, it offers fertile ground for understanding why and how people do and do not choose to become parents today. Unlike most heterosexuals or even lesbians, gay men have to struggle for access to "the means of reproduction" without benefit of default scripts for achieving or practicing parenthood. They encounter a range of challenging, risky, uncertain options—foster care, public and private forms of domestic and international adoption, hired or volunteered forms of "traditional" or gestational surrogacy, contributing sperm to women friends, relatives, or strangers who agree to co-parent with them, or even resorting to an instrumental approach to old-fashioned heterosexual copulation.

Compared with maternity, the social character of paternity has always been more visible than its biological status. Indeed, that's why prior to DNA testing, most modern societies mandated a marital presumption of paternity. Whenever a married woman gave birth, her husband was the presumed and legal father. Gay male paternity intensifies this emphasis on social rather than biological definitions of parenthood. Because the available routes to genetic parenthood for gay men are formidably expensive, very difficult to negotiate, or both, most prospective gay male parents pursue the purely social paths of adoption or foster care.[6]

Stark racial, economic, and sexual asymmetries characterize the adoption marketplace. Prospective parents are primarily white, middle-class, and relatively affluent, but the available children are disproportionately from poorer and darker races and nations. Public and private adoption agencies, as well as birth mothers and fathers, generally consider married heterosexual couples to be the most desirable adoptive parents.[7] These favored straight married couples, for their part, typically seek healthy infants, preferably from their own race or ethnic background. Because there are not enough of these to meet the demand, most states and counties allow single adults, including gay men, to shop for parenthood in their overstocked warehouse of "hard to place" children. This is an index of expediency more than tolerance. The state's stockpiled children have been removed from parents who were judged to be negligent, abusive, or incompetent. Disproportionate numbers are children of color, and the very hardest of these to place are older boys with "special needs," such as physical, emotional, and cognitive disabilities.

The gross disjuncture between the market value of society's adoptable children and the supply of prospective adoptive parents allows gay men to parent a hefty share of them. Impressive numbers of gay men willingly rescue such children from failing or devastated families. Just as in their intimate adult relationships, gay men more readily accept children across boundaries of race, ethnicity, class, and even health.[8]

The multi-racial membership of so many of gay men's families visually signals the social character of most gay fatherhood. In addition, as we will see, some gay men, like single-mother-by-choice Christie Malcomson, willingly unhitch their sexual and romantic desires from their domestic ones in order to become parents. For all of these reasons, gay men provide frontier terrain for exploring noteworthy changes in the meanings and motives for paternity and parenthood.

Finding Pop Luck in the City of Angels

Gay paternity is especially developed and prominent in L.A.—again, not the environment where most people would expect to find it, but which, for many reasons, became a multi-ethnic mecca for gay parenthood. According to data reported in Census 2000, both the greatest number of same-sex couple households in the United States and of such couples who were raising children were residing in Los Angeles County.[9] It is likely, therefore, that the numbers there exceeded those of any metropolis in the world.

Local conditions in Los Angeles have been particularly favorable for gay and lesbian parenthood. L.A. County was among the first in the United States to openly allow gay men to foster or adopt children under its custody, and numerous local, private adoption agencies, lawyers, and services emerged that specialized in facilitating domestic and international adoptions for a gay clientele. In 2001 California enacted a domestic-partnership law that authorized second-parent adoptions, and several family-court judges in California pioneered the still-rare practice of granting pre-birth custody rights to same-sex couples who planned to co-parent. Gay fatherhood became exceptionally institutionalized and visible in Los Angeles, as I indicated in chapter 1. The City of Angels became the surrogacy capital of the gay globe, thanks especially to Growing Generations, the world's first

Author marching with Pop Luck Club in Gay Pride Parade, West Hollywood, June 2002.

gay- and lesbian-owned professional surrogacy agency founded to serve an international clientele of prospective gay parents.[10] The thriving Pop Luck Club (PLC), also mentioned earlier, sponsored monthly gatherings, organized special events, and provided information, referrals, support, and community to a membership that by the time I concluded my field research in 2003 included more than two hundred families of varying shapes, sizes, colors, and forms. A PLC subgroup of perhaps ten at-home dads and their children met for a weekly play date in a West Hollywood playground, followed by a "pop luck" lunch. Doting dads taught their young children to dig, slide, swing, teeter-totter, take turns, and make friends while swapping parenting advice, baby clothes, toys, and equipment and building a sustaining community. Single gay dads and "prospective SGDs seeking to meet others who understand how parenting affects our lives" held monthly mixers that featured "friendly folks, scintillating snacks, and brilliant banter—about the best brand of diapers!"[11] Additional PLC focus groups, for prospective gay dads or adoptive dads, for example, as well as satellite chapters in neighboring counties continually emerged.

The gay men I studied, as the stories in chapter 1 revealed, were among the first cohort of gay men young enough to even imagine parenthood outside heterosexuality and mature enough to be in a position to choose or reject it. I intentionally over-sampled for gay fathers. Nationally 22 percent of male same-sex-couple households recorded in Census 2000 included children under the age of eighteen.[12] However, fathers composed half of my sample overall and more than 60 percent of the men who were then in same-sex couples. Depending on which definition of fatherhood one uses, between twenty-four and twenty-nine of my fifty primary interviewees were fathers of thirty-five children, and four men who were not yet parents declared their firm intention to become so.[13] Only sixteen men (32 percent), in contrast, depicted themselves as childless more or less by choice. Also by design, I sampled to include the full gamut of contemporary paths to gay paternity. Although most children with gay fathers in the United States were born within heterosexual marriages before their fathers came out, this was true for only six of the thirty-four children that the men in my study were raising. All of the others were among the pioneer generation of children with gay dads who chose to parent after they had come out of the closet. Fifteen of the children had been adopted (or were in the process of becoming so) through county and private agencies or via independent, open adoption agreements with birth mothers; four were foster-care children; five children had been conceived through surrogacy contracts, both gestational and "traditional"; and four children had been born to lesbians who conceived with sperm from gay men with whom they were co-parenting. In addition, five of the gay men in my study had served as foster parents to numerous teenagers, and several expected to continue to accept foster placements. Two men, however, were biological but not social parents, one by intention, the other unwittingly.[14]

The fathers and children in my study were racially and socially diverse, and their families, like gay-parent families generally, were much more likely to be multi-racial and multi-cultural than are other families in the United States, or perhaps anywhere in the world. Two-thirds of the gay-father families in my study were multi-racial. The majority (fifteen) of the twenty-four gay men who were parenting during the time of my study were white, but most (twenty-one) of their thirty-four children were not.[15] Even more striking, only two of the fifteen children they had adopted by 2003 were white, both of these through open adoption arrangements with birth mothers; seven adoptees were black or mixed race, and six were Latino. In contrast, nine of the twelve adoptive parents were white, and one each was black, Latino, and Asian American.

It is difficult to assess how racially representative this is of gay men, gay parents, and their families in the city, the state, or the nation. Although the dominant cultural stereotype of gay men and gay fathers is white and middle class, U.S. Census 2000 data surprisingly report that racial minorities represented a higher proportion of same-sex-couple-parent households in California than of heterosexual married couples.[16] The vast majority of the

children in these families, however, were born within their gay parents' former heterosexual relationships.[17] Contemporary gay paths to paternity are
far more varied and complex.

The Passion-for-Parenthood Continuum

The fifty gay men I interviewed in Los Angeles expressed attitudes toward
parenthood that ranged from religious vocation to unabashed aversion. On
one end of the passion-for-parenthood continuum clustered men I think
of as "predestined parents." Compelled by a potent, irrepressible longing,
these men said that they had always known that they wanted to become
parents and that they had been prepared to move heaven and earth to do
so. Few, if any, predestined parents consciously sought single parenthood,
but like Christie Malcomson, they were willing to brave this trying trail
rather than miss out on parenthood entirely. In fact, their desire to parent
often trumped their desire for a partner, and a predestined parent would
forsake a mate who forced him to choose between the two.

On the far opposite end of the spectrum lay the absolute "parental refuseniks," for whom parenthood held less than no appeal. A few gay men
even viewed their freedom from the pressure to parent to be one of the
compensatory rewards of their stigmatized sexual identity. With exactly inverse priorities to a predestined parent, a pure refusenik's aversion to parenthood was so potent that he would forfeit his couple relationship rather
than go along with his mate's unequivocal yearning to become a parent. Ar-
rayed between these two poles was a broad spectrum of inclinations held
by less determined souls. Persuasive life partners or circumstances could
recruit or divert these potential "situational parents" into or away from the
world of Pampers and playgrounds that the two other groups fervently
embraced or eschewed.

Predestined Progenitors

Of the men I interviewed, eighteen who had become dads and four who
planned to do so portrayed their passion for parenthood in terms so ardent
that I classify them as predestined parents. A shared craving for parenthood united three fortunate pairs in my study, including Ossie and Harry,
whom we met in chapter 1. Five men sought to become parents without

an intimate partner; five others persuaded situational partners to support their quest; and primordial parental desires had led two men to create married heterosexual-parent families before they came out—families that they later left. The following two stories illustrate typical challenges and triumphs of different paths to predestined parenthood. The first depicts another blessedly compatible and privileged couple, and the second is about a courageous, much less affluent gay man who was "single by chance, parent by choice," to paraphrase the title of a book about single women who choose to become mothers.[18]

Predestined Pairing

Eddie Leary and Charles Tillery, a well-heeled, white, Catholic couple, had three children born through gestational surrogacy. Their firstborn was a genetic half-sibling to a younger set of twins. The same egg donor and the same gestational surrogate conceived and bore the three children, but Charles is the genetic father of the first child, and Eddie's sperm conceived the twins. At the time I first interviewed them in 2002, their first child was three years old, the twins were infants, and the couple had been together for eighteen years. Eddie told me that they had discussed their shared desire to parent on their very first date, just as Ossie and Harry had done. In fact, by then Eddie had already entered a heterosexual marriage primarily for that purpose, but he came out to his wife and left the marriage before achieving it. Directly echoing Christie Malcomson, Eddie claimed that he always knew that he "was meant to be a parent." He recalled that during his childhood whenever adults had posed the clichéd question to him, "What do you want to be when you grow up?" his ready answer was "a daddy."

Charles and Eddie met and spent their first ten years together on the East Coast, where they built successful careers in corporate law and were gliding through the glamorous DINC (double income, no children) fast lane of life. By their mid-thirties, however, they were bored and began to ask themselves the existential question, "Is this all there is?" They had already buried more friends than their parents had by their sixties, which, Eddie believed, "gives you a sense of gravitas." In addition, he reported, "My biological clock was definitely ticking." In the mid-1990s, the couple migrated to L.A., lured by the kind of gay family life style and the ample job opportunities it seemed to offer. They spent the next five years riding an emotional roller coaster attempting to become parents. At first Eddie and Charles considered adoption, but they became discouraged when they learned that then-governor Pete Wilson's administration was preventing

joint adoptions by same-sex couples. Blessed with ample financial and social resources, they decided to shift their eggs, so to speak, into the surrogacy basket. One of Charles's many cousins put the couple in touch with
her college roommate, Sally, a married mother of two in her mid-thirties
who lived in Idaho. Sally was a woman who loved both bearing and rearing
children, and Charles's cousin knew that she had been fantasizing about
bestowing the gift of parenthood on a childless couple. Although Sally's
imaginary couple had not been gay, she agreed to meet them. Eddie and
Sally both reported that they bonded instantly, and she agreed to serve as
the men's gestational surrogate.

To secure an egg donor and manage the complex medical and legal
processes that surrogacy requires at a moment just before Growing Generations had opened shop, Eddie and Charles became among the first gay clients of a surrogate parenthood agency that mainly served infertile heterosexual couples. Shopping for DNA in the agency's catalog of egg donors,
they had selected Marya, a Dutch graduate student who had twice before
served as an anonymous donor for married couples in order to subsidize
her education. Marya had begun to long for maternity herself, however,
and she was loathe to subject her body and soul yet again to the grueling
and hormonally disruptive process that donating ova entails. Yet when she
learned that the new candidates for her genes were gay men, she found
herself taken with the prospect of openly aiding such a quest. Like Sally,
she felt an immediate affinity with Eddie and agreed to enter a collaborative egg-donor relationship with him and Charles. When she had served
as egg donor for infertile married couples, Marya explained, "the mother
there can get a little jealous and a little threatened, because she's already
feeling insecure about being infertile, and having another woman having
that process and threatening the mother's role, I think is a big concern."
With a gay couple, in contrast, "you get to be—there's no exclusion, and
there's no threatened feelings."

Because Eddie is a few years older than Charles, he wanted to be the
first to provide the sperm, and all four parties were thrilled when Sally became pregnant on the second in-vitro fertilization (IVF) attempt. Elation
turned to despair, however, when the pregnancy miscarried in the thirteenth week. Eddie described himself as devastated, saying, "I grieved and
mourned the loss of my child, just as if I'd been the one carrying it." In
fact, Sally recovered from the trauma and was willing to try again before
Eddie, who said, "I couldn't bear the risk of losing another of my children."
Instead, Charles wound up supplying the sperm for what became the

couple's firstborn child, Heather. Two years later, eager for a second child, the couple had persuaded both reluctant women to subject their bodies to one more IVF surrogacy, this time with Eddie's sperm. A pair of healthy twin boys arrived one year later,[19] with all four procreative collaborators, as well as Sally's husband, present at the delivery to welcome the boys into what was to become a remarkable, surrogacy-extended family.

Occasionally Marya, the egg donor, continued to visit her genetic daughter, but Eddie and Sally quickly developed an extraordinary, deep, familial bond. They developed the habit of daily, long-distance phone calls that were often lengthy and intimate. "Mama Sally," as Heather started to call her, began to make regular use of the Leary-Tillery guest room, accompanied sometimes by her husband and their two children. Often she came to co-parent with Eddie as a substitute for Charles, who had to make frequent business trips. The two families began taking joint vacations skiing or camping together in the Rockies, and once Marya had come along. Sally's then ten-year-old daughter and eight-year-old son began to refer to Heather as their "surrogate sister."

Eddie and Charles jointly secured shared legal custody of all three children through some of the earliest pre-birth decrees granted in California. From the start, the couple had agreed that Eddie, a gourmet cook who had designed the family's state-of-the-culinary-art kitchen, would stay home as full-time parent, and Charles would be the family's sole breadwinner. After the twins arrived, they hired a daytime nanny to assist Eddie while Charles was out earning their sustenance, and she sometimes minded the twins when Eddie and Heather joined the weekly playgroup of PLC at-home dads and tots. Charles, for his part, blessed with Herculean energy and scant need for sleep, would plunge into his full-scale second shift of baby feedings, diapers, baths, and bedtime storytelling the moment he returned from the office. Although Eddie admitted to some nagging concerns that he "may have committed career suicide by joining the mom's club in the neighborhood," he also believed he'd met his calling: "I feel like this is who I was meant to be."

When I contacted Eddie again in late October 2008, he reported that he and Charles were among those thousands of same-sex couples in California who had just rushed to register their "shotgun weddings" before the November election. They would have preferred to wait until the following spring to celebrate the twenty-fifth anniversary of their union with a big wedding. Instead, they acted on what proved to be their prescient fear that voters would take away their new right to marry by passing Proposition 8, the initiative to insert a ban on same-sex marriage into the state constitution. Other than the hastily staged marriage, Eddie said that he had no momentous family changes to report:

> We are another of those boring families where little has changed other than our children are more beautiful and a little older, and Charles and I have more gray hair and feel a lot older. We live in a neighborhood filled with children (fifty of whom were here with their parents on Halloween night for our annual open house), and as far as I know, none of them have been traumatized living near a family headed by two gay men. Charles still works, and I still see my job as taking care of my family. We are fortunate to be able to afford this choice.

Of course, few readers would agree with Eddie that his is a boring family. In fact, its surrogacy-extended kin ties had expanded and deepened in the years since my research. Egg donor Marya was now a married mother of two after she too had held a shotgun wedding, but of a more old-fashioned sort. A few years earlier Marya had found herself accidentally, but not unhappily, pregnant after her fourth date with a lover who proved willing to jump-start a family. So the three Tillery-Leary children had acquired two more genetic half-siblings. Marya and her family were living in New Mexico and were about to come visit again, because, Eddie wrote, "Mama Marya and her husband believe it is important for the five kids to know they are siblings and that Marya is one of our three children's moms." In addition, Eddie announced that the children's other, more actively involved mom, gestational surrogate Mama Sally, and her husband were coming for Thanksgiving: "because we like spending as much time together as possible." The two surrogacy-linked couples and children celebrated holidays together regularly and had taken to spending their summers together as well on a ranch in south Texas that Sally and her husband had purchased.

Eddie and Charles were no longer active in the PLC, because they had neither time nor need for such organized support. Their children now went to school with several kids from the old PLC at-home dads' playground group. Their family and community life were so full, rich, rewarding, and integrated that being gay dads rarely seemed much of an issue anymore. In fact, Eddie reported that recently his aging Catholic mother had told him that he was the only person she knew who had gotten everything he had ever wanted in life.

Parent Seeking Partner

Armando Hidalgo, a Mexican immigrant, was thirty-four years old when I interviewed him in 2001. At that point, he was in the final stages of adopting his four-year-old black foster son, Ramón. Armando had been a teenage sexual migrant to Los Angeles almost twenty years earlier. He had run away from home when he was only fifteen in order to conceal his unacceptable sexual desires from his large, commercially successful, urban Mexican family. The youthful Armando had paid a coyote to help him cross the border. He had survived a harrowing illegal immigration experience which culminated in a Hollywood-style footrace across the California desert to escape an INS patrol in hot pursuit. By working at a Taco Bell in a coastal town, Armando put himself through high school. Drawing upon keen intelligence, linguistic facility, and a prodigious work ethic and drive, he had built a stable career managing a designer furniture showroom and he had managed to secure U.S. citizenship as well.

Four years after Armando's sudden disappearance from Mexico, he had returned there to come out to his family, cope with their painful reactions to his homosexuality and exile, and begin to restore his ruptured kinship bonds. He had made annual visits to his family ever since, and on one of these he fell in love with Juan, a Mexican language teacher. Armando said that he told Juan about his desire to parent right at the outset, and his new lover had seemed enthusiastic: "So, I thought we were the perfect match." Armando brought his boyfriend back to Los Angeles, and they lived together for five years.

However, when Armando began to pursue his lifelong goal of parenthood, things fell apart. To initiate the adoption process, Armando had enrolled the couple in the county's mandatory foster-care class. However, Juan kept skipping class and neglecting the homework, and so he failed to qualify for foster-parent status. This behavior jeopardized Armando's eligibility to adopt children as well as Juan's. The county then presented Armando with a "Sophie's choice." They would not place a child in his home unless Juan moved out. Despite Armando's primal passion for parenthood, "at the time," he self-critically explained to me, "I made the choice of staying with him, a choice that I regret. I chose him over continuing with my adoption." This decision ultimately exacted a fatal toll on the relationship. In Armando's eyes, Juan was preventing him from fulfilling his lifelong dream of having children. His resentment grew, but it took another couple of years before his passion for parenthood surpassed his diminishing passion for his partner. That is when Armando moved out and renewed the adoption application as a single parent.

Ramón was the first of three children that Armando told me he had "definitely decided" to adopt, whether or not he found another partner. His goal was to adopt two more children, preferably a daughter and another son, in that order. Removed at birth from crack-addicted parents, Ramón had lived in three foster homes in his first three years of life, before the county placed him with Armando through its fost-adopt program. Ramón had suffered from food allergies, anxiety, and hyperactivity when he arrived, and the social worker warned Armando to anticipate learning disabilities as well. Instead, after nine months under Armando's steady, patient, firm, and loving care, Ramón was learning rapidly and appeared to be thriving. And so was Armando. He felt so lucky to have Ramón, whom he no longer perceived as racially different from himself: "To me he's like my natural son. I love him a lot, and he loves me too much. Maybe I never felt so much unconditional love."

In fact, looking back, Armando attributed part of the pain of the years he spent struggling to accept his own homosexuality to his discomfort with gay male sexual culture and its emphasis on youth and beauty. "I think it made me fear that I was going to grow old alone," he reflected. "Now I don't have to worry that I'm gay and I'll be alone." For in addition to the intimacy that Armando savored with Ramón, his son proved to be a vehicle for building much closer bonds with most of his natal family. Several of Armando's eleven siblings had also migrated to Los Angeles. Among these were a married brother, his wife, and their children, who provided indispensable back-up support to the single working father. Ramón adored his cousins, and he and his father spent almost every weekend and holiday with them.

Ramón had acquired a devoted, long-distance *abuela* (grandmother) as well. Armando's mother had begun to travel regularly from Mexico to visit her dispersed brood, and, after years of disapproval and disappointment, she had grown to admire and appreciate her gay son above all her other children. Armando reported with sheepish pride that during a recent phone call his mother had stunned and thrilled him when she said, "You know what? I wish that all your brothers were like you. I mean that they liked guys." Astonished, Armando had asked her, "Why do you say that?" She replied, "I don't know. I just feel that you're really good to me, you're really kind. And you're such a good father." Then she apologized for how badly she had reacted when Armando told the family that he was gay, and she told him that now she was really proud of him. " 'Now I don't have to accept it,' " Armando quoted her, " 'because there's nothing to accept. You're natural, you're normal. You're my son, I don't have to accept you.' And she went on and on. It was so nice, it just came out of her. And now she talks about gay things, and she takes a cooking class from a gay guy and tells me how badly her gay cooking teacher was treated by his family when they found out and how unfair it is and all."

Although Armando had begun to create the family he always wanted, he still dreamt of sharing parenthood with a mate who would be more compatible than Juan: "I would really love to meet someone, to fall in love." Of course, the man of his dreams was someone family-oriented: "Now that's really important, family-oriented, because I am very close to my family. I always do family things, like my nephews' birthday parties, going to the movies with them, family dinners, etcetera. But these are things that many gay men don't like to do. If they go to a straight family party, they get bored." Consequently, Armando was pessimistic about finding a love match. Being a parent, moreover, severely constrained his romantic pursuits. He didn't want to subject Ramón, who had suffered so much loss and instability in his life, to the risk of becoming attached to yet another new parental figure who might leave him. In addition, he didn't want Ramón "to think that gay men only have casual relationships, that there's no commitment." "But," he observed, with disappointment, "I haven't seen a lot of commitment among gay men." Armando took enormous comfort, however, in knowing that even if he never found another boyfriend, he will "never really be alone": "And I guess that's one of the joys that a family brings." Disappointingly, I may never learn whether Armando found a coparent and adopted a sister and brother for Ramón, because I was unable to locate him again in 2008.

Adopting Diversity

While Eddie, Charles, and Armando all experienced irrepressible parental yearnings, they pursued very different routes to realizing this common "destiny." Gestational surrogacy, perhaps the newest, the most high-tech, and certainly the most expensive path to gay parenthood, is available primarily to affluent couples, the overwhelming majority of whom are white men who want to have genetic progeny.[20] Adoption, on the other hand, is one of the oldest forms of "alternative" parenthood. It involves bureaucratic and social rather than medical technologies, and the county fost-adopt program which Armando and six other men in my study employed is generally the least expensive, most accessible route to gay paternity. Like Armando, most single, gay prospective parents pursue this avenue and adopt "hard-to-place" children who, like Ramón, are often boys of color with "special needs."

The demographics of contrasting routes to gay parenthood starkly expose the race and class disparities in the market value of children. Affluent, mainly white couples, like Charles and Eddie, can purchase the means to reproduce white infants in their own image, or even an enhanced, eugenic one, by selecting egg donors who have traits they desire with whom to mate their own DNA. In contrast, for gay men who are single, less privileged, or both, public agencies offer a grab bag of displaced children who are generally older, darker, and less healthy.[21] Somewhere in between these two routes to gay paternity lie forms of "gray market," open domestic or international adoptions, or privately negotiated sperm-donor agreements with women, especially lesbians, who want to co-parent with men. Independent adoption agencies and the Internet enable middle-class gay men, again typically white couples, to adopt newborns in a variety of hues.

Bernardo Fernandez, a middle-class, black Latino, took the gray-market route to parenthood, and with intimate consequences almost opposite to Armando's. Bernardo adopted the first of two mixed-race children while he was single, but then he had the great fortune of falling in love with a gay man who also had always wanted to parent. Less fortunately, however, Bernardo's beloved was an Australian visitor to the United States, and U.S. immigration law does not grant family status to same-sex partners. His partner therefore applied for a work visa so that he could stay in the United States, but his tourist visa had expired, and he had been forced to return home. The prospects of receiving a work visa were not looking good, and Bernardo feared that in order to live together as a family, he and the children were going to have to migrate to Australia, because it did admit same-sex partners. In the meantime, Bernardo was spending the months between his lover's regular visits parenting alone.

Price does not always determine the route to parenthood that gay men choose, or the race, age, health, or pedigree of the children they agree to adopt. During the period of my initial research, only one white, middle-class couple in my study had chosen to adopt healthy white infants. Some affluent white men enthusiastically adopted children of color, even when they knew that the children had been exposed to drugs prenatally. Drew Greenwald, a very successful architect who could easily have afforded assisted reproductive technology (ART), was the most dramatic example of this. He claimed, "It never would have occurred to me to do surrogacy. I think it's outrageous because there are all these children who need good homes. And people have surrogacy, they say, in part it's because they want to avoid the complications of adoption, but in candor they are really in love with their own genes. . . . I just think there is a bit of narcissism about it." An observant Jew and the son of Holocaust survivors, Drew found gestational surrogacy particularly offensive. "The idea of having a different genetic mother and birth mother is a little too Nazi-esque for me, a little too much genetic engineering for me. I feel somewhat uncomfortable with that. I mean, someone can be good enough to carry the baby, but their genes aren't good enough? That's outrageous."

Drew had opted for independent, open, transracial adoption instead. When I first interviewed him in 2002, he had just adopted his second of two multi-racial babies born to two different women who both had acknowledged using drugs during their pregnancies. Drew, like Bernardo, had been single when he adopted his first child, and parenthood proved to be a route to successful partnership for him as well. Soon after adopting his first infant, Drew reunited with James, a former lover who had fallen "wildly in love" with Drew's new baby. James moved in while Drew was in the process of adopting a second child, and they have co-parented together ever since. Indeed, parenthood is the "glue" that cemented a relationship between the couple that Drew believed might otherwise have failed. Shared parenting provided them with a "joint project, a focus, and a source of commitment." Drew acknowledged that he was not a romantic. He had questions, in fact, "about the very term *intimacy*" and considered sex to be an important but minor part of life. He and James were very "efficient" in servicing their sexual needs, he quipped. They devoted perhaps "a few minutes" of their over-stuffed weekly schedule to this activity, "mainly on Shabbas, and then we're back to our family life."

I was indulging in my guilty pleasure of reading the Style section of the Sunday *New York Times* one morning in the fall of 2008, when I stumbled across a wedding photo and announcement that Drew and James, "the parents of five adopted children," had just married. Several weeks later, on a conference trip to Los Angeles, I visited the bustling, expanded family household. I learned that the white birth mother of their second child had since had two more unwanted pregnancies, one with the same African American man as before and one with a black Latino. She had successfully appealed to Drew and James to add both of these mixed-race siblings to their family. After the first of these two new brothers had joined their brood, Drew and James began to worry that because only one of their children was a girl, she would find it difficult to grow up in a family with two dads and only brothers. And so they turned to the Internet, where they found a mixed-race sister for their first daughter. Three of the five children suffered from learning or attention-deficit difficulties, but Drew took this in stride. He was well aware, he said, that he and James had signed on "for all sorts of trauma, challenge, heartache" in the years ahead. He was both determined and financially able to secure the best help available for his children. Nonetheless, Drew acknowledged, "I fully expect that the kids will break my heart at some point in various ways, but it's so worth it." It was sufficiently worth it, apparently, that the year after my 2008 visit, I received an email from Drew announcing that their child head count had climbed to six, because their "jackpot birth mom" had given birth yet again. "We're up to four boys and two girls," Drew elaborated. "It's a lot, as you can imagine, but wonderful."

Two other predestined parents in my study were co-parenting with lesbian friends children who had been conceived through donor insemination.[22] Both have created multi-gay-parent families that I describe later in this chapter.

Dads-in-Waiting

The final category of predestined parents consists of four men who were not yet parents but expressed irrepressible parental yearnings and had begun to actively weigh their options. Three of these men were white, and one black; two were coupled, and two single. And these social statuses influenced how they calculated the opportunities and risks that different strategies seemed to pose. Damian, for example, a thirty-four-year-old, white observant Catholic, was still struggling in 2001 to make his peace with what he viewed to be his "homosexual nature" and the barrier it posed to his potent conventional familial longings and values. Once again, like Christie Malcomson, Damian was unhappily single and discouraged about the prospects of finding the sort of committed relationship he desired, but he refused to forfeit his parental desires. He had been sorely tempted by the option of entering a heterosexual marriage of convenience. "I have a very close female friend," Damian reported, "who would marry me in a heartbeat if I wanted to marry and have a kid. I've actually thought about it, but then if I had a kid with Colleen, I'd have to share. And what if we broke up, or things fell apart? Then what?" To achieve a more secure form of primary parental status, Damian had decided to pursue some form of adoption, but he was not yet in a financial situation to attempt single parenthood at that point.

When I spoke with Damian again in October 2008, he was thrilled to report that he had achieved his goal. Three years earlier, he had adopted an infant white son through independent adoption. After he became a single parent, Damian found that he had to seek a more child-friendly work environment than the one he had been in. He considered himself blessed to have found an employer who allowed him to bring his infant to the office. He had also successfully converted a former lover into a best friend who had become part of a chosen, supportive, extended family for him and his son. Damian dearly wished that he could afford to adopt a baby sister or brother for his son, but the recent economic crisis had placed him in such precarious circumstances that he was worrying about continuing to earn enough to support the one child he already had.

Michael David, the black single man we met in chapter 1, arrived at a similar parental goal through a somewhat different calculus. He confessed with some embarrassment that his desire to parent was so compelling that he had contemplated engaging in closeted heterosexual courtship in the hope of impregnating an unsuspecting prospective co-parent. Michael found the ethics of that strategy troubling, "but the problems of doing that seem less than the problem of not to have a kid at all." He had rejected this prospect in favor of adoption, however, because like Damian, he was not interested in a parenting relationship that might not allow him to live with his children full-time.

When Michael attended a PLC orientation meeting with me just before I left Los Angeles in 2003, I introduced him to Bernardo, who was then awaiting the birth of the second child he had arranged to adopt. Inspired by the model of this black gay dad who had been single when he adopted his first child, Michael assured me that he would soon initiate his own parental quest. His commitment to children seemed so powerful that I was surprised to learn in the fall of 2008 that, unlike Damian, Michael seemed to have evaded his parental "destiny." By then his avuncular caseload had expanded from eight nieces and nephews to fifteen. Michael reported that the copious experiences he had had observing and assisting the single parents among his sisters and cousins had dampened his determination to assume similar financial and emotional challenges. Michael still held out some hope that he might find a mate to co-parent with him someday, but otherwise, he had decided that being a beloved uncle to multitudes might prove a sufficient compromise. Predestination is an imperfect science.

Refuseniks

The alter image of a predestined parent is someone born to be child-free. This is the dominant stereotype of gay male culture, of course, but in fact, only a minority of contemporary gay men declare themselves categorically opposed to parenthood. For example, a study of the desire to parent among ninety-four gay men in New York conducted in the mid-1990s found that only eleven of them (12 percent) expressed clearly negative attitudes toward children.[23] I classify men as refuseniks if, had they been asked the question posed in that study, "How do you feel about raising children?" they would most likely have echoed the reply, "Not in a million years!"[24] By this standard, only two of my fifty primary informants unambiguously qualified as refuseniks.

Angel Lopez was the more unequivocal of these. A bohemian artist who had migrated to the United States from Argentina in 1997 in search of professional rather than sexual opportunities, Angel was single and child-free, and both by firm choice. His chosen lifestyle came closer to dominant stereotypes of gay male sexual freedom, or even excess, than did anyone else's in my study. Angel exuded native good looks and sex appeal, honed by a gym-sculpted physique of the sort that elicits the clichéd straight woman's lament that all the good-looking men are gay. He boasted a lusty sexual appetite and résumé to match. Committed to maintaining his personal independence and sexual freedom, Angel frequented the city's gay baths and sex clubs two or three times a week to indulge his desire for recreational sex without strings.

I characterize Angel as child-free rather than childless, because he actually was a genetic father but not a social one. In fact, the birth of an unintended biological child twenty years earlier had been a factor in Angel's shift from his bisexual erotic orientation to a gay sexual career. Angel's self-described bisexual appetites and history probably would have earned him a score of three or four in the middle of the Kinsey scale (which goes from zero to six). However, his experience with unsought paternity contributed to his decision to avoid future heterosexual intimacies. He had decided to escape from the kinds of emotional demands and family "dramas" that he associated with women. Angel had been a sexually precocious adolescent rebel against the social norms of his bourgeois, conservative, Catholic family and community, when he met Alina, who was then a twenty-eight-year-old married woman. Angel claimed that Alina had seduced him into what soon became a passionate, clandestine relationship that lasted nearly five years. "She was really sexual too," Angel recalled, "and she showed me everything. I was sixteen; I was a young horse, just ready to go all the time."

Alina's marriage broke up after her husband discovered the affair, and then, when Angel was nineteen years old, she became pregnant. Angel was not certain that the pregnancy was accidental. He had been using condoms, but Alina had wanted children and had frequently told him that she wanted to have his baby. Angel claimed that he had always told her that given his age and their situation, he didn't think this was a good idea. He knew that their relationship was never going to be public and that in a few years he would permanently leave town. At the same time, however, Angel said that he told Alina that she was free to "do whatever": "It's your body, and you have all the right to have it." He didn't mind her getting pregnant with his sperm, if she wanted to do it anyway, because, he said, "I don't have those feelings about my genetic material." Being a parent is a social relationship, in Angel's view, not a biological one.

Alina went ahead and had the baby, and for a while their clandestine affair continued. Initially, "she was very happy," Angel claimed, "but then she started to get a little more, you know how women get—after they have a baby? You know—they want a man all the time to be there, to protect it, all that thing. And they don't want the man at all. They get with the kid and forget about, you know—that whole psychological thing!"

No one ever learned that Angel was the biological father, and " 'til the kid was one year old," the couple had continued their affair, with Angel visiting Alina and the baby, as though he was "a friend of the family." But Alina wanted more from him. Angel said that he "warned her not to push, but she pushed and pushed and pushed and pushed—'you didn't come today to see the guy,' etcetera." In this way, it seems, Alina inadvertently "pushed" Angel into exploring his latent homoerotic desires.

One night Angel went along with some friends to a gay bar "just to have some fun." There, a gay man twenty years his senior "hit on" Angel and invited him to lunch the next day. Angel remembered feeling nervous, and his instinct was to refuse: "but then I thought about my fucked-up life with Alina and the kid, and all the secrets and problems." So, he figured, "What do I have to lose—a couple hours in an afternoon? I want to see what it's like." That fateful lunch proved to be the start of "a deeply neurotic" four-year relationship that nonetheless initiated Angel into what became an enduring homoerotic preference. Laughing, he explained, "I find it easier with men." Although he still was attracted to women as well, he claimed,

"It's too much work. You know, I go to the sex club, I get ready in five minutes. And I don't have to promise anything, I don't have to do anything. They don't feel bad because they've been used. I mean, you know, if it was a little more equal in that way, you know, I would play with women too, and I will enjoy it, I think." In my view, Angel's shift from what appears to be a rare fully bisexual erotic predisposition to exclusively homosexual practice expressed more of a gender preference than a sexual one. He chose to pursue his ecumenical erotic desires exclusively among men, because he found it easier to avoid pressures for emotional commitment, monogamy, and, perhaps above all, parenthood.

Through extensive psychotherapy, Angel had come to terms with some of the familial sources of his antipathy to parenting. For many years he had been estranged from his own father, who had deserted Angel's mother and the couple's five children for a younger woman when Angel was a teenager. Therapy enabled him to understand, forgive, and reestablish contact with his father. "I even like him now," Angel acknowledged, claiming that he had realized that his father had "never wanted to have five kids and have to work to feed them": "Who wants to? Not me, and not him. He was not a family man." Neither is Angel.[25]

The sole other man in my study who was unambiguously determined not to parent did not share Angel's more general aversion to love, domesticity, or family life. Luíz Gonzalez, a forty-year-old, undocumented Mexican immigrant who worked as a gardener, and his partner of ten years, also an undocumented Mexican immigrant, were renting a small house in a family-centered Latino enclave. Both men had grown up in poor, huge families of migrant farm workers. Even though Luíz had suffered years of homophobic rejection by his parents and many of his eleven brothers and sisters, he continued to contribute some of his scant earnings to his ever-expanding and struggling family of origin.

Luíz was determined, however, not to acquire dependents of his own. In fact, he reported that his opposition to parenthood had become a major source of conflict with his partner, who was eager to have a son. Because of this and waning sexual attraction, Luíz confided that he had already decided to break up with his longtime companion and to seek a new romance. However, he had not yet found the courage to inform his partner or his family of this decision. Paradoxically, Luíz feared facing the disappointment and disapproval that he anticipated receiving from his parents and other relatives. Despite their strong disapproval of homosexuality, they had gradually integrated his gay partner into *la familia,* and they enjoyed his company and support. Luíz believed that his relatives would be very upset and critical of him if he were to rupture that bond.

Although only two of my fifty principal research subjects themselves qualified as refuseniks, several of the predestined dads spoke of failed relationships they had experienced with other gay refuseniks. Like Armando, the single adoptive dad mentioned earlier, they described former partners who had jumped ship before or shortly after an adoption was under way. Nonetheless, the ranks of genuine parental refuseniks in my sample, and in the broader society, are surprisingly thin. There is no evidence that much of the growing incidence of "fatherlessness" or male childlessness in advanced industrial societies can be explained by an increasing aversion to paternity.[26]

Situational Parents

Despite the fact that I over-sampled for gay parents, the majority of men in my study fell into the intermediate range on the passion-to-parent continuum. I would classify twenty-six of my fifty primary research subjects as having been situationally with or without children. Nine men whose personal desire to parent had ranged from reluctant, unenthusiastic, or indifferent to ambivalent, hesitant, or even mildly interested became situational parents after they succumbed to the persuasive entreaties of a fervently motivated mate, or if they fell in love with a man who was already a parent. Sixteen men who had remained childless expressed a similar range of sentiments, and in one case even a portion of regret. These men would have agreed to co-parent with a predestined partner or, in some cases, with even just a willing one. They had remained childless, however, either because they were single or because their partners were refuseniks or other "situationists." None of them had a passion for parenthood that was potent enough to overcome the resistance of a reluctant mate or to confront alone the formidable challenges that prospective parents, and especially gay men, must meet.

Persuasive Partner

Glenn Miya, a Japanese American who was thirty-six years old when we first met, liked children enough to spend his workaday life as a pediatrician. Nonetheless, he had not felt an independent desire to fill his home life with them as well. His long-term partner, Steven Llanusa, a

Cuban-Italian elementary school teacher, however, was a predestined parent who, eight years into their relationship, had given Glenn an ultimatum to co-parent with him or part. Glenn's initial misgivings had been serious enough to rupture the couple's relationship for several months. Looking backward on this period, Glenn thought that he had been "suffering a bit of pre-parental panic," while Steven felt that he "was being forced to make a choice between his partner or being a parent," just the way Armando had felt. Although Steve had not wanted to face this choice, he had been determined that he "was not going to renege" on his commitment to parenthood. Fortunately for both men and, as it turns out, for the three Latino brothers whom they later adopted, couples counseling helped Glenn to work through his reservations and to reunite the couple.

Their co-parenting career began, Glenn said, by "parenting backwards." First they had signed up with a foster-care-parent program and taken in several teenagers, including one who was gay. Both the positive and negative aspects of their experiences as foster parents convinced them that they were ready to make a more permanent commitment to children. The couple's combined income was clearly sufficient to cover the expense of independent adoption, and perhaps even surrogacy, had they wished to pursue these options. Instead, however, they had enrolled in the county's fost-adopt program, choosing "very consciously to adopt elementary-school-age kids," because they believed that they could not afford to stay home as full-time parents and did not want to hire a nanny to take care of infants or toddlers. They chose, in other words, to undertake what most authorities consider to be the most difficult form of adoptive parenthood. Nor had they chosen to start, or to stop, with one "difficult-to-place" child. Rather, they had accepted first a set of seven-year-old Mexican American twin boys and their five-year-old brother soon afterword. The county had removed the three boys from drug-addicted parents. Both twins had acquired learning disabilities from fetal alcohol syndrome, and one had a prosthetic leg. All three boys had suffered parental neglect and been physically abused by their father, who was serving a prison sentence for extensive and repeated domestic violence.

Despite the formidable challenges of transracially adopting three school-age abused and neglected children with cognitive, physical, and emotional disabilities, or perhaps partly because of these facts, the Miya-Llanusa family had become a literal California poster family for gay fatherhood. Both parents and their three sons played active leadership roles in the Pop Luck Club; they all participated in public education and outreach within the gay

With their three sons as their best men, Steven Llanusa and Glenn Miya are married in California by the Rev. Dr. Homer D. Henderson, during the summer before the passage of Proposition 8 in November 2008. Photo courtesy of Steven Llanusa and Glenn Miya.

community and beyond; they spoke frequently to the popular media; they hosted massive community and holiday parties; and they served as general goodwill ambassadors for gay and multi-cultural family values in the boys' schools, sports teams, and dance classes and in their Catholic parish and their white, upper-middle-class suburban neighborhood.

Although Steve had been the predestined parent, and Glenn initially had been a reluctant, situational one, Glenn was the one who told me that he wouldn't mind emulating Eddie Leary's pattern of staying home to parent full-time, if his family had been able to afford forgoing the ample income that his pediatric practice earned. Ironically enough, the family probably could have afforded to forgo Steve's much less ample, middle-school teacher's salary. Steve, the predestined parent, however, loved his job and had no desire whatsoever to trade it in for full-time parenthood.

The Miya-Llanusa clan was still going strong and still going public with their enduring love and family story when I caught up with them again in October 2008. Love certainly had come first for this family, but it had taken twenty-two years before the state of California briefly allowed marriage to follow. In August 2008, Steve and Glenn had seized the moment and held a glorious, almost-traditional, religious and legal wedding ceremony, with all three, now teenage sons as ushers, and more than one hundred of their beaming family and friends in attendance. By then, Proposition 8 was on the California ballot, and Glenn and Steve had contributed their time, resources, and a photo-album slide show portraying the history of their love, marriage, and family to that unsuccessful political campaign to keep marriage legal for other California families like theirs.

Franny Has Five Gay Uncles

I never met three-year-old Franny, but I heard quite a bit about her from five men in my study who all qualified as situational non-parents. Franny had acquired five proud gay uncles because her married heterosexual parents, Sophia (predestined) and Jerry (situational), each had a gay brother who was in a committed, long-term partnership. A fifth bonus uncle appeared in Franny's deck because her father's gay brother is a member of the remarkable triad of committed mates we met in chapter 1. Franny's five uncles exhibited the full intermediate range of sentiments toward parenthood—from mild enthusiasm to mild discomfort. None expressed greater reluctance to parent or reservations that were graver than those Glenn Miya had overcome, and all agreed that a determined mate could have persuaded them to co-parent without provoking a crisis in the relationship. Instead, all five men had mated with other situational non-parents.

Sophia's brother Matt, the "sex pig," and his older partner, Robert, had never seriously considered adding children to their cozy domestic life. Playing an occasional avuncular role in Franny's world and doting daily on their beloved schnauzer amply satisfied this couple's modest parental libido. All three members of the gay trio, on the other hand, were more activist, engaged uncles to Franny and to two nephews who were related to them via other adult siblings. They happily babysat regularly, sometimes pinch-hitting for as long as a week so that their nieces' and nephews' parents could take child-free vacations. Unlike Matt and Robert, the triad had actively considered the question of adding a younger generation to their family. "We all like kids," the most enthusiastic of the three volunteered, "and we engaged in a lot of talk about it, about whether to try to adopt or something."

Social sensitivity had snuffed their insufficient ardor. They were realistic enough to grasp that "the irregular character" of their family would have geometrically expanded the difficulties that routinely confront gay men who seek children to adopt. They themselves even had worried that their unconventional brand of intimacy just might be "an unfair level of difference, of deviance to saddle on a kid." Given these serious concerns, their hands-on experiences with substitute parenting proved decisive, just as it had done with Michael David. Much as they loved the time they spent with Franny and with their nephews, they realized that "it's great being an uncle, and it's great being able to hand the kid back at the end of the visit." The last time that they had spent a week babysitting Franny full-time had tipped the scales away from seriously attempting parenthood. All three mates endorsed my belief that they would have been likely paternal prospects had they been heterosexual, or even if they had been more conventionally gay. Instead, Franny, her parents, and the rest of their extended families reap indirect kinship benefits from the situational childlessness of her five iconoclastic, but all happily mated, gay uncles. The trio was celebrating their tenth "triplet" anniversary and Matt and Robert their twenty-third as a couple when I reconnected with them in the fall of 2008.

Poly-Parent Families

Although the trio chose not to try to become a three-parent family, gay paternity often does lead to plural forms of parenthood and innovative family forms. Recall, for example, how gestational surrogacy generated a rich set of brave new extended kin for Eddie and Charles and their three children. When Bernardo, the black Latino with the white Australian lover, adopted his first biracial child, he developed a close, familial relationship with his social worker at the independent adoption agency—a white, straight woman. At her encouragement, he decided to move across country to her northeastern community to make his second adoption easier and because she offered to become a back-up child-care provider during the regular trips home that Bernardo's Australian partner had to make to renew his tourist visa.

Independent adoption often generates complex family ties. Many pregnant women choose this option so that they can select adoptive parents whom they like for their babies and who will maintain contact with them after the adoption has been finalized. That is one of the reasons for the steady growth in the number of children Drew and James were raising. Although there are no reliable data on this, gay men seem to have an advantage over lesbian or single straight women who seek gray-market babies, because some birth mothers find it easier to relinquish their babies to men than to women, just as Marya had felt about donating her eggs.

A pregnant woman who chooses gay men to adopt her offspring can hold on to her maternal status and avoid competitive, jealous feelings with infertile, adopting mothers.

It is true that most of the men in my study who adopted children through the gray market wanted their children to stay in touch with their birth mothers, and sometimes with their birth fathers as well. Drew and James even chose to operate "on a first-name basis" with their six (so far!) adopted children in order to reserve the terms *Mommy* and *Daddy* for their children's various genetic parents. Poly-parenting families do not always spring from such contingencies, however. Pursuing parenthood outside the box inspires some people to create intentional multi-parent families. As I foreshadowed earlier, three gay men in my study collaborated with lesbian friends to carefully design the following three- and four-parent families.

Front House/Back House

After thirteen years of close friendship, Paul (a white gay man) and Nancy (a white lesbian) decided to try to start a family together through alternative insemination. The two self-employed professionals spent the next two years carefully discussing their familial visions, values, expectations, anxieties, and limits. In October 1999, when Nancy began attempting to conceive their first child, they composed and signed a co-parenting agreement. They understood that the document would lack legal force but believed that going through the process of devising it would lay a crucial foundation for co-parenting. This agreement could serve as a model of ethical, sensitive planning for egalitarian, responsible co-parenting. In fact, it has already done so for several lesbian and gay friends of Paul's and Nancy's, and for two of mine. I do not know of any heterosexual couples who have approached the decision to parent together so thoughtfully. Perhaps this agreement can inspire some of them to do so too (see appendix for document).

Nancy and Paul were delighted, devoted biological and legal co-parents of a preschool-age son and an infant daughter when I interviewed them in 2001. They were not, however, the children's only parents. Before Nancy became pregnant with their first child, Cupid tested Paul's ability to live up to the sixth of the pair's prenatal pledges. Nancy had met and entered a romantic relationship with Liza, a woman who long had wanted to have children. Paul had risen to the challenge of supporting and incorporating Liza into his parenting alliance with Nancy, and so their son and daughter were born into a three-parent family. Nancy and Paul more than honored all of the pertinent terms in their shared parenting plan. Jointly they had purchased a duplex residential property. During the period of my study, Nancy and Liza lived together in the front house, Paul inhabited the back house, their toddler was sleeping alternate nights in each, and the breast-fed infant still was sharing her two mothers' bedroom every night. Paul and Nancy, the two primary parents, were fully sharing the major responsi-bilities and expenses along with the joys of parenthood. Both had reduced their weekly work schedules to three days so that each could devote two days weekly to full-time parenting. A hired nanny cared for the children on the fifth day. Liza, who was employed full-time, did early evening child care on the days that Nancy and Paul worked late, and she fully co-parented with them on weekends and holidays.

This three-parent family enjoyed the support of a thick community of kith and kin. One of Paul's former lovers was godfather to the children, and he visited frequently. The three-parent family celebrated holidays with extended formal and chosen kin, including another gay-parent family. Paul had been one of the core members of the Pop Luck Club and of its sub-group of perhaps ten or so at-home dads. On Fridays, Paul brought the children to the group's weekly play date in the Weho playground, where they often found Ossie and his two children and Eddie with his three.

The family was still intact when I contacted Paul and Nancy again in October 2008. Nancy and Liza had just celebrated their tenth anniversary as a couple, and Paul was still single. All three were then involved in the unsuccessful campaign to defeat Prop 8, even though Nancy and Liza had chosen not to get married themselves during the legal interval. Over the intervening years, Liza had survived a life-threatening illness and gradu-ally expanded her role as a third parent. After her recovery, she found work close to home, which allowed her more time with the children. The chil-dren attended school with several of their former PLC play-group friends, including Eddie and Charles's three children. All three parents would have preferred a bit more living space, but they were not willing to move unless they could find a larger, affordable duplex habitat nearby.

Nancy and Paul had not bothered to renegotiate the original co-parent-ing agreement to reflect Liza's expanded role as a third parent. In fact, they had never even referred to the written document, because, as Nancy wrote, "We're often too busy parenting!" The agreement had served its purpose as an effective launching pad for discussing and initiating their shared par-enting framework. Once launched, however, successful parenting did not need to be codified. In Nancy's wise words, "Parenting has to be kept flexible so it can live and breathe over time."

Careful Fourplay

A second successfully planned poly-parent family included two moms, two dads, and two homes. Lisa and Kat, a monogamous, white lesbian couple, had initiated this family when after fifteen years together, they had asked their dear friend and former housemate, Michael Harwood, to serve as the sperm donor and an acknowledged father to the children they wished to rear. It had taken Michael, a white gay man who was single at that time, five years of serious reflection and discussions before he finally agreed to do so. "There is really no way to express the complexity of my journey," Michael related in an account he wrote for a gay magazine, "or to impart the richness of the experience. Given the rare opportunity to truly think about whether or not I wanted to be a parent (as opposed to having it sprung upon me), I left no rock unturned—no hiking trail was untread."[27]

Gradually Michael had realized that he did not wish to become a parent unless he too had a committed mate: "I told them that I could not do it alone (without a partner). I thought about what it would be like going through parenthood without a significant partner with whom to discuss and share things. It seemed too isolating."[28] Fortuitously, just when his lesbian friends were reaching the end of their patience, Michael met and fell in love with Joaquín, a Chicano, gay predestined parent who had always wanted children. The new lovers asked Lisa and Kat to give them a year to solidify their union before embarking on co-parenthood. Both couples reported that they spent that year in a four-way parental courtship:

> Joaquín and I had many talks and all four of us were, quite frankly, falling in love with each other in a way that can only be described as romantic love. There were flowers, there were candlelight dinners, and there were many beach walks and much laughter. There were many brave conversations about our needs and our fears and our excitement. There was nothing that could prepare us for the first night when Joaquín and I went to Lisa and Kat's home to make love and leave a specimen. . . . By the way, it is NOT a turkey baster but a syringe that is used. Love was the main ingredient, though, and Joaquín and I experienced a transcendent epiphany as we walked along the beach after the exchange. We knew that our lives

and our relationship to Lisa and Kat would never be the same even if the conception did not happen. We shared, perhaps, the most intimate of experiences with Lisa and Kat.[29]

Since that magical night, the two couples also had shared many of the intimate joys and burdens of parenting two children. Unlike Nancy and Paul, however, they did not try to equalize parental rights and responsibilities. Lisa and Michael are the children's biological and legal parents, with both of their names on both of the birth certificates. The children resided, however, with Lisa and Kat, who are their primary, daily caretakers and their chief providers. Lisa, who gave birth to and breast-fed both children, also spent the most time with them, primarily because Kat's employment demanded more time outside the home. Although Michael and Joaquín lived and worked more than seventy-five miles away, they had visited their children every single weekend of the children's lives as well as on occasional weeknights. They also conferred with the co-moms and spoke, sang, read, or sent emails to their preschooler almost daily. In addition, the adults consciously sustained, monitored, and nurtured their co-parenting alliance and friendship by scheduling periodic "parent time" for the four adults to spend together while the children slept.

This four-parent family, like the three-parent front-house/back-house family and like the surrogacy-extended family that Eddie and Mama Sally nurtured, regularly shared holidays and social occasions with a wide array of legal and chosen kin. They too were immersed in a large local community of lesbian- and gay-parent families, a community which Lisa had taken the initiative to organize. Three proud sets of doting grandparents were constantly vying for visits, photos, and contact with their grandchildren. In painful contrast, Kat's parents had rejected her when she came out, and they refused to incorporate, or even to recognize, their grandchildren or any of their lesbian daughter's family members within their more rigid, ideological understanding of family.

I was able to meet with Michael again when we were both visiting the Bay Area in August of 2009. He had no major changes to report about his poly-parenting family. They had gone through "some rough patches" and dealt with thorny issues, predictably enough, in the intervening years. But, he said, "things are still pretty solid," and the basic patterns and understandings of both their couple and parenting relationships were the same as before. Michael's and Joaquín's employment situations had both improved, and they were contributing more financial support to the kids.

They were no longer visiting them every single weekend because of the toll the weekly trips had begun to take on their own relationship, work, and friendships. However, they never let more than two weeks pass without a visit, and now they had one or both children alone with them on school vacations. Their older son, now ten years old, had begun to seek out some private paternal time, especially with Michael. Lisa and Kat had married during the California window, but Michael and Joaquín had chosen not to follow suit.

The Contingency of Contemporary Parenthood

This colorful quilt of lucky, and less lucky, gay pop stories from my research opens a window onto the vagaries of contemporary paths to parenthood generally and to paternity specifically. Because I intentionally over-sampled for fathers when I was recruiting participants for my study, I wound up including a disproportionate number of predestined parents. Their stories help us to understand some complex connections between romantic partnership and parenthood today. Most, if not all, of the fervently motivated dads strongly wished to combine the two forms of intimacy. Some even had made parenthood a pivotal courtship criterion, and the luckiest of these, like Eddie and Charles and Ossie and Harry, found compatible predestined partners. However, if push comes to shove for a predestined parent, children will trump coupledom and can even thwart it, as we have seen. Although Armando deeply desired and attempted to combine partnership with parenthood, he was ultimately unwilling to sacrifice the latter on the pyre of adult intimacy. On the other hand, parenthood can prove a pathway to coupling for a fortunate few who, like Drew and Bernardo, find that their parental status enhances their appeal to other predestined parents.

Although gay male culture conjures up anti-familial images of sexual and personal self-indulgence to critics, including to some gay fathers like Armando, I encountered very few parental refuseniks during my research. The majority of the gay men I studied neither avidly yearned for parenthood nor categorically spurned it. Most agreed that they would have been likely to succumb, with varying levels of resistance or grace, to the entreaties or demands of a determined partner, as Glenn Miya had done when his partner, Steve, issued his ultimatum.[30] Without facing such pressure, however, most gay men seem able to forgo parenthood without serious regrets.

A study of the desire to parent among ninety-four gay men in New York reported that nineteen of the men proclaimed a desire to parent and eleven rejected it, but the vast majority (fifty-eight) expressed ambivalence.[31] Ambivalence seems to describe the dominant parental outlook of most contemporary men, whatever their sexual desires.

Although women and men occupy all points along the spectrum of parental desire, clearly they do not do so equally. Men and women display average differences here, as they do with most traits and preferences. For example, a Dutch study that compared planned lesbian and heterosexual two-parent families found that, on average, the heterosexual fathers scored the lowest in the strength of their desire to have children. Lesbian biological mothers earned the highest scores on this measure, followed next by lesbian social mothers and then by heterosexual mothers.[32] Many other social indices imply that women handily dominate the predestined end of the parental yearnings arc, while men would win a refusenik derby with their hands tied behind their backs.

Increasing numbers of single women today who are disappointed in love nonetheless, like Christie Malcomson, "choose to be a parent."[33] In contrast, the ranks of straight men who emulate Armando, Damian, Bernardo, or Drew by pursuing parenthood solo are thin indeed.[34] Of course, male biology erects a significant barrier to gender equity here, but one that gay men appear more motivated than their straight counterparts to hurdle. Straight men also are less likely than gay men like Eddie to regard full-time at-home parenting as their calling. In fact, an analysis of data in the 2000 Census found that families headed by two gay dads were even a bit more likely than those headed by lesbian co-moms or married moms and dads to include a full-time at-home parent.[35] And as the marriage-promotion movement emphasizes, data on the comparative weakness of paternal ties to children after divorce are disturbingly strong.[36]

There are numerous reasons to believe that fewer straight men than gay men feel a predestined urge to parent. For one thing, by definition, if not by disposition, gay men are already gender dissidents. Living without wives or girlfriends, they have to participate in caretaking and domestic chores more than straight men do and are less likely to find these activities threatening to their masculine identities. Second, gay men are more likely to be single than are straight men or than are women of whatever sexual orientation.[37] That translates into a higher percentage of men like Armando, Damian, and Michael David who are apt to feel drawn to seek compensatory intimacy through parenthood. On the carrot side of the ledger, gay dads enjoy easier access than most straight dads do to primary parenting status and its rewards and to support networks for their families, like the PLC, COLAGE, or Family Week in Provincetown.

Gay men also face less pressure to conform to gender scripts for parenting or to defer to women's biological and cultural advantages for nurturing young children. Gay fatherhood, that is to say, occupies terrain more akin to conventional motherhood than to dominant forms of paternity. In fact, many of the sporadic debates that erupted on the PLC listserv over appropriate parenting standards (including nutrition, bedtime rituals, discipline, toy weapons, cloth vs. disposable diapers, and TV fare) were so familiar to me that I dubbed them the "Mr. Mommy Wars." The month before the annual Gay Pride parade in 2002, however, a less generic internal conflict broke out on the list over plans for a PLC contingent to march in the parade. Several member dads did not approve of the parade's sexualized displays. Others debated the pros and cons of exposing their children to gay sexuality or to hostility from potential anti-gay protestors whom the march was likely to attract.

The unmooring of masculinity from paternity exposes the situational character of contemporary fatherhood and fatherlessness. No longer a mandatory route to masculine adult social status, paternity today is increasingly contingent on the fate of men's romantic attachments. In fact, to attain any form of parenthood today requires either the unequivocal yearning of at least one adult or a more or less accidental pregnancy, like egg donor Marya's. In other words, contemporary maternity has also become increasingly situational, a fact that is reflected in declining fertility rates and is satirized in popular culture. An ironic feminist greeting card that circulated widely in the late 1970s, for example, featured a Warhol-style female character who laments, "Oh dear, I forgot to have children!"

Nonetheless, the majority of women still skew toward the predestined pole of the desire-to-parent continuum. Men, in contrast, regardless of their sexual inclinations, generally cluster along the situational bandwidth. Heterosexual "situations" lead most straight men into paternity (and straight women to maternity). Homosexual situations, on the other hand, lead most gay men to forgo parenthood. (Lesbian situations likely lie somewhere in between.)[38] If this contrast seems obvious, even tautological, it was not always the case. Instead, most contemporary gay fathers became parents while they were enmeshed in closeted homosexual "situations." *Far from Heaven,* a popular 2002 film about the unraveling of a picture-perfect 1950s marriage, and the recent political sex scandals involving former New

Jersey governor Jim McGreevey and U.S. senator Larry Craig, among others, remind us of the intense pressure men with homoerotic desires long have felt to suppress or shield their stigmatized yearnings by entering into heterosexual marriages.[39] The past few decades of hard-won gains in gay struggles for social acceptance have diminished the need for men with homoerotic desires to resort to this ruse.

Paradoxically, the same shift from closeted to open homosexuality which has made gay fatherhood so visible might also reduce its incidence. Beyond the closet, far fewer gay men than before will become situational parents because they entered heterosexual marriages to pass as straight. Openly gay paternity, by definition, is never accidental. It requires the determined efforts of at least one gay man, like Armando, Eddie, Steven, Damian, or Harry, whose passion for parenthood feels predestined—a man, that is, whose parental desires more conventionally might be labeled maternal rather than paternal. "For most heterosexual men," gay author and situational dad Jesse Green observes, "the birth of a child, a son especially, seems to confirm their masculinity, however idiotic the connection may be. Was it possible that, for a gay man, adopting a son would have the opposite effect? A single father would be first a mother, and thus, in a way, *less* of a man."[40]

The gay dads I studied did not feel that parenting made them less, or more, of a man. Instead, most felt free to express a full palette of gender options. As Drew put it, "I feel that I have a wider emotional range available to me than maybe most of the straight men I know. And I feel comfortable being mother, father, silly gay man, silly queen, tough negotiator in business. I feel like I'm not bound by rules." Rather than a bid for legitimate masculine status, or a rejection of it, intentional gay parenthood represents a search for enduring love and intimacy in a world of contingency and flux.

Of course, there is nothing distinctively gay or masculine about this quest. Heterosexual masculinity also no longer depends upon marriage or parenthood. Indirectly, therefore, gay male paths to planned parenthood highlight the waning of traditional incentives for pursuing the status of fatherhood as we knew it. Parenthood, like marriage and mating practices, has entered contingent terrain. The facetious observation about our endangered species in the first epigraph to this chapter may be halfway accurate. Without "masculine" cravings for sex and "feminine" yearnings for babies, paternity, but not male or female parenthood, might wither away. That form of "fatherlessness" should not be cause for alarm.

How the Gender and Sexual Orientation of Parents Matter

The fact that gay men now pursue parenthood outside social conventions of gender, marriage, and procreation catapults them into the vanguard of contemporary parenting. Just as gay men are at once freer and more obliged than most of the rest of us to craft the basic terms of their romantic and domestic unions, so too they have to make more self-conscious decisions about whether to parent, with whom, and how. I hope that the thoughtful, magnanimous, child-centered co-parenting agreement that Paul and Nancy devised will inspire throngs of prospective parents to undertake similar discussions before deciding whether baby should make three, or four or more, for that matter.

Like Nancy and Paul, most lesbians and gay men who choose to co-parent favor comparatively egalitarian and flexible approaches to sharing child care and breadwinning.[41] They presume, quite correctly, that an individual parent's character, capacities, and foibles count for more than biology or gender conventions do in shaping parenting behaviors. Gay male and female parents alike nurture, discipline, socialize, subsidize, organize, challenge, comfort, delight, and inspire their children, as well as disappoint, disturb, frustrate, neglect, and abuse them. Gay parenting gives the lie to the popular, but misguided, naturalist belief that women and men are inherently different kinds of parents.[42] This is not to deny the likelihood that even if we were to achieve a fully egalitarian feminist utopia, more women than men still might discover their inner at-home parent, like Eddie has done. The crucial point, however, is that already today, men like Eddie, Paul, Ossie, Harry, and their friends in the PLC at-home dads group are eagerly investing more of their lives taking care of their children than do the vast majority of contemporary mothers in advanced industrial democracies.

Most opponents of gay parenting, however, subscribe to pervasive, "commonsense" prejudices about gender differences in parenting. They often claim that social science research supports their conviction that women and men are distinctly different kinds of parents, that nature makes women more nurturing and men better disciplinarians, and that it is rational, therefore, to conclude, as the 2006 New York State court ruling against same-sex marriage did, "that it is better, other things being equal, for children to grow up with both a mother and a father."[43] Thus, former president George W. Bush defended Florida's ban on gay adoption rights by contending that "studies have shown that the ideal is where a child is raised in a married family with a man and a woman."[44] Similarly, an expert witness testifying against legal same-sex marriage in the state of Washington stated that his "extensive review of the published research on the need that every child has for both a mother and a father" confirmed that "children not raised by their own married mother and father are subject to increased risk of disadvantage and harm."[45]

This appeal to social science, however, commits two of the most common misuses of statistics. It confuses correlation with causation, and it mistakes average differences for dichotomous ones. Women, *on average*, do seem to be more likely than men, *on average*, to feel themselves predestined to parent, for example, and to become emotionally close to their children.[46] However, just as with gender differences in height, speed, or a yen for action films, these are not gender-exclusive monopolies. We all know many women who are taller or run faster than many men, and some of us even know straight men who admit to enjoying chick flicks. So, too, when it comes to parental passions. Some women are absolute refuseniks (in fact, increasing numbers, now that women are freer to refuse), while some men, like Eddie, Ossie, Harry, Armando, Steven, and Bernardo, yearn for and delight in parenthood just as much as Christie Malcomson did.

The contemporary marriage-promotion movement in the United States commits both methodological errors when it identifies fatherlessness as "the leading cause of declining child well-being in our society" and as "the engine driving our most urgent social problems, from crime to adolescent pregnancy to child sexual abuse to domestic violence against women."[47] I agree that there are good reasons to worry about men's declining involvement in parenthood, but the impact of fatherlessness on children who have gay dads or lesbian moms clearly is not one of them. And even though we do not yet have much research on how children develop in planned gay-male-parent families, so far nothing indicates that their children are suffering harmful effects from this kind of "motherlessness."

We do, however, have dozens of studies conducted over more than three decades on "fatherless" children raised by lesbian co-moms. By now social scientists have achieved overwhelming consensus that these children turn out at least as well as children who grow up with their married moms and dads.[48] Apart from matters related to social stigma and discrimination, the studies find very few measurable differences between children raised by lesbian or straight couples, and the rare differences that show up in this research more often favor the children with two lesbian moms.[49] Most likely, this is not because lesbianism per se makes a woman a better parent. Instead, differences in the ways lesbian and straight couples become parents and how they share the work and play lead to some advantages through what social scientists call "selection effects." It generally augurs well for children when they have comparatively mature and educated parents who deeply desired them and carefully planned for parenthood. Intentional lesbian co-parenting "selects" for these auspicious factors. Gay men, of course, face even higher entry bars to parenthood than do lesbians, and so their children seem certain to reap benefits from these stringent selection effects. The many hours over several years that I spent observing gay dads with their children in their homes, at parties, in churches, marches, and meetings, on playgrounds, in restaurants, and at the beach in Los Angeles gave me great confidence that future research will find that these (not always) "motherless" children fare at least as well as their conventionally mothered peers.

Of course, it should go without saying that not all gay parents are saints or wizards, and, unlike the kids in Garrison Keillor's mythical Lake Wobegone, not all of their children are above average. Just as with straight parents, a few gay parents in my study had survived traumatic, messy breakups before I met them, and some were struggling to cope with disturbed, disabled, and hostile children. A few parents struck me as over-protective, overly indulgent, or too demanding. However, a remarkable proportion of the families in my study seemed to have achieved enviable harmonious, loving, responsible, committed, ethical, and enduring bonds with their children, their co-parents, and their communities.

In the fall of 2008, I was able to locate nine of the eleven families from my original study that had included gay men who had been co-parenting by 2003. Defying the cultural odds, all of these relationships and families were still intact, and seven of the co-parenting couples within these families had married over the prior few months. In fact, as I mentioned before, I learned of only two couples among all of the participants in my original study who had broken up since 2003 — Jake and Shawn and a closeted African American gay couple who had asked me not to write about their relationship. Neither of these couples had been among the co-parents.

Protecting Marriage Won't Protect Enough Children or Families

It is not easy to understand why advocates of heterosexual marriage promotion imagine that denying marriage to same-sex parents constitutes a pro-child goal. As frustrated gay parents often point out, preventing them from marrying certainly does not benefit their children. How other children gain from such exclusion is neither apparent nor just.[50] Even if it were true, as the New York State court reasoned, "that it is better, other things being equal, for children to grow up with both a mother and a father,"[51] maintaining a heterosexual monopoly over marriage will not increase the ranks of children who will grow up that way. In any case, it is not true, and other things are certainly not equal. As I have discussed, "fatherless" children who have lesbian parents fare just as well as children of heterosexual children, and the same most likely will prove true for "motherless" children growing up with dads like Eddie, Charles, Ossie, Harry, Armando, Damian, Drew, Bernardo, Steven, Glenn, and so many others.

On the other hand, although I support same-sex marriage on equal-rights grounds, I do not agree with gay-marriage advocates that this is a genuinely pro-child platform either. True, it would admit children with two married lesbian or two gay male parents into the privileged family circle, but only by helping to justify discrimination against many other children and parents—children with gay single parents like Armando, gay and lesbian poly-parents like Paul, Nancy, and Liza, and children and loved ones in millions of other contemporary families that do not include married parents, whether gay, straight, or otherwise. Gay men generate only a small fraction of these families, but as we have seen, some of those offer unusually creative and successful models of alternative domesticity.

The contemporary gay rights movement's focus on marriage as the crucial gateway to family equality and as the way to protect children who have gay parents threatens to curtail and penalize such creativity. When Michael Howard (one of the two gay dads in the four-parent family discussed earlier) and I conversed again in 2009, he confessed to feeling disappointed that he wasn't seeing many younger gay men who were following the path to poly-parenthood that he and Joaquín had embraced, or who were devising other new forms of family. Michael wondered whether "queerer" families like his "may have been a historic blip" now that so many younger gay men and lesbians seem eager to replicate the heterosexual model of married, nuclear family life.

Unfortunately, many of the impressive, innovative parenting relationships in my study remain invisible and vulnerable because of the massive disjuncture between their lived and legal statuses. Family law, social science research, and public policy often echo and reinforce a hurtful, exclusionary definition of family rather than the more generous, pragmatic, and creative understandings of family I have described in this chapter. Census data and most demographic surveys, for example, would have recorded the three-parent family consisting of Paul, Nancy, Liza, and their children as two un-related households, one headed by a same-sex female couple, the other by a single man.[52] Paul and Nancy would each have appeared to be unmarried parents who shared legal and physical custody of their biological children. Although Liza had served as an active third parent to both children since their birth and contributed financial support along with daily care, her pa-rental role is legally and linguistically invisible. She possesses no rights or responsibilities. No kinship terms identify her relationships to her children or to Paul.

The same is true for the four-parent, geographically dispersed family crafted by Lisa, Kat, Michael, and Joaquín. To a census taker, these would have appeared to be two unrelated households in distinct census tracts. One household might be recorded as including an unmarried mother, her two biological children, and her same-sex, registered domestic partner; the second, as housing a domestic partnership between a non-residential fa-ther and a childless man. Yet Kat and Lisa had spent five years jointly plan-ning for their children, and they have co-parented them from the get-go. Kat also had been her children's principal breadwinner for several years. Nonetheless, Kat, like Liza, was a legally invisible parent. Even though Kat and Lisa had joined the thousands of same-sex couples in California who rushed to marry while it was briefly possible in 2008, California law would treat Kat as a married step-parent, because Michael did not relinquish legal paternity. Judicial precedents do not recognize the poly-parenting arrange-ment that Lisa, Kat, Michael, and Joaquín devised. They would offer Kat no clear grounds to petition for child custody or visitation in the event of a custody conflict or if Lisa dies. Kat could only be legally recognized as her children's co-parent if Michael were to relinquish his legal paternal rights and responsibilities.[53]

Of the seven parents in these two poly-parent families, Joaquín was by far the most invisible and unprotected. He had matched Michael's love, attention, and commitment to their children in every possible way since before they were conceived. His three co-parents all reported that their firstborn found Joaquín's infectiously warm, playful, and easygoing charm so irresistible that he seemed to favor Joaquín a bit over Michael. Yet, be-cause Joaquín was not a biological, residential, or adoptive parent of either child, he had no legal claim to paternity whatsoever. In addition, the vis-ible physical contrast between Joaquín's dark Latino features and those of his tow-headed, blue-eyed, fair-skinned, Anglo kids immediately signaled their racial-ethnic difference and often evoked confusion, discomfort, and worse from strangers who encountered this father out alone with his children in playgrounds and other public spaces.

All of the gay and lesbian parents in my study whom I was able to contact in 2008 were actively supporting the campaign to defeat Proposition 8. Five of the original eight co-parenting gay couples I located, including Eddie and Charles, Drew and James, Steven Llanusa and Glenn Miya, and Lisa and Kat (but not Michael and Joaquín), had rushed to hold gay "shotgun" weddings during California's brief window of legal opportunity. Legal marriage held potent symbolic and emotional meaning for them and for most of their children in addition to the significant material benefits it bestowed. Legal marital status, however, would have done nothing to recognize or protect the complex parenting and kin relationships in several of the families I have described. It would not have conferred parental status on Kat, Joaquín, or Liza, for example, or legitimated the deep family bonds that Eddie and Charles and their three children have forged with gestational surrogate Mama Sally and her husband and two children, or the genetic half-sibling relationships between egg donor Mama Marya's two youngsters and the three she helped create for Eddie and Charles.

Legal marriage offers no benefits to the children of gay or straight single parents like Armando or Damian. And, of course, it would have been utterly irrelevant to the mutually sustaining intergenerational bonds Mother Randolph had formed with Dino and the other "boys," or to all of the heroic networks of care that gay men and their allies created in response to the catastrophic impact of AIDS. In fact, legalizing same-sex marriage would do more to exacerbate the invisibility of parents and kin in these families. As Nancy Polikoff methodically documents in *Beyond (Straight and Gay) Marriage,* it would also reinforce pervasive discrimination against all unmarried adults and the people they nurture.

I believe that Liza, Kat, and Joaquín deserve better than that. Armando and his son Ramón deserve better. Christie Malcomson and her children do too. And so do the rest of us. In chapter 1, I described the creative terms of erotic intimacy devised by gay men like Franny's five gay uncles—Matt and Robert and the indomitable trio—in order to inspire us to redefine fidelity. I hope equally that the inventive kaleidoscope of planned parenting patterns that gay fathers in this chapter pioneered will help to move our public conversations about the best way for children to grow up well beyond the flawed concept of "fatherlessness" as well as beyond marriage, whether gay or straight.

3

A South African Slant on the Slippery Slope

Among the likeliest effects of gay marriage is to take us down a slippery slope to legalized polygamy and "polyamory" (group marriage).
— Stanley Kurtz, "Beyond Gay Marriage," 2003

Anyone else bored to tears with the "slippery slope" arguments against gay marriage? Since few opponents of homosexual unions are brave enough to admit that gay weddings just freak them out, they hide behind the claim that it's an inexorable slide from legalizing gay marriage to having sex with penguins outside JC Penney's.
— Dahlia Lithwick, "Slippery Slop," 2004

It's only a matter of time before the homosexual agenda in South Africa reaches an even more radical level, as it already has in the USA, where certain groups are seeking to legalize pedophilia, polygamy and polyandry.
— James Dobson, "An Open Letter to South Africans on Same-Sex Marriage," 2005

IN THE SPRING of 2008, two remarkable interventions in U.S. family life riveted the mainstream media and the blogosphere.[1] On April 3, state authorities raided the Yearning for Zion (YFZ) Ranch in Eldorado, Texas, in what they described as "the largest child-welfare operation in Texas history."[2] The ranch was the polygamous Fundamentalist Latter Day Saints (FLDS) compound founded by Warren Jeffs, who now is serving a prison sentence for compelling a fourteen-year-old girl to marry her nineteen-year-old cousin, and the raid was the most coercive state offensive against polygamy to take place in the United States in over fifty years. In an action that the Texas Supreme Court later judged illegitimate, the Lone Star State forcibly removed hundreds of children from their mothers and families without any specific complaints that they had been abused or neglected.[3]

Six weeks later, on May 15, 2008, the California Supreme Court issued the fateful decision in favor of same-sex marriage that incited thousands of gay and lesbian couples, including Eddie and Charles, Drew and James, Steven and Glenn, and Lisa and Kat, to wed during the six months before passage of Prop 8 snuffed out their chance to do so.

These two compelling events in U.S. family politics were unrelated. Nonetheless, California Chief Justice Ronald George felt the need in his majority opinion to specify that the court's ruling for the right to same-sex marriage "does not affect the constitutional validity of the existing legal prohibitions against polygamy and the marriage of close relatives."[4] The chief justice's gratuitous caveat testifies to the cultural influence of slippery slope arguments against same-sex marriage, like the one in the first epigraph to this chapter, by conservative Hoover Institute scholar Stanley Kurtz. Similarly, when the U.S. Supreme Court overturned laws against sodomy in *Lawrence v. Texas* in 2003, Justice Scalia issued a stinging dissent that charged the Court with paving a "slippery slope" to legal gay marriage, bigamy, bestiality, and the end of all laws based on moral choices.[5] The excesses of the Eldorado raid and of the language in the California decision that associated plural marriage with incest both indicate the extremity of cultural antipathy to polygamy in the United States.

Small wonder, therefore, that so many U.S. advocates for same-sex marriage take great pains to distance their cause from the slightest taint of association with polygamy. Immediately after the California decision, for example, a prominent gay newspaper, the *Washington Blade,* published an article titled "Will Gay Marriage Lead to Legalized Polygamy? Legal Experts Respond to Arguments of Conservative Activists," which featured reassurances "that the California Supreme Court ruling has nothing to do with polygamy."[6] Most gay rights supporters, like Dahlia Lithwick in the second epigraph to this chapter, dismiss warnings that same-sex marriage will pave the way for polygamy as mere rhetorical ruses for homophobia.[7] Some legal scholars have addressed the genuine constitutional questions raised by the slippery slope argument.[8] Curiously, however, public discussions of this topic ignore the fact that the relationship between legal same-sex and plural marriage is no longer exclusively hypothetical. There actually is one nation in the world in which both forms of marriage are legal.

Just a few months before the two U.S. events, polygamy and same-sex marriage attracted public attention in another liberal democracy a distant hemisphere away. Two high-profile weddings on the same day shared front-page mainstream media coverage in South Africa. On January 5,

High Court of Appeal Justice Edwin Cameron officiating at the wedding of Zackie Achmat and Dali Wyers, Cape Town, January 5, 2008. Reprinted by permission of the *Sunday Times*; photo by Esa Alexander.

2008, Zackie Achmat, a Nobel Peace Prize nominee and arguably the most prominent AIDS activist in Africa, married his longtime companion, Dalli Wyers, an HIV/AIDS researcher. High Court of Appeal Justice Edwin Cameron, who has since been appointed to the Constitutional Court, proudly officiated over the interracial, same-sex wedding. Justice Cameron, who like his good friend Achmat is openly gay and HIV positive, described the wedding as "not just an intimate act of love, it's also a political affirmation."[9] Yet unlike Justice Roberts in California, Cameron felt no need to distance the ceremony from another notable South African wedding that was taking place that day. Also on January 5, 2008, Jacob Zuma, who had just been elected president of the African National Congress (ANC) Party and is now the president of South Africa, celebrated a customary Zulu wedding ceremony for his polygynous marriage to the mother of two of his many children.[10] Post-apartheid South Africa is the only nation in the world where these concurrent weddings could legally occur, because it alone recognizes both plural and same-sex marriages.

I doubt that many people noticed the convergence of any of these four events or that I would have connected them either had I not already been studying family diversity in South Africa and the United States. In

President-elect Jacob Zuma in a traditional Zulu wedding ceremony marries one of his plural wives on January 5, 2008. Reprinted by permission of AP Photo/Simphiwe Nkwali —The Times.

the 1980s, I was among thousands of people who participated in the international divestment campaigns against the apartheid regime and who were later inspired by South Africa's relatively peaceful transition to a constitutional democracy. In the wake of the disappointing defeat of the Equal Rights Amendment in the United States, it was particularly stirring for feminists of my generation when the new South African constitution of 1996 became the first in the world to ban discrimination on grounds of gender and sexual orientation, as well as race.[11] It was only by my chance attendance at a plenary session held at a family research conference in Kansas City in 1996, however, that I discovered that South Africa had also embarked upon a vanguard experiment in family democracy. Invited speaker Nontombi Naomi Tutu, the daughter of Archbishop Desmond Tutu, alluded to anguishing conflicts over family policy that the South African law-reform commission had confronted during its deliberations over the new constitution. Ms. Tutu described bitter clashes between traditional leaders who demanded constitutional protections for customary African

marriages, which included polygyny, and activists committed to full gender and sexual equality, including same-sex marriage and gay family rights.

This serendipitous event stoked my curiosity about gender and sexual
politics in the new South Africa. Nearly a decade passed, however, before
I decided to reconsider U.S. hostility to polygamy, as well as our pitched
battles over same-sex marriage and gay parenthood, by way of a comparative detour through the thickets of South African family politics. It took
only cursory study to realize that de jure and de facto support for family
diversity generally, and for same-sex marriage and polygamy specifically,
were as upside down in South Africa and the United States as is our geography. South Africa sets the gold standard for pluralist family law, including
legal recognition for both same-sex and plural marriage. However, de facto
conditions of inequality in South Africa are still among the steepest in the
world, and an entrenched culture of patriarchal domination and virulent
homophobia visit severe, sometimes deadly consequences upon many who
seek to exercise their rights. Directly inverse, the United States leads the
world in de facto family diversity. Our national family history encompasses
a cornucopia of experimentation, including polygamous and same-sex
unions.[12] Ever since the federal government forcibly abolished Mormon
polygamy more than a century ago, outlaw communities of fundamentalist
Mormon, polygynous families, like the residents of YFZ, have persisted as
open secrets in Utah, Arizona, and adjacent states, while gay and lesbian
unions and parenting enjoy increasing national visibility and acceptance.

Paradoxically, however, contemporary family law in the United States
could snare a rearguard crown among liberal democracies, albeit with
significant local inconsistencies, because the U.S. Constitution allocates
family law to the states. Just when campaigns for same-sex marriage were
tallying stunning victories in unlikely nations like South Africa and Catholic Spain, as well as in northern Europe and Canada, the U.S. government
was promoting major efforts to reverse the trend at home, including the
Defense of Marriage Act (DOMA), a proposed Federal Marriage Amendment, and the Federal Marriage Initiative. In addition, scores of states were
instituting bans against same-sex marriage, like Prop 8 in California in
2008.[13] Recently too, after a fifty-year hiatus, two U.S. states initiated criminal prosecutions for bigamy, and Texas is prosecuting several residents of
the YFZ compound.[14]

These provocative contrasts convinced me that South Africa offered a
unique, instructive opportunity to scrutinize family debates in the United
States from an alternative, and salutary, slant. After an exploratory visit to

South Africa in 2004, I conducted background research on post-apartheid family and sexual jurisprudence, legislation, activism, and public discourse. In June and July of 2007, I returned to South Africa to conduct two months of field research on family practices and politics, including extensive interviewing and observations of public figures, private families, relevant organizations, activities, and events. I conducted lengthy interviews with Constitutional Court justices and their law clerks, gay activists and lawyers, ANC elected officials, and officers of the National House of Traditional Leaders (NHTL) and Contralesa (Congress of Traditional Leaders). I also visited and interviewed members of polygynous families in Johannesburg and in rural Kwa-Zulu Natal.

This chapter and the next draw on this research to take the slippery slope argument seriously. I compare the links between legal and popular treatment of same-sex marriage and polygamy in the two nations to gain fresh perspectives on whether these divergent alternatives to monogamous, heterosexual marriage share significant social sources, affinities, or fates. This chapter considers whether dropping gender restrictions on who can marry creates pressures to shed numerical constraints as well. The next chapter draws on recent South African experience with polygamy to reconsider the potent aversion to it in the United States. Is plural marriage incompatible with democracy and inherently oppressive to women and children, as U.S. policies, as well as most feminists, seem to presume? Does criminalizing polygamy serve women's interests? Would legalizing plural marriage promote or constrain promiscuity? What impact, if any, would legal polygamy be likely to have on monogamous marriage? Who would gain and who would lose if plural marriage ever were to become legal in the United States? A close look at the contrasting de jure and de facto experiences with marital diversity in South Africa and the United States suggests some unexpected answers to these questions.

South Africa

Vanguard Family Pluralism De Jure

If judged only by the letter of the law, post-apartheid South Africa looks like a human rights utopia. Determined to repudiate the evils of apartheid, the Founding Provisions of the new 1996 constitution enshrined human dignity, equality, and human rights, as well as non-racialism and non-sexism, as the core values of the new republic. To great international acclaim, the constitution became the first in the world to ban discrimination based not only on race but also on culture, gender, and sexual orientation. Less noticed, the expansive equality clause of the Bill of Rights also explicitly forbids discrimination on grounds of marital status: "The state may not unfairly discriminate directly or indirectly against anyone on one or more grounds, including race, gender, sex, pregnancy, marital status, ethnicity or social origin, colour, sexual orientation, age, disability, religion, conscience, belief, culture, language and birth."[15] These constitutional commitments to honor both culture and sex equality produce a prickly paradox, however, because many of the protected indigenous African cultures include deeply patriarchal practices, like polygyny. South African courts must continually struggle to reconcile patriarchal customs with sex equality principles.[16]

Polygamy and same-sex marriage both have gained legal status since 1996, but not in the order that the U.S. slippery slope argument predicts. Legalizing same-sex marriage did not open the marital floodgates to plural marriage in South Africa. Instead, the post-apartheid state legalized customary polygamy *before* it accepted gay unions. In 1998, Parliament passed the Recognition of Customary Marriages Act (RCMA) after complex political negotiations. The RCMA represents an uneasy compromise between feminists, who sought to outlaw polygyny, and traditional African leaders, who continue to resist subjecting their customary cultural practices to gender equality principles.[17] The RCMA aims to ensure that women consent to customary African marriages and to protect their rights to property within these marriages. To guard the monogamous character of civil marriage, however, it forbids spouses in a civil marriage from registering additional customary marriages. To promote women's rights, it requires customary wives to give their consent before their husbands can take another bride, and it provides community property rights to women within customary marriages.[18]

Most South African feminists wanted the new society to abolish polygyny, but feminist organizations went along with the RCMA compromise in order to gain women's property and custody rights within customary marriages and in exchange for the hard-won agreement to formally subject customary law to the gender equality clause. Traditional leaders, on the other hand, fought adamantly, but unsuccessfully, to exempt customary law from the gender equality principle. An officer of the National House of Traditional Leaders (NHTL) complained to me that the new constitution represented "a threat to [South African] culture and . . . traditions," because it

is rooted in "lots of Western cultural thinking rather than African thinking."
He told me that the NHTL is opposed to provisions of the RCMA that
require a husband to secure the consent of his first customary wife before
he can marry additional women. The organization objects to a wife's "being given that authority and power of determining whether [a man] should
marry another wife or not," because, this officer explained, "obviously, she
wouldn't agree." Consequently, in his view, "you are restricting another
person from practicing his custom," and this just encourages the man "to
have another woman on the side." In short, feminists and traditional leaders alike correctly understand that the RCMA legalized polygyny in order
to regulate and ultimately erode it. They simply have opposing sentiments
about this prospect.

What is truly startling from a North American perspective, however, is
the fact that polygamy in South Africa is legal only for indigenous black Africans. The RCMA defines as customary "a marriage negotiated, celebrated
or concluded according to any of the systems of indigenous African customary law which exist in South Africa" and specifies "that this does not
include marriages concluded in accordance with Hindu, Muslim or other
religious rites."[19] For most of the twentieth century, South African civil law
refused to recognize even monogamous Muslim marriages because of their
"potential" for polygamy.[20] The post-apartheid regime has not yet managed to negotiate a law to recognize Muslim marriages among its substantial Indian and South Asian minorities, also due partly to their potentially
polygynous nature.[21]

In 1998, the same year that Parliament approved the RCMA, South
Africa's Constitutional Court overturned sodomy laws, handing gay rights
advocates the first in a rapid series of stunning judicial victories. In decisions that granted lesbians and gays equal employment, immigration, and
parenting rights, domestic-partner rights, and ultimately the right to marry,
the court rebuffed the justifications that U.S. courts have used to deny them
these rights. Countering the popular claim that procreation is the central
purpose of marriage, the court found that, "from a legal and constitutional
point of view, procreative potential is not a defining characteristic of conjugal relationships."[22] It rejected the view put forth by U.S. opponents of
same-sex marriage that excluding such couples from legal status and benefits protects the family lives of heterosexuals, and it deemed gays and lesbians "capable of constituting a family, whether nuclear or extended, and
of establishing, enjoying and benefiting from family life which is not dis-
tinguishable in any significant respect from heterosexual spouses."[23] The

Constitutional Court boldly insisted that LGBT citizens deserve respect and support for their relationships whether they are queer by biology or by choice, for a day or for a lifetime.

In December 2005, the Constitutional Court issued its historic ruling in the *Fourie* case that same-sex couples must receive equal marriage rights by the following year's end. During the challenging year of emotional hearings and negotiations that followed, an "unholy alliance,"[24] of a sort scarcely thinkable in the United States, formed to oppose same-sex marriage. Conservative Christians (led by the African Christian Democratic Party and with links to some evangelical Christian groups in the United States)[25] linked elbows with traditional leaders from polygamous South African cultures (led by Contralesa and the NHTL). The former argued that homosexuality is un-Christian, while the latter insisted that it is un-African. In vivid contrast, right-wing Christian forces in the United States often wield the specter of polygamy as a trump card in their campaigns against same-sex marriage.

After the year of raucous hearings and contentious debates, Parliament negotiated a delicate compromise between gay activists and religious and cultural conservatives. It declined to expand the existing civil Marriage Act to include same-sex couples, as gay right advocates wanted it to do, or to restrict same-sex couples to civil unions, as the traditional forces preferred. Instead, Parliament reserved the Marriage Act for heterosexual couples, but it granted same-sex couples the right to choose to register their unions as either a marriage or a civil union under the Civil Union Act.[26]

The Civil Union Act provides couples with the identical rights and responsibilities as the Marriage Act, and it allows straight as well as gay couples to choose to marry or to enter a civil union under its aegis. However, opponents of same-sex marriage succeeded in inserting a clause that allows public officials to "opt out" of conducting ceremonies for same-sex couples on grounds of conscience. Also, efforts by feminists and gay activists to make domestic-partnership status available to both same- and different-sex couples failed during fraught deliberations.[27] In the end, South African opponents of same-sex marriage managed to extract a few significant concessions from Parliament, but they failed to prevent passage of a law which, when it took effect on November 30, 2006, made South Africa the fifth nation in the world and the first in the Southern Hemisphere to legalize same-sex marriage.

How stupendously ironic, therefore, that marriage laws remain baldly and legally segregated by race and sexuality in officially anti-racist and

South African cartoon during the national debate over the Constitutional Court's same-sex-marriage decision, 2006.

anti-sexist new South Africa, despite, and partly because of, constitutional commitments to both multiculturalism and sex equality. The civil Marriage Act from the apartheid era continues to govern heterosexual monogamous marriages, which historically were exclusively for whites de jure and remain disproportionately so de facto. The right to plural marriages, on the other hand, belongs exclusively to black, heterosexual men, like President Zuma, because of its cultural legitimacy as an African tradition. A Constitutional Court justice I interviewed affirmed its normative African stature: "I'm not aware of any African culture that doesn't accommodate it—polygamy. Polygamy is an African cultural phenomenon. It's an African cultural idea."[28]

I was repeatedly struck during my field research in South Africa by how little public discussion, concern, or even mention the racial character of legal polygamy seemed to provoke. According to informants on the South African Law Commission, it was not a contentious issue during their deliberations over the RCMA. Nor does the topic seem to attract very much political discussion today. The four Constitutional Court justices of different racial (and gender) identities whom I interviewed seemed scarcely to have noticed, let alone worried, about the racial character of legal polygamy. One white and one black justice assured me that whites could agree to participate in customary marriages if they had integrated into a traditional culture. One justice described a white woman acquaintance who had received *lobola* (bridewealth) and entered an interracial, "customary" marriage knowing that it was potentially polygynous. Perhaps a bit defensively, three justices reminded me that customary marriages are subject to the constitution's gender equality clause.

The justices' apparent lack of concern about the racial character of the right to plural marriage reflects a widespread expectation in South Africa, one shared by feminists and traditionalists alike, that polygyny will continue to erode as the society modernizes. Although the post-apartheid state sought to accommodate indigenous African marital traditions, it did not wish to encourage plural marriage. The justices I interviewed had no desire to extend polygamy to other racial groups.

Unequal Family Prospects De Facto

Post-apartheid South Africa boasts the most pluralist and egalitarian gender, sex, and family laws on the planet, but securing access to many of these rights is quite a different story. Poignantly, South Africa is still among the most unequal societies in the world, and the gap between rich and poor has actually worsened since the fall of apartheid.[29] The new regime had the historical misfortune to assume power in the 1990s, during the unlucky conjuncture of global developments that doomed the new government's ambitious, redistributive development goals and mocked its egalitarian family principles. The demise of the Soviet Union made it easier for global capitalist forces to impose stringent constraints on the state's economic development strategies.[30] Worse, by the 1990s, the global AIDS epidemic was taking its severest toll on the peoples of sub-Saharan Africa.[31] Sustaining any sort of family life remains a formidable challenge for masses of South Africans, particularly among the black racial majority.

Although blacks, Coloureds (the South African term for mixed-race heritage), and white women have achieved striking gains in political representation in the new South Africa, stark race and gender inequality endures.[32] Southern Africa suffers the world's highest HIV infection rates, and these expose harsh race and gender disparities. By 2005, official estimates placed the HIV prevalence rate among South African adults between 16.8 and 20 percent, which represented 10 percent of the world's reported cases.[33] The vast majority of South African AIDS victims are black, and women suffer twice the infection rates as men. AIDS had orphaned more than one million, primarily black, South African children by 2003, and given the tragic denialist policies of former president Mbeki's regime, experts were bracing for increases in all of these dismal statistics.[34]

Contemporary family patterns are indeed diverse and often innovative, but grim necessity rather than individual choice or newly garnered rights explains most of the family changes under way. Declining marriage rates are no more race-blind in South Africa than in the United States. In 2001, 54 percent of black African women ages fifteen and older had never married, compared with 44 percent of colored women, 31 percent of Indian/Asian, and 25 percent of white women.[35] However, unwed teen pregnancy had "become virtually institutionalized" among black rural South Africans, due to men's sexual abuse much more than to young girls' passion for parenthood.[36] The severe double standard of a brutal patriarchal sexual culture also underwrote the disproportionate AIDS burden that black women suffer.[37]

Apartheid exacerbated male dominance in South Africa, and black women had always suffered its heaviest abuses. Severe poverty and unemployment in the African "homelands" had compelled black men to migrate to mines and cities in search of work. The sex-ratio imbalance they left behind magnified women's economic dependence and shrunk their marital options. In contrast, lengthy absences from wives, families, and villages expanded men's sexual freedom and gave them access to multiple partners, including male youth, whom many workers in the single-sex mining communities took as their "boy wives."[38] Meanwhile, back in the rural villages, women often had to enter polygynous marriages if they were to marry at all and obtain the crucial, if meager, supplies of housing and co-workers that marriage might provide.[39]

Contemporary examples of polygyny are on prominent, unapologetic display in post-apartheid South Africa. During my fieldwork in June 2007, a colorful photo of a beaming African father surrounded by most of his twenty-four children from his four wives emblazoned the first page of the Father's Day edition of *The Star*, a South African newspaper. "We are very organized," the news-route driver dad boasted, "and even have a timetable for chores, meal times, bathing, and even which wife can stay with me. It's part of my religion, and I am happy to have such a big family around me. It makes me feel strong."[40] As President Zuma's weddings demonstrate, some black men among the political elite share his feelings. The sixty-five-year-old Zuma had already fathered at least eighteen children with at least four or five women when he took thirty-three-year-old Nompumelelo Ntuli as a plural wife in January 2008. Since then, he has married another woman,

WHO'S YOUR DADDY?

Father's Day will be a day of great celebration and dancing for Zibonele Moses Khuzwayo. Father of 24 children, guardian to three grandchildren and a husband to four wives, the Shembe devotee said he was excited about spending time with his huge brood. A driver at Independent Newspapers in Greyville, Khuzwayo (50) said people were always amazed when they discovered how large his family was. "They always think I'm lying when I tell them about the children, and when they hear about the number of wives I have, they are completely astounded," he said. His children, ranging in age from 6 to 30, all live with him in Ndwedwe, near Durban, with three of his grandchildren, his wives and his brother. As the only breadwinner in the family, Khuzwayo said it was by the "grace of God" that his family had everything they needed. The family survive on bare essentials. The children sleep in rondavels built next to the main house, which is reserved for Khuzwayo and his wives, who surprisingly are extremely close to each other. "We are very organised and even have a timetable for chores, meal times, bathing and even which wife can stay with me. It's part of my religion and I am happy to have such a big family around me. It makes me feel strong," he said. – Tash Reddy   Photograph: Sherelee Clarke

Father's Day feature photo of Johannesburg father and children, *Saturday Star,* June 16, 2007.

with whom he had fathered children, and he has been rumored to be planning to marry another woman as well.[41]

Nonetheless, economic conditions, women's resistance, and perhaps symbolic effects of the new legal principles seem to be taking a collective toll on the incidence and character of customary polygynous marriages. Despite the legal option, few South Africans formally register their plural marriages, as I discuss in the next chapter. Between 1996 and 2001, the percentage of South Africans classified by the census in customary marriages declined from 12 to 10.2 percent. The vast majority of these citizens were black, of course, but the 2001 census also classified 36,775 whites in customary marriages and 1,366 whites in polygamous ones.[42] Likely, most of the unconventional white South Africans who are in these "customary" and polygamous marriages are women whose presence alone renders the marriages decidedly uncustomary. South Africa's severe sexual double standard also undergirds a continuum of contemporary sexual practices by men that blur the line between philandering, open marriage, and polygyny, as I discuss in the next chapter.

Several scholars maintain that employment, residence, and marriage policies under apartheid deepened and distorted customary patriarchal marriage practices.[43] According to these scholars, historically, polygynous marriages had been relatively rare, but the Transkei Marriage Act of 1978 entrenched polygyny in that region. The first foreign minister of Transkei rationalized that "the African is by nature a polygynist."[44] Xhosa men interviewed in an Eastern Cape township in that period justified their sexual behavior in these terms. Amanda Gouws argues that colonial authorities and African male elders colluded in codifying a rigid form of "defensive customary law" out of gender and family practices that earlier had been fluid, more communitarian, and more respectful of women.[45] The traditional leaders I interviewed uniformly held rigid, sexist views of African customary marriage. They found the very concept of polyandry to be preposterous. An NHTL officer insisted that a woman with multiple husbands "is something that has never happened before. It never happened before on this earth."

Scholars also have documented occasional instances of same-sex unions that took place within plural marriage systems in traditional African cultures.[46] Insufficient cultural memory of these unions survived the apartheid era, however, to prompt the Law Commission even to consider including homosexual polygamy among the customary practices protected by the RCMA.[47] My attempt to discuss some of the documented customary African traditions that allowed for same-gender unions aroused hostile denials from traditional leaders. "According to our customs and culture in South Africa," an NHTL officer insisted, "we don't have these things at all. Traditionally, if a woman couldn't get pregnant, then a woman—let's say my sister, who did not have children—she could go out and marry a lady," who would serve as a surrogate to produce an heir to keep the chieftainship in the lineage. "This, however, had nothing to do with homosexuality," which, he repeated, is un-African.

The claim that homosexuality is un-African enjoys official status within the NHTL and Contralesa. Both organizations submitted documents to Parliament that vehemently condemned not only same-sex marriage but also homosexuality itself. According to the NHTL,

> The practice of same-sex marriages is against most of African beliefs, cultures, customs and traditions, and this in turn goes against the mandate of

traditional leaders which is to promote and protect the customs of communities observing a system of customary law.

Traditional leaders have vowed to make it their mission for the coming
five years to campaign against this wicked, decadent and immoral Western practice.[48]

Contralesa's submission went so far as to insist that some of the founda-
tional principles of the South African constitution were alien to African
culture:

> As traditional leaders we have had occasion to raise the matter of homo-
> sexuality in several of our forums. . . . All those present were agreed that
> homosexuality is neither condoned nor promoted by any of their cultures.
> . . . We object to the certification of the Constitution on the basis that it is
> Eurocentric and will lead to undesirable consequences such as the Consti-
> tutional court judgment in question.[49]

Arguably, nonetheless, black gays and lesbians have a constitutional
basis to press for a right to plural marriage. Scholars claim that during the
colonial period, patriarchal African leaders may have suppressed evidence
that some traditional black southern African polygamous family systems
included the practice of same-sex marriage.[50] All of the Constitutional
Court justices I interviewed gave impressively informed responses about
indigenous African traditions of same-sex marriage. Two justices even discussed queer scholarship about such traditions that they had consulted
while they were conducting research for their decision on the same-sex-
marriage case. All four were open to the possibility that the historical record might be able to sustain a bid for including same-sex marriage within
the definition of an indigenous African tradition. If so, black lesbians and
gays would be able to seek access to polygamy, not only under the equality clause but also as a customary practice. They have not yet done so, nor
does a legal appeal of this sort seem likely soon.[51]

Instead, for most non-white South African gays, lesbians, and trans-
people, securing access to the most basic of their unambiguous legal rights
remains a daunting challenge. The breathtaking constitutional commitments to gender and sex equality did not stem from grassroots struggles
that gradually won over the hearts and minds of the people. Rather, the
ANC leadership largely imposed these humanitarian principles on an un-
sympathetic populace, because of the influence of key individual leaders

of the anti-apartheid struggle and of the international human rights movement that supported them. A survey of 2,163 South African individuals
from all races and regions was conducted in 1995, just before the new constitution was adopted. It found that 44 percent were opposed to including equal rights for gays in the constitution, 64 percent opposed equal
partner rights for same-sex couples, and 68 percent opposed allowing gays
the right to adopt children.[52] Though the Constitutional Court has now
granted these rights, the government has done very little to change such
social views. A Human Sciences Research Council survey of five thousand
South Africans conducted in 2005 found the persistence of overwhelming
disapproval of homosexuality. More than three-fourths of those surveyed
claimed that sexual relations between adults of the same gender are "always
wrong."[53] As South African sociologist Jacklyn Cock summarizes, "Homophobia is intense and widespread in post-apartheid South Africa."[54]

The state is not collecting racial data on same-sex marriages registered
under the Civil Union Act, but anecdotal evidence and public perception
strongly indicate that most of these are white weddings.[55] In fact, in some
(overwhelmingly black) rural areas, no Home Affairs officers are willing
to perform marriages under the Civil Union Act.[56] Their refusal reflects a
firmly held African belief that homosexuality is an unnatural perversion
that white, Western colonials imported to Africa. According to a Contralesa official I interviewed, for example, "if people sleep with their own
sex, it's witchcraft, evil and not natural." When I asked him if there had
been any changes in marriage in the new South Africa, he immediately and
angrily identified same-sex marriage and issued a popular African version
of the slippery slope logic: "Nonsense! It doesn't make sense. Bestiality
will be next."

Despite official government support for sexual equality, some public
figures echo dictatorial President Mugabe of Zimbabwe when they politically exploit this popular African prejudice. During Winnie Mandela's
trial for kidnap and assault, she appealed to homophobia, and her supporters waved banners outside the court announcing that "homosex is not in
black culture."[57] More alarming to South African lesbians, gays, and human rights supporters, current president Jacob Zuma made a homophobic
speech at a Heritage Day celebration in his home province of KwaZulu-
Natal during the parliamentary debate on same-sex marriage in 2006.
Zuma called same-sex marriage "a disgrace to the nation and to God" and
boasted, "When I was growing up an ungqingili (a gay) would not have
stood in front of me. I would knock him out."[58] Finally, Trewhela suggests

that former president Mbeki's tragic capitulation to AIDS "denialism" was rooted in an Africanist genre of homophobia.[59] Not only does this anti-colonial discourse deny black gays and lesbians their de jure family rights, but also it threatens the survival of AIDS-afflicted families among South Africa's black racial majority.

Virulent homophobia entwines with brutal patriarchal sexuality in contemporary black South African culture. Gangs of youth engage in violent gay bashing, including "curative" rapes of lesbians and occasional murders, with little fear of prosecution. In 2006, Zanele Muholi, co-founder of the Forum for the Empowerment of Women (FEW), a support network for black gay women, recorded fifty cases of black lesbians who had been raped in black townships because of their sexual orientation.[60] According to the director of the Triangle Project, the principal GLBT organization in Cape Town, appearing to be a butch lesbian or an effeminate male arouses violence even more than sexual orientation does: "Lesbians who mimic men are seen to be challenging male superiority. Rape and violence against lesbians is common. . . . The men who perpetrate such crimes see rape as curative and as an attempt to show women their place in society."[61] "The fact that we have one of the most advanced constitutions," Muholi points out, "has had little impact on mind-sets in townships. Members of our community are celebrating the Constitution, but it is very different in the society."[62] After three black lesbians were murdered in hate crimes during the two-month period of my fieldwork in 2007, the Joint Working Group (an alliance of LGBT activist organizations across the country) agreed to make violence against black lesbians their priority issue.[63]

South African gender, family, and sexual relationships today bear the weighty imprint of the nation's violent colonial history and its legacy of patriarchal cultures. Even though most rapes go unreported, in 1996 South Africa held unenviable first place for rate of reported rapes among eighty-nine Interpol states.[64] Research conducted in Soweto and surrounding townships between 1997 and 2000 found that 59 percent of women considered a sexually violent man to be more powerful, 32 percent of male youth did not consider it to be violence if a man forces a woman he knows to have sex, and almost as many of the female youth agreed.[65] Survey data in the early 1990s reported that 62 percent of women in KwaZulu-Natal believed that their male partners had a right to multiple sexual partners, 49 percent did not believe that women had a right to refuse sex with their partners, and 51 percent stated that asking their partners to use condoms would anger them and risk provoking violence or desertion.[66] Throngs of

African women as well as men demonstrated to support Jacob Zuma in 2006 when he was acquitted of raping a thirty-one-year-old lesbian friend of his family's. Zuma acknowledged that he had had unprotected sex with the woman despite the fact that he knew that she was HIV-positive. However, he argued that she had invited his advances by wearing a short skirt and that he would have been culturally remiss to refuse her invitation. He testified too that he had taken a shower after they had sexual intercourse in order to reduce his risk of HIV.[67] De facto gender and family relationships in South Africa bear scant resemblance to the lofty intentions of the constitution.

United States

Rearguard Family Pluralism De Jure

Quite unlike South Africa's family pluralism, U.S. family law has always upheld a singular commitment to monogamous, heterosexual marriage. Throughout U.S. history, courts and legislatures have claimed the natural superiority of this family form to justify suppressing other brands of intimacy and kinship, particularly plural and same-sex marriage. Slaves were denied the legal right to marry outright, and the Supreme Court did not overturn state bans on interracial marriage until the historic *Loving v. Virginia* decision in 1967. Over the past century, however, the laws governing heterosexual marriage evolved from racist patriarchal principles to gender and race neutrality. Feminist struggles gradually sheared marriage laws of male privileges, and civil rights struggles overturned anti-miscegenation laws. Nevertheless, U.S. family rights continue to splinter along lines of class, sexuality, and geography. U.S. family law is mainly state law and wildly inconsistent across state lines. Federal and state courts and legislatures wrestle, often incompatibly, to address the changing realities of American family life

The U.S. Constitution does not protect nearly so many identities from discrimination as South Africa's does. The civil rights movement won the right to apply the judicial standard of strict scrutiny to cases that charge race discrimination, but no such protections apply to gender, sex orientation, or culture, and certainly not to marital status. The feminist struggle to add an Equal Rights Amendment to the Constitution failed in 1982, and the U.S. Supreme Court was five years behind its South African counterpart before it finally overturned laws against sodomy in *Lawrence v. Texas* in 2003. The Supreme Court has found a fundamental right to monogamous heterosexual marriage but not to family life more generally. U.S. family jurisprudence promotes marital relationships that involve childrearing, often presuming that married co-parents are legitimate, even if one parent lacks biological ties to the child. State courts battle fiercely over how to define a parent, particularly when a non-biological parent wants to be recognized.[68] LGBT parents find their rights deeply implicated in these struggles.

In contrast with South Africa, U.S. family law displays a checkered pattern of gains and losses for gay family rights. Because states control most family law, gays and lesbians have to cope with incoherent, contradictory circumstances if they relocate across state lines. Lesbigay family law emerged in the 1970s when a burgeoning gay rights movement ushered a generation of people out of the closet. The first wave of case law featured battles by newly out lesbian and gay parents to retain custody and contact with their children after divorce. At first, these pioneers suffered devastating defeats, but gradually courts began to award visitation and custody rights to lesbian and gay parents. However, judges often imposed restrictions on co-habiting, social behavior, or even the mere presence of a same-sex romantic partner visiting the home.

As the lesbian "gayby boom" flourished in the 1980s, the immorality rationale for discriminating "per se" against lesbigay parents began to wane. States and courts now differ widely in their use of a "best interests of the child" standard. At present, only Florida explicitly prohibits all homosexuals from adopting children, but several other states ban adoption by same-sex or unmarried couples. In November 2008, Arkansas voters passed a ballot initiative that excluded unmarried couples from adopting or foster parenting, and groups opposed to gay parenthood have introduced similar proposals in additional states.[69]

After same-sex couples adopt or give birth to a child, they generally have to apply for second-parent adoptions so that both can be legal parents. Here, too, state laws on second-parent and co-parent adoption differ vastly, and law has yet to catch up with the science of assisted reproductive technology (ART). The bedrock principle of legal parentage is "the presumption of legitimacy" (the assumption that a woman's husband is the natural and legal father of any child she bears in wedlock). It does not apply to same-sex couples who cannot marry in most of the United States.[70]

In addition to the lesbian gayby boom, the outbreak of the AIDS epidemic in the 1980s heightened a sense of urgency in the struggle to secure gay family rights. Soon many gay rights organizations were focusing their energies on marriage rights, which seemed to provide a quick fix for many legal problems that lesbigay relationships face. *Lawrence v. Texas* (2003), the Supreme Court decision that overturned same-sex sodomy laws, was a watershed event in contemporary U.S. gay rights jurisprudence. The ruling inflamed cultural and legal combat over same-sex marriage. Though many gay advocates scoffed at the claim of dissenting Justice Scalia that the decision would lead to legal gay marriage, as it turned out, he may have been partly right. Massachusetts became the first U.S. state to legalize same-sex marriage soon after, with its state supreme court decision in the 2004 *Goodridge* case. The proposed Federal Marriage Amendment, which sought to enshrine the heterosexuality of marriage into the U.S. Constitution, failed to pass in 2006. Then in May 2008, the California Supreme Court ruling for same-sex marriage that promptly provoked Prop 8 was followed by a sudden wave of gay marriage victories in Connecticut, Iowa, Vermont, New Hampshire, and Maine.[71]

South Africa's equality principle led to fully equal legal parenting and partner rights for LGBT individuals. The United States is still squabbling over whether gays can parent or sustain intimate relationships and whether the law should recognize those relationships. Courts sometimes adopt and sometimes reject the analogies to racial equality precedents that gay family rights advocates frequently, and sometimes insensitively, offer.[72] LGBT families find themselves awash in a confusing morass of law.

Though the two stories are rarely read in tandem, the history of marriage inequality in the United States is inextricably bound up with the legal suppression of Mormon polygamy.[73] Mormon plural marriage was a racial anomaly in Western family history when it suddenly surfaced in the nineteenth century, because white Christian and Jewish communities in Europe and North America had abandoned the Old Testament practice of polygyny centuries before. Western marriage systems have been exclusively and intolerantly monogamous ever since. Few U.S. citizens today are aware of the racist rationale that the government used to justify harsh actions to eradicate Mormon polygamy. As historian Nancy Cott has demonstrated, nineteenth-century white Americans believed that voluntary monogamous marriage signaled the political superiority of their democracy and the racial superiority of its practitioners.[74] Therefore, when the practice of Mormon polygamy appeared among white Christians in the mid-nineteenth century, it directly threatened this self-conception. Legal scholar Martha Ertman demonstrates that opponents of the new religion portrayed Mormon

Racist sheet-music cover associates Mormon polygamy with black racial inferiority.

polygamists as race traitors.[75] Eradicating plural marriage became crucial to establishing a uniquely American (coded white and Christian) national identity. Rendering Mormons "metaphorically nonwhite," Cott suggests, the federal government relentlessly pursued this goal with extreme, punitive measures.[76]

In 1856, the new Republican Party pledged to extinguish the "twin relics of barbarism," polygamy and slavery. Between 1854 and 1887, Congress passed a series of acts to criminalize bigamy and disenfranchise the Mormon Church and its followers. In the historic *Reynolds* case in 1878, the Supreme Court outlawed bigamy as an "offense against society." Associating it with "barbaric African and Asiatic practices . . . odious to the northern

and western nations of Europe," the Court denied Mormon polygamy constitutional protection as a free exercise of religion.[77] After the federal government refused to grant statehood to Utah unless it repudiated polygamy, Church officials finally capitulated. In 1890, Wilford Woodruff, the fourth president of the Church of Latter-Day Saints (LDS), received a "revelation" that led the Church to rescind "the principle" of plural marriage. The now-infamous Yearning for Zion Ranch in Texas descends from the breakaway, underground LDS sects that spawned to preserve polygamy.

Three-quarters of a century after the *Reynolds* decision, even liberal Supreme Court Justice William Douglas employed racial rhetoric when he upheld the conviction of a Mormon polygynous husband under the Mann Act (prohibiting prostitution) in 1946: "The organization of a community for the spread and practice of polygamy is, in measure, a return to barbarism. It is contrary to the spirit of Christianity and of the civilization which Christianity has produced in the Western world."[78]

A paternalist patina of feminist sentiments often consorts with this racially tinged rationale for criminalizing polygamy as an un-American activity. Since the mid-nineteenth century, most critics have associated polygamy with male domination and sexual promiscuity and portrayed it as abusive to women. A prominent nineteenth-century anti-polygamy crusader, the Reverend John W. Mears, condemned Mormon plural marriage as "the manifest degradation of woman."[79] He influenced Chief Justice Waite to describe polygamy not only as patriarchal but as barbaric as well.[80] In the late nineteenth century, Congress funded a home to shelter women who were escaping polygynous marriages. Although few Mormon women sought refuge, the government prosecuted and imprisoned polygynous men. Sporadic government interventions culminated in the notorious Short Creek raids on FLDS communities in 1953 to rescue women and children from the polygynous families the raids disrupted.[81] In a similar manner, Texas authorities justified the 2008 raid on the YFZ compound as an attempt to rescue girls from statutory rape and polygamy.

Today, plural marriage is illegal in all fifty states. State bigamy offenses range from misdemeanors that impose small monetary fines to felonies mandating prison sentences.[82] Some statutes also forbid a married person from co-habiting with another person and from "aiding and abetting" bigamy by marrying someone who is already married to someone else. These laws are ubiquitous but rarely enforced.[83] Just as Justice Scalia predicted, however, soon after the *Lawrence v. Texas* decision, legal interest in polygamy revived. The next year, Brian Barnard, a civil rights attorney, cited the *Lawrence* decision in a federal suit he filed to overturn Utah's ban on polygamy on behalf of a married couple who wanted to enter into a plural marriage with another woman.[84] In a different case, in 2006, the Utah Supreme Court upheld the conviction of Rodney Holm for bigamy and sexual conduct with a minor, but Chief Justice Christine Durham issued a strong dissent against the bigamy conviction. Raising issues I pursue in the next chapter, Durham pointed out the hypocrisy of confining the *Lawrence* decision to specific sexual acts. She argued that the Utah ruling codified in law "mere moral disapproval of an excluded group."[85]

In short, the United States is a stubborn laggard when it comes to legally recognizing different family forms. The singular fixation that U.S. family law has had on promoting heterosexual, monogamous marriage does not contrast only with South Africa. It is also increasingly out of step with the ways in which most liberal democracies, including its northern neighbor, Canada, are responding to the reality of family diversity.

Vanguard Family Diversity De Jure

When it comes to the lived experience of family diversity, however, the United States has few peers. No society has spawned more vibrant grassroots movements to transform intimacy. Family innovations in South Africa came from top-down initiatives or from desperate strategies to survive extreme poverty and the AIDS catastrophe. However, from the nineteenth-century utopian communities until the present, family experimentation in the United States has always sprouted from the bottom up.[86] The United States is the global headwaters of personal identity politics. In the decades since the 1960s, the sexual revolution, the counter-culture, and movements of women, LGBT, and disabled people have inspired throngs to radically transform the visible shapes of love, sex, and family lives. Youth rebelled against sexual repression, hypocrisy, and bourgeois propriety; feminists assailed men's sexual privilege and coercion and denounced "the feminine mystique" of domesticity; lesbians, gays, and bisexuals rejected "compulsory heterosexuality;"[87] a trans movement refused gender conformity or destiny; and disabled people challenged notions of the normal body. Free-market access to reliable contraception, sperm banks, and reproductive technology also unhitched the links between sex, love, marriage, pregnancy, and parenting.

Despite dazzling changes in the timing, meaning, stability, and substance of marriage, and despite chronic breast-beating over its decline, it remains far more prevalent in the United States than it is in South Africa or in most Western nations. To be precise, marriage is far more common among whites. For in the United States, as in South Africa, the history of marriage is deeply racialized, as we have seen. In stark contrast with South Africa, polygamy in the United States has been mainly white and racist. Despite its "metaphorically nonwhite" history, the LDS Church doctrine was white supremacist. Brigham Young taught that whites were "pure" and "delightsome," but blacks were the "unrighteous," "despised," and "loath-some" descendants of Cain, the cursed murderer of Abel. State coercion convinced the LDS Church to modernize its marriage doctrine in 1890 by repudiating polygamy, but the state did not demand or invite the Mormons to repudiate their racism. The LDS "revelation" that ended racial apartheid in the church did not occur until 1978.[88] It provoked another schism, and a small exodus of believers joined the lily-white FLDS communities. In the 1990s, FLDS patriarch Warren Jeffs warned his followers against inter-racial relationships and contended that blacks "are low in their habits, wild and seemingly deprived of nearly all the blessings of the intelligence that is generally bestowed upon mankind."[89]

Even now that marriage laws in the United States are racially neutral, marriage rates still vary starkly by race, as in South Africa. Whites are twice as likely as blacks to tie the legal knot.[90] Even more than in South Africa, white gays and lesbians dominate U.S. campaigns for same-sex marriage and gay family rights, which too often do not seem sensitive to the fraught racial history of marriage in the United States.[91] Although gays and lesbi-ans of color have organized their own advocacy groups, social networks, and institutions, these groups rarely fight for same-sex marriage. Black gay journalist Kenyon Farrow asks, "Is gay marriage anti-black?" and criticizes the implicit whiteness and racial insensitivity of the campaign.[92] For dec-ades social science research and "family values" rhetoric have stigmatized black families for failing to conform to the monogamous marital ideal.[93] The campaign for same-sex marriage generally ignores this history and fails to address the core concerns of poor, black Americans—housing, health care, employment, and the over-incarceration of black men—that under-mine black heterosexual marriages and families to begin with. This places black churches and communities in the ideological crosshairs of a battle between white religious conservatives on the one hand and primarily white gay activists on the other.

In the United States, as in South Africa, many people of color consider gay to be an immoral white identity that is alien to their traditional cul-ture.[94] Survey data report stronger opposition to same-sex marriage among blacks than among whites.[95] Higher percentages of black voters supported Prop 8 in California. This was mainly due to their higher rates of religiosity and lower levels of education, which correlate with opposition to gay marriage.[96] However, weaknesses in the racial and religious politics of the gay marriage campaign played a part in black support for Prop 8 as well. Gay family rights can seem a white, affluent agenda to less privileged constituencies, whether gay or straight.[97]

Of course, in the United States, unlike in South Africa, marriage also remains a bastion of explicit sexual privilege. The 2008 victories of Prop 8 and similar initiatives in Florida and Colorado, followed by the repeal of same-sex marriage in Maine in 2009, should remind us that a passionate backlash against gay rights continues to tally wins in its drive to preserve a heterosexual monopoly on marriage. In contrast, since Anita Bryant's "Save the Children" crusade helped to pass Florida's categorical state ban on gay adoption in 1977, the anti-gay backlash has paid less attention to preventing gay parenthood through banning adoption, access to fertility services, or child custody. However, recently it has begun to make gay parenthood the target of a second front. Buoyed by the victory of the 2008 Arkansas initiative that restricted adoption and foster care to married couples, the movement plans to promote similar campaigns in numerous red (and some purple) states.[98]

Despite political setbacks, lesbian and gay couples and parents have won far greater social acceptance in the United States than the reactionary legal landscape implies, and certainly greater than in South Africa. In the United States, gay and lesbian couples and their children are almost literally "everywhere," as the slogan boasts. The 2000 Census recorded 1.2 million individuals residing in households headed by same-sex couples in 99 percent of U.S. counties.[99] One in four of these households included children, and 12–15 percent of the couples were biracial.[100] Because the census only counts the relationships of people who live together, these data under-estimate and provide misleadingly static portraits of lesbian and gay family formations. They miss the creative panoply of forms of intimacy and kinship that Paul, Nancy, and Liza crafted, for example, as well as those in many of the other families I described in chapters 1 and 2. As we saw, the United States remains the global epicenter of planned lesbian and gay parenting. It boasts an elaborate infrastructure of commercial sperm banks, assisted reproduction centers, and adoption agencies and lawyers devoted to serving them, as well as countless gay community and support groups like the Pop Luck Club.[101]

Today only a comatose resident of the United States can avoid encountering positive and even multi-racial images of gay family relationships. Projected onto the silver and the electronic screen, broadcast on the airwaves and into earbuds, plastered on billboards and blogs, advertised in classified pages, and celebrated in wedding announcements in the *New York Times,* images of gay family life now saturate U.S. popular culture. To be sure, vicious hostility, harassment, rape, bashing, and even homicide against gays also persist, sometimes incited by such exposure. Still, gays and lesbians and their families have won huge gains in public acceptance. Popular opposition to gay relationships is notably less widespread in the United States than in South Africa, and it seems to be waning at a rapid clip. National Opinion Research Center poll data reported an 18 percent drop in the percentage of Americans who said that "homosexual relations are always wrong," from 73 percent in 1973 to 55 percent in 2002.[102] A 2009 national Gallup Poll reported that 57 percent of adults were opposed to "extending marriage to include same-sex couples," and 40 percent were in favor.[103] And if the majority of Americans still oppose same-sex marriage, polls consistently show that a majority of younger adults support it along with gay rights in general.[104] This arc of history is bending toward social acceptance.

"Such a day of social acceptance will never come for polygamists," a prominent U.S. law professor predicted in 2004. "It is unlikely that any network is going to air *The Polygamist Eye for the Monogamist Guy* or add a polygamist twist to *Everyone Loves Raymond.*"[105] National aversion to polygamy in the United States is so robust that few would have challenged Professor Turley's prophecy at the time. Indeed, 92 percent of Americans surveyed in a 2005 Gallup Poll viewed polygamy as "morally unacceptable."[106] Remarkably, however, less than a year after this survey, U.S. cable TV channel HBO premiered just such a script. The surprise hit series *Big Love* sympathetically portrays a fundamentalist Mormon husband and his three wives navigating the emotional, sexual, and social complexities of their closeted polygamous family life in suburban Utah.

Advocates for same-sex marriage and for polygamy are unlikely, mutually suspicious, political bedfellows. Nonetheless, contests over same-sex marriage inadvertently have revived long-dormant conflicts over fundamentalist Mormon polygyny, disrupting the wink-wink accommodation between the sect and the state that had been in effect since the political debacle of the 1953 Short Creek raids. The slippery slope argument that links gay marriage to polygamy has borne some ironic fruit. *Big Love,* perhaps the most unlikely of these, was written and produced by a gay male screen-

A *New Yorker* cover, depicting a newly wed man and his three
brides, that appeared right after the debut of *Big Love* in 2006.
Some readers mistook the image to depict a joint wedding of
a straight and a lesbian couple.

writer couple, Mark V. Olsen and Will Scheffer. When Terry Gross interviewed the couple on her popular *Fresh Air* National Public Radio program
in 2007, they credited the Republican campaign against same-sex marriage
with seeding their concept for the series. They were offended by statements
that former president George W. Bush made soon after his second inauguration in 2004 about what makes a proper family and who can and cannot
get married. And so they conceived the idea to explore such issues through
the struggles of a fictional fundamentalist Mormon polygamist family.[107]

Big Love characters frequently adopt the idiom of the closet to describe their family circumstances, and they draw analogies between social stigma and discrimination against polygamous and gay families.[108] The series has inspired small polygamy-rights groups to adopt these rhetorical devices as well. The clearinghouse website for polygamy advocacy groups credits media interest in *Big Love* with reporting "around the world" their conviction that "polygamy rights is the next civil rights battle."[109] In August 2006, after the series's first season, the pro-polygamy group Principle Voices organized a protest rally in Salt Lake City at which youth from polygynous families echoed children of gay parents as they spoke about the prejudice and pain they suffer trying to conceal from peers, neighbors, and authorities their parents' non-normative marriages.[110]

On the other hand, *Big Love* also has exposed FLDS abuses against women and children to a broad viewing public. Roman, the sinister patriarchal leader of "Juniper Hill," the fictional sectarian compound portrayed on the program, unmistakably was inspired by Warren Jeffs, the now imprisoned founder of the YFZ ranch in Eldorado. It seems more than coincidental that the FBI placed Jeffs on its "Ten Most Wanted Fugitives" list (along with Osama bin Laden) in 2006 soon after *Big Love* first aired. Likewise, one cannot but wonder about the program's indirect impact on the Texas authorities who organized the televisual spectacle of the Eldorado raid. In turn, the punitive raid prompted principal legal allies for gay family rights, such as the ACLU, to join efforts to secure due process for the YFZ children and their mothers.[111]

Because polygamy is illegal in the United States, unlike in South Africa, the practice has been driven underground, where it survives primarily in outlaw communities, like the YFZ ranch, but located mainly around the border of Utah and Arizona. Scholars estimate that there are between eleven thousand and fifty thousand members of Mormon offshoots like the FLDS, the fundamentalist splinter group of the LDS which rejected as heresy the Church's 1890 pragmatic decision to renounce plural marriage.[112] A smaller number of non-Mormon, self-described Christian polygamists also believe that the Old Testament mandates "The Principle" of patriarchal polygyny, and an assortment of polygamists who distance themselves from the FLDS make up a small pro-polygamy constituency that I discuss in the next chapter.

Political fallout from the 1953 Short Creek raids dampened the government's appetite for prosecuting polygynists.[113] A half century passed before the state again took legal action. By driving polygyny underground, the

United States enabled patriarchal sexual abuses to proliferate unregulated. Dictatorial, self-proclaimed prophets, like Warren Jeffs, have been able to rule renegade communities with impunity. Jeffs and his ilk appropriate as many women and underage girls for themselves as they wish, assign and reassign brides to men who fall in and out of their favor, and banish from the community adolescent "Lost Boys," who represent competition for women, or anyone who threatens their authority.[114]

If slavery was the barbaric twin of polygamy for many nineteenth-century U.S. Christians, same-sex marriage seems to have filled its vacated shoes for contemporary Christian conservatives. Christian opponents lump gay marriage with polygamy because they mistakenly associate both with promiscuity. While many queer critics view the demand for gay marriage to be a conservative bid to assimilate into a suspect regime of bourgeois propriety,[115] Christian conservatives fear that gay marriage will subvert that regime. Stanley Kurtz, for example, warns, "Up to now, with all the changes in marriage, the one thing we've been sure of is that marriage means monogamy. Gay marriage will break that connection. It will do this by itself, and by leading to polygamy and polyamory. What lies beyond gay marriage is no marriage at all."[116] Kurtz predicts that the sympathetic treatment of polygamy on *Big Love* by gay male screenwriters, as he unfailingly underscores,[117] will undermine cultural taboos against polygamy and foster support for pluralist definitions of marriage and family. "At the heart of the show," Kurtz worries, is the claim "that, so long as people love each other, family structure doesn't matter."[118]

Kurtz has grounds for this fear. Although *Big Love* is fictional and parodic, the well-researched TV series has revived national attention to polygamy in the United States, and, as I discuss in the next chapter, a few mainstream voices have dared to call for decriminalizing polygamy. Tellingly, however, Utah House Speaker Marty Stephens warned that tampering with anti-polygamy laws could "open up a Pandora's Box." His Pandora reverses the conventional slippery slope argument: "If we are going to argue people ought to be able to marry who they want and have plural marriage, how different is that from saying you ought to allow homosexual marriages?"[119] Employing similar logic, Vicky Prunty, director of the anti-polygamy group Tapestry Against Polygamy, labels LDS leaders who protest gay marriage "shamefully hypocritical" for failing to mobilize against polygamy as well. "Let there be no mistake: Passing a marriage amendment to stop gay marriages or any other form of marriage including polygamy is putting false hopes in a bogus amendment. Polygamy has been illegal for decades while some of the strongest proponents of the [anti-gay-]marriage amendment are our nation's gravest enablers of polygamy."[120]

In a sense, Prunty's complaint was that conservative Christians in the United States also had forged an "unholy alliance" with (in this case, tacit) supporters of polygamy. Two years after she issued this charge, many political analysts credited passage of the Prop 8 ban on same-sex marriage in California to the tremendous infusion of volunteers and finances donated by the (now anti-polygamist) Mormon Church. Of course, this victory did nothing to expand the practice of monogamous heterosexual marriage, to reduce same-sex intimacies or gay parenthood, or to retard the dynamic diversity of family life in the United States.

Different Slopes for Different Folks

Studying the contrasts between de jure and de facto support for same-sex and plural marriage in these two societies led me to shift my perspective on whether legitimating the former alternative to heterosexual monogamy would lead inexorably toward legalizing the latter. The (too) simple verdict is no, "not guilty as charged." Clearly, there is no predestined link and no unidirectional chute that joins these two forms of marriage in South Africa, the United States, or anywhere else. Their intersecting trails are unpredictable, alternately slippery or pocked with moguls.

Polygamy appeared long before gay marriage in both South Africa and the United States. Therefore, one could more credibly conclude that a slope tilts from plural to same-sex marriage than the other way round. However, few would or should make this claim. Historically, polygyny was a pre-modern, patriarchal institution that mainly served the desire of a husband's family for heirs, workers, and alliances. Same-sex marriage, in contrast, springs from the modern egalitarian, romantic ideal that encourages individuals to seek the emotional and erotic rewards of "the pure relationship," as sociologist Anthony Giddens called it.[121] That is why few people would have dreamed that same-sex couples would win the right to marry in under-developed South Africa long before they are likely to do so in the affluent global superpower, the United States.

South Africa, as we have seen, had a history of race-based legal pluralism in its marriage laws. Polygyny and monogamy co-existed under apartheid, but the former was governed by customary law for black Africans only, and whites regarded this as a sign of their racial superiority. The post-apartheid regime instituted a radical shift in values from state-sponsored, patriarchal racism to the constitution's utopian commitments to social justice and equality. That is why it seems so startling to learn that marital pluralism in South Africa retains a racial basis. Same-sex marriage and full gay family rights rapidly won civil legal status under the equality clause, but the legacy of anti-colonial homophobia makes it very difficult for black gays and lesbians to exercise these rights. Legal plural marriage, on the other hand, still is available exclusively to black South African men.

Nevertheless, my research convinced me that the 1998 RCMA was an attempt to regulate rather than to endorse polygyny. It tried to subject this patriarchal form of marriage to the equality clause, despite the fact that the two seem fundamentally incompatible. Constitutional commitments to gender and sexual equality made legal same-sex marriage inevitable in South Africa. Wherever same-sex marriage appears in the world, it builds upon a long historical drive toward gender equality in civil marriage. The slope of marriage laws in South Africa slid swiftly from the equality principle to legal same-sex marriage. It more haltingly lists toward either eroding legal polygamy or shearing it of patriarchal and racial privileges. Unfortunately, however, widespread popular support for male dominance and homophobia make the prospects for realizing the egalitarian family ideals promised by the South African Bill of Rights seem distant and dim.

Historical connections between plural and same-sex marriage in the United States are nearly the mirror image of those in South Africa. Neither plural marriage nor a pluralist definition of marriage has ever enjoyed legal status in the United States. Historians have demonstrated that a single-minded "deployment of monogamous [heterosexual] conjugal norms" promoted "the imperial consolidation of the nation-state."[122] The defeat of Mormon struggles for the right to practice plural marriage long preceded contests over same-sex marriage in the United States, and the rhetoric about equality and liberty that was used *against* polygamy then appears now in campaigns *for* gay marriage. In fact, the conservative Christian pro-polygamy movement argues that "anti-polygamy is the real 'slippery slope,'"[123] because it abandoned biblical teachings and allowed government to define marriage. In the process, the state arrogated to itself the power to legalize same-sex marriage if and when it chooses.

I agree that the history of anti-polygamy in the United States bends toward same-sex marriage, but my reasoning is secular. When the U.S. state suppressed Mormon plural marriage in the nineteenth century, it brandished voluntary monogamous marriage as a badge of national and racial superiority. Casting polygamy as a barbaric, African, Asiatic, and "Mohammaden" practice helped to justify the imperialist nineteenth-century doctrine of Manifest Destiny.[124] Gradually our radical modern expectation that an individual should freely seek a beloved soulmate to wed has vanquished pre-modern patriarchal notions of marriage.[125] This modern "transformation of intimacy" from meeting the needs of families to the quest to fulfill individual desires is the ideological foundation for same-sex marriage. Once an ideal marriage becomes a freely chosen love match, the state has lost any rational grounds for dictating the gender of the match that anyone freely "chooses" to love.

If the ideology that the United States uses to suppress polygyny and that South Africa employs to regulate and erode it helps to propel the case for gay marriage, this seems to flip the slippery slope analysis belly up. It supports the verdict that gay marriage is not guilty as charged by Scalia, Kurtz, Dobson, and many of its opponents. However, I am not willing to dismiss the slippery slope case quite so quickly. Though I believe that anti-polygamy efforts performed historical spade work for legitimating same-sex unions, this might not turn out to be the end of the story.

Legalizing gay marriage in the contemporary period still could weaken the legal grounds for ruling all forms of plural marriage beyond the pale, just as Scalia warns. By conceding this point, I am not endorsing the view of the small, primarily religious pro-polygamy movement in the United States that polygamy is "the next great civil rights issue." However, I do believe that if a constituency were to mobilize in the United States—or in South Africa, for that matter—whose goal was to make plural marriages legal for consenting adults *of any gender,* it could make rational appeals to the same love-based ideology that now serves plaintiffs for same-sex marriage. Franny's unusual triumvirate of "duogamous" uncles, for example, could mount a compelling case for this sort of plural marriage if they wished. There are very few plural mates like those three in either nation, however, and, as I discuss in the next chapter, there is no reason to expect their ranks to balloon in any imaginable future.

In the end, the fate of legal gay or plural marriage or of any state-sponsored brand of marriage will not hinge on abstract logic or on legal precedents but on complex social forces and political alliances that are either painstakingly forged or foolishly foresworn. As we have seen, vexed racial histories distort the politics of marriage and family in both nations.

Notions of racial and religious purity helped to justify the modern model of monogamous marriage that both nations still favor. Unless advocates for racial, sexual, and economic rights join forces to support family diversity, few forms of kinship will enjoy both de jure and de facto success. The politics of family change is never a smooth slide down a slippery slope.

4

Paradoxes of Polygamy and Modernity

Polygamy is a divine institution. It has been handed down direct from God. The United States cannot abolish it. No nation on earth can prevent it, nor all the nations of the earth combined.

—John Taylor, January 4, 1880, quoted in Krakauer,
Under the Banner of Heaven, 2003

With Barack Obama's election, African Americans have successfully travelled the road from oppression to president, thereby giving hope to still-oppressed polygamous Americans that, one day, a consenting-adult polygamist might also be elected to the highest office of the land.

—Pro-Polygamy.com, "Obama's Historic Election Gives
Hope to Polygamous Americans," 2008

You'd think the family values branch of the Republican Party would have this down pat: Americans disapprove of adultery. They disapprove of it so much that they rank philandering as less morally acceptable than the death penalty, cloning humans or suicide. . . . Only one behavior came close to the disapproval of adultery in the Gallup poll. Polygamy—deemed wrong by 91 percent of Americans.

—Eduardo Porter, "Tales of Republicans,
Bonobos and Adultery," 2009

People are naturally polygamous.

—David P. Barash and Judith Eve Lipton,
Strange Bedfellows, 2009

ON MAY DAY 2008, less than a month after the raid on the polygamous YFZ ranch in Texas and two weeks before the California Supreme Court issued its ruling in favor of same-sex marriage, one of the ubiquitous sex scandals that incessantly spice up U.S. political life clocked its fifteen minutes of fame. U.S. Congressman Vito Fossella of Staten Island, New York, a married father of three children and staunch Republican proponent of family values, was arrested in Washington, D.C., for driving under the influence. When Fossella told the arresting officer that he was hurrying home to the bedside of his sick three-year-old daughter, he inadvertently exposed his clandestine, second family life with Laura Fay, a former air force officer, and their "love child." Fossella thereby joined the popular scarlet parade of fallen conservative politicians and preachers who had built their careers as defenders of the sanctity of heterosexual marriage.[1]

Fossella's voting record on gay rights had earned him a perfect goose egg from the mainstream gay-advocacy organization the Human Rights Campaign. He had voted, for example, for the failed Federal Marriage Protection Amendment to make same-sex marriage unconstitutional and, closer to home, for a bill to refuse funding for gay parents who adopt children in Washington, D.C. The former congressman's opposition to gay family rights seems to have been as personal as it was political. Investigative journalists soon revealed that his sister Victoria is a lesbian and an adoptive co-parent of two children born to her partner through donor sperm. Reportedly, Vito refuses to attend family gatherings if his sister and her family will be present.[2]

It would have been easy to overlook Fossella's misadventure amid the bumper crop of higher-profile political sex scandals that vied for public opprobrium that spring—among them the salacious exposés involving New York's then governor Elliot Spitzer and Democratic presidential candidate John Edwards.[3] Fossella's denouement caught my attention, however, because it spoke so directly to the moral disconnect between the ideological claims of marriage-promotion politics and the living practice of family diversity today. Vito's version of closeted, informal polygyny and his sister Victoria's out-and-proud, gay-parent family life offer useful "tools to think with" about the bad faith embedded in official U.S. sexual mores and the sheer irrationality of many of our family policies.

Vito and Victoria Fossella represent two of the decidedly unwitting bedfellows who jostle uncomfortably beneath the patchwork quilt of contemporary family forms and values. The family lives of both of these estranged siblings violate the monolithic definition of monogamous heterosexual marriage which historians have shown to be central to U.S. national republican identity.[4] In opposite ways, Vito's and Victoria's families expose the massive chasm between mainstream sexual and familial ideology and widespread intimate practices in the United States. The odds are strong, however, that Vito and his sister share their culture's entrenched aversion to polygamy and the popular prejudice that believes monogamy is not only morally superior but a natural human preference.

And yet, historically, many more societies have practiced polygamy than have prohibited it. Before the era of Western colonialism, according to one scholarly estimate, "more than three-quarters of all human societies were polygynous. Monogamy was the preferred norm in fewer than one-quarter of human societies."[5] Even today, polygamy is a regular, legitimate practice in more than fifty countries, and nations like Russia, Mongolia, and even Canada are deliberating proposals to make it legal.[6] As we saw in chapter 3, modernity and globalization tend to undermine traditional polygamous marriage systems and to unleash demands to open the marital gates to same-sex couples, like Victoria and her partner.

Contemporary marital practices are quite another story, however, as demonstrated by the scandals involving Vito Fossella and his many more prominent political brethren whom I refer to as the Scarlet Lettermen. In the United States, as elsewhere, informal versions of polygamy persist and proliferate. Once again, my research in South Africa allows me to probe more deeply into the changing character and fate of polygamy in the modern world and to provoke serious consideration of the ways we respond to it. Building on my analysis of the messy links between the politics of plural and same-sex marriage in chapter 3, here I examine what family practices like Fossella's reveal about our culture's actual gender, sexual, and family behaviors, values, and confusions.

Post-apartheid Plural Marriages, Black and White

Although South Africa passed the RCMA in 1998 in order to recognize and regulate customary marriages, the law seems to have fostered some unanticipated effects on post-apartheid practices of polygamy. During the apartheid era, polygamy was illegal in urban areas, and most urban black Africans considered it a backward cultural phenomenon. However, the post-apartheid commitment to multi-culturalism, which led the new regime to pass the RCMA, also helped to revive social respect for the traditional practice. Even so, as I indicated in chapter 3, few contemporary black South African men bother to register their plural marriages, despite the new legal option. In part, this is because the law does not allow participants in a civil marriage to register a later customary one. As explained by Walter Luzama, the head of the first of several unregistered polygynous families I describe in this chapter, "Most couples start with a civil marriage, because the first time a man marries he doesn't realize that he'll later want to have a second wife."

Few black South African men who belatedly discover their appetite for additional wives seem to lose much sleep over the legal impediment, however. Instead, like Walter Luzama and unlike Congressman Fossella, many now openly practice unregistered versions of polygyny. Some of these genres do follow customary African traditions, others adapt traditional practices to untraditional circumstances, and a few are decidedly modern and innovative, incorporating interracial and even bisexual intimacies.

Thanks to the RCMA, some elite black South African men have elevated their long-term mistresses to the status of second wives. Clearly breaking with tradition, occasionally these plural unions cross racial borders. One particularly flamboyant, prominent, interracial polygynist, Jeri Ngomane, an ANC officer of royal Swazi descent in Mpumalanga province and a former mayor of one of its districts, traveled openly together with his black Swazi first wife and his white Afrikaans second wife. He lived jointly with them and their nine children, black and white. The co-wives both maintained significant paid careers, chose to live together, and claimed to feel close to each other.[7] There are no reliable data on the incidence of interracial polygamy in South Africa, but the fact that this case attracted media attention indicates its relative novelty.

More common than formal polygyny, other married men among the new black elite have adopted a stereotypically French style of modern plural marriage by participating unapologetically in the open secret of the long-term, extra-marital affair. Some of the men have children with their mistresses, but unlike Americans such as Vito Fossella, they often introduce them to their wives and other relatives and openly divide their time between their two families.[8] Some less affluent black men who entered monogamous civil marriages during apartheid now transition openly to unregistered plural marriages by taking additional wives in religious or customary ceremonies. The character of the unregistered plural marriages I encountered in urban centers like Johannesburg seemed to differ substantially from more customary unions in rural areas like Kwa-Zulu Natal.

A Tour Guide Keeping Two Trailers in Line

Walter Luzama was forty-two years old and a self-employed tour guide when I interviewed him in July 2007 in one of the two Johannesburg households in which he resided on alternate weeks. With a toddler astride his hip, Walter greeted me and my South African male research assistant at the urban apartment complex's security gate and led us to the small, clean, modern apartment where he spent every other week with his senior wife and their four children. I shook hands and chatted briefly with his wife and teenage daughter before Walter dismissed them so that he could be interviewed privately. He then shook hands with my male research assistant but declined my offered palm, because, he explained, physical contact with an unrelated woman violates the moral doctrine of the International Pentecostal Church (IPC), which he had joined five years earlier. The IPC can scarcely be termed an African customary religion. Founded in Soweto in 1964, it is a messianic black Christian Zionist denomination that endorses patriarchal polygyny on Old Testament grounds. With over 165 branches, and a stadium built near Johannesburg to seat twenty thousand, it is one of the largest and fastest-growing indigenous churches in South Africa today.

Walter and his first wife had been legally married for seventeen years when in 2006 he wed his second, younger bride in an elaborate IPC church ceremony. Because his first union was a registered civil marriage, Walter could not register this second marriage under the RCMA. This was a mere legal technicality, as far as he was concerned, without practical effects. It might have been a bit of a problem if he owned property, he allowed, because then he would have had to draw up a will to protect his second wife. Lacking property, however, he perceived no impact of the unregistered status of his second marriage on him or his family. Walter embraced the IPC's explicitly patriarchal and naturalist view of male sexuality as the prime justification for polygyny. It was natural, he explained, that some men "want more than one wife, some want only one, and some don't want any. That's how God created men." My query about whether some women might want more than one husband seemed as preposterous to Walter as it had to the NHTL official I quoted in chapter 3. "Men should always be on top," he asserted. "This is a man's world," in his unapologetic view, as well as one with a surplus of black women who need husbands, because "being a woman and unmarried is like a curse. God says you're untrustworthy if you're unmarried."

Walter's new wife, a divorced mother of two, had been engaged to marry a second time, but her fiancé had died, "and so it was important for her to get married, even if she had to share her husband," Walter explained. He conceded that "it probably wasn't her first choice" to share a husband, nor was it something that his first wife had wanted. "I don't think it's any woman's wish to have her husband take a second wife," he candidly acknowledged, but given male sexual nature, polygyny offers women some "peace of mind." In Walter's view, it is a plain matter of fact that "the majority of men philander," just as he had done before he joined the IPC, "and that's what puts women at risk." Polygyny offers women relief from the worry that their husbands are cheating, and it protects them from AIDS, he incorrectly asserted.

It turned out that converting from philandering to patriarchal polygyny actually had bestowed some peace of mind (and matter, as we shall see) on Walter, whatever its effect on his wives. Walter claimed that his first wife used to give him a hard time about his mistresses, but she had accepted his second wife, because the church practices polygyny and "people know that." In fact, the IPC pastor had arranged and officiated over the second union, which was consecrated in a large church wedding. Walter proudly produced for my perusal a wedding album that documented the event and displayed Walter's first wife and the couple's four children participating prominently in the bridal party. It was a relief to Walter that in plural marriage "you don't have to lie about your whereabouts," and his second marriage offered some domestic and kinship benefits to his children, and perhaps to his first wife, as well. For example, his younger children enjoyed visiting their new step-siblings and staying over with them occasionally in their new co-mother's home. Perhaps his senior wife considered this to be a benefit as well.

Most scholars believe that a key reason why polygamy declines in industrializing societies is that few male wage earners can afford to support more than one wife and children.[9] Walter looked at it differently. Given his belief that men are naturally non-monogamous, polygamy struck him as a financial bargain. "If you have a mistress, you spend more than on a wife!" he explained. Working as a tour guide, he had been hired by many relatively affluent married men from around the world whose extra-marital relationships proved far more costly than Walter's plural marriage. A married Japanese professor who was touring South Africa with his mistress, for example, told Walter that he was spending millions of Rand on her. In contrast, although Walter was the sole breadwinner for his homemaker senior wife and their four children, his second wife was a teacher who independently supported herself and her children from her prior marriage. Walter only felt obliged to make occasional modest contributions to her household expenses. Curiously, he did not seem to have considered future financial costs that this second marriage seemed likely to impose. His new wife had already suffered a miscarriage during the first year of their marriage, but Walter fully expected that she would successfully bear additional children of his before long. Most likely he will feel some pressure and obligation to contribute to his future children's support.

Although Walter believes monogamy is unnatural for most men, the IPC had taught him to condemn both adultery and divorce. In the church's view, they too are unnatural, as well as immoral, un-African products of a legacy of Western colonialism. Walter scorned the hypocrisy of Western norms that make it illegal to have more than one wife but not to have mistresses, when "it should be the other way round." He echoed the moral logic expressed by the officer of the NHTL I described in chapter 3: "Those people who are so critical of polygamy, if you can check them, what they are doing outside. It's terrible, terrible! You'll find a man with ten, fifteen girlfriends throughout the country. When he's in Durban, he's got a girlfriend; when he's in Cape Town, he's got a girlfriend; when he's in Johannesburg, he's got a girlfriend; in Pretoria, he's got a girlfriend—all over the country!"

Polygyny, in the view of its religious advocates in the United States as well as in South Africa, imposes a higher moral standard on men than monogamy requires. Before Walter became a Zionist, he confessed, he too used to take mistresses without ever considering marrying them. In the IPC, however, he proclaimed with righteous pride, marriage is "for life! We don't divorce, and we don't keep mistresses." Walter cited rising levels of divorce in South Africa as one of many negative effects of what he considers to be misguided, un-African features of the country's transition to democracy. "Divorce has gone up" since the new government took power, he argued, with undisguised indignation, "because women have been empowered." When women gain economic power, Walter complained, they "expect men to take responsibility for doing things at home. Women go to classes taught by women who've been to the United States or England, and they get unreasonable expectations of what's possible. My woman is not equal to me. We're like a king and a queen, not equals. How can you be equal? It's ridiculous. A queen is to be pampered, taken care of, respected, but I'm the head. Women will rule you if you're not careful."

Walter was careful. Despite the IPC's support for polygyny, he often found it challenging to handle jealousy and competition between his wives. For example, recently Walter's second wife had conveyed an anxiety dream in which he was building a big house for his first wife, and there was "a bit of stress around that." To cope with such stress, Walter and his wives attended gender-segregated marriage classes that their church provided to help congregants negotiate the pitfalls of polygyny. There men learned that the cardinal rules for successful plural marriage were "to split your time as equally as possible" among wives and "that you don't say anything about this one to the other one. *Never, ever!*" Employing a metaphor that sounded like it might have been borrowed from an IPC marriage-class instructor, Walter summed up the responsibilities of a polygynous husband: "If a truck is pulling two trailers and it drives straight, the trailers will follow in line, but if it doesn't drive straight, there's trouble. His job is to drive the truck straight."

Even within the IPC, it turned out, few men seemed eager to put their driving skills to such a road test. Perhaps only 10 percent of the men in the congregation, Walter estimated, had more than one wife. "Some men are too scared," he explained, "or just too weak" to handle its complex demands. "It's not for boys. It's for men."

Altruistic Polygyny

Starkly different circumstances and values generated the unregistered polygynous families I visited in an arid, poor village in rural Kwa-Zulu Natal (KZN). Whereas Walter Luzama spoke to me on behalf of his wives, I was unable to interview, or even to meet, Marshall Silongo, the head of one plural family. Instead I interviewed his two wives, forty-eight-year-old Nobunto and thirty-eight-year-old Lindiwe, and met the five children that Marshall was supporting by commuting weekly to his job as a maintenance worker at a hotel located one hundred kilometers away from the village.

Marshall and his first wife, Nobunto, had been married and monogamous for more than twenty years before he initiated his second customary union with Lindiwe. Both women had suffered family traumas that made Marshall's decision to take a second, younger wife seem almost partially altruistic. Nobunto and Marshall Silongo had had four children together, but all four died in infancy, rendering Nobunto a tragic local figure facing a dire social fate as she aged. Marshall met Lindiwe several years before my visit, when she was working in a *shebeen* (informal tavern) that he frequented near the hotel where he worked and lived during the week. When they met, Lindiwe was a destitute single mother. Years earlier, she had been literally seduced and abandoned in Johannesburg by a man who had promised to marry her but left her alone with two young children instead. Unable to support her children alone in the city, Lindiwe had returned to KZN to share a cramped residence and resources with her sister, her sister's boyfriend, and their children. She had taken the job in the *shebeen* to supplement the household's meager earnings.

A flirtation gradually developed between Marshall and Lindiwe, and when it blossomed into romance, Marshall told Lindiwe about his marriage to Nobunto and about the tragic death of their children. Lindiwe recounted how deeply disappointed she had been when she learned that Marshall already had a wife. However, by then she had begun falling in love with him, she told me, and because she felt so sorry for his childless first wife, she decided not to break off the romance. Marshall assured her that he loved both her and Nobunto, and, Lindiwe explained, "because I also loved him, we came to an agreement." She would marry him too after he had saved enough money to pay *lobola* to her family.

Soon Lindiwe became pregnant with his child, and Marshall introduced her to Nobunto. "We didn't have a problem with each other," Lindiwe reported matter-of-factly. Earlier, I had asked Nobunto how she had felt about her co-wife when they first met. Her response was equally pithy: "I liked her because she had children." Scarcely one year later, when Lindiwe was pregnant once again, Marshall proposed inviting her and the children to move into the household with Nobunto. Despite some feelings of jealousy and loss, Nobunto agreed to share her husband and home with a customary co-wife in exchange for becoming co-mother to Lindiwe's children.

Nobunto's natal family history had prepared her for sharing marriage and motherhood and extended family living. Her polygynous father had died when she was very young, leaving three widows with twelve children between them. None of the co-widows ever married again. Collectively, the women raised and supported their children by subsistence farming, making grass mats and mealie, selling pumpkins, and the like. "It was as if we were from one mother," Nobunto reminisced, as she described her close ties to all of her mothers and siblings. When she was eighteen years old, Nobunto married Marshall and moved into his extended family, sharing a household with his parents, his two brothers, his sister-in-law, and his young nieces and nephews. Like vast numbers of married black South Africans during apartheid, the newlyweds quickly had to adjust to living apart. During the early years of their marriage, Marshall found work in a milling factory in distant Johannesburg. Because apartheid laws did not grant residency permits to the families of black migrant workers, the young wife saw her husband only when he could arrange a weekend visit home every two months or so. Nobunto did not ask and does not know whether her husband had lovers in the city during those years.

Lindiwe's parents, in contrast, had a monogamous marriage, but before she met Marshall, she too had accrued close personal experience with shared parenthood. When Lindiwe was four years old, her parents had sent her, the youngest of their eleven children, to be raised by an aunt and uncle in a distant village. She had not returned to her parental home until her father died when she was a teenager. Still, Lindiwe admitted to having had strong misgivings when Marshall invited her and her growing brood to share the close quarters of her senior wife's modest cottage, particularly since he would be present only on the weekends. However, by then both women had already gotten used to sharing Marshall in a weekend, commuter, conjugal arrangement. Besides, Lindiwe keenly wanted to exit the joint household she had been sharing with her sister and her boyfriend and their children. And so, even though Marshall had not yet been able to accumulate the money for *lobola*, she consented to the move.

Traditional Zulu culture endorses polygyny, as Jacob Zuma seems to enjoy reminding the public, with his recurrent Zulu wedding ceremonies.

President Jacob Zuma's three co-wives nap during his inauguration ceremony in Pretoria on May 9, 2009. Reprinted by permission of Gallo Images/Nardus Engelbrecht.

Marshall Silongo, however, was a member of the lay clergy in a local Christian denomination that condemns the practice. Consequently, he agreed to pay *lobola* to Lindiwe's relatives but did not register his second customary union, although it would have been legal under the RCMA to do so. His co-wives spent an emotionally challenging year sharing their husband's attentions on alternate weekend nights in the crowded three-room residence, until Marshall finished building a separate structure for his junior wife. By then, Lindiwe had given birth to three of his children, and she moved with them into the adjacent cabin but left her two teenage daughters residing with Nobunto, their new *umamkulu* (senior mother). Nobunto, for her part, loved having all of the children in her life, and she appreciated the domestic help and company her teen step-daughters provided. Without the plural marriage, Nobunto would have remained childless, and, in her view, "A house without children is not a good house."

Due to Marshall's distant employment, the co-wives spent more family and daily life with each other than with their shared mate, occasionally eating supper together, if one of them had "cooked something good." Yet I did not get the impression that much affection had developed between them. Still, both Nobunto and Lindiwe claimed that they loved and felt loved by their husband. Separate residences had made it much easier to cope with the alternate weekend-night conjugal visits, but it seemed clear that, given their druthers, both women would have chosen a life of monogamous marriage and parenthood with Marshall. The harsh patriarchal legacy of apartheid, poverty, and AIDS grants few black South African women such druthers. Nobunto and Lindiwe both judged sharing this husband and these children a far better bargain than their former circumstances without children or without a husband and father, respectively. "He was sent from God for me," Lindiwe said of their husband. And Nobunto, thanks to her co-wife's children, lived in "a good house" at last. I did not need to be a fan of polygyny to deduce that both women and all five children were better off than they would have been had Marshall still been married only to one childless wife.

In fact, even though Lindiwe would have preferred to be Marshall's sole spouse, she had discovered some compensatory benefits to plural marriage. Subscribing to a view of men's non-monogamous sexual nature similar to that espoused by Walter and the IPC, Lindiwe believed that having two wives "stops him from going around looking for other women." And even though Lindiwe and Nobunto both depicted harmonious spousal relationships with Marshall, Lindiwe counted it a blessing that in those inevitable moments when "there's conflict in one house, he can go cool off at the other house." The quality of the man that a woman marries is immeasurably more significant, in her view, than the quantity of women this man weds. That is why Lindiwe would not object to polygyny for her own daughters, she claimed, "so long as the husband was a good man."

In light of Nobunto's fond memories of being raised by three co-mothers, she surprised me by sharply rejecting Lindiwe's views. Not only would Nobunto advise her daughters against entering a plural marriage, but she claimed not to "know anyone who thinks polygamy is a good idea." It was fortunate in her view that "polygamy is dying out. People today are civilized, and besides it's too expensive." "The problem today," Nobunto explained, "is that the men don't support all of their wives." She agreed with Walter Luzama that men, like the Japanese professor he had described, give their mistresses preferential treatment. Nobunto had personally witnessed the troubling fact that "men support their mistresses better than their legal wives." Her own brother-in-law had one wife and two mistresses, but instead of supporting his wife and their children, he chose to support only his newer mistress and the children she had before he met her. However, Nobunto doesn't buy the widespread claim that plural marriage makes a man more responsible or reliable morally, materially, or sexually. Polygyny is no deterrent to philandering. "Even if he marries the second wife," Nobunto observed cynically, "he'll still have so many mistresses."

Big Brother (and Other) Love

Grounds for Nobunto's skepticism took little effort to locate amid the potpourri of informal polygamous family patterns in contemporary South Africa.[10] Take, for example, the case of Thabo Mabuza, a sixty-seven-year-old retired electric-company worker in rural Kwa-Zulu Natal. Thabo had two wives, more than fifteen surviving children, and almost as many grandchildren. Thabo had married his first wife in a customary wedding more than forty years earlier but later registered this marriage in a civil ceremony. However, when a younger brother of his was killed during the armed clashes between the ANC and Inkatha (IFP) in the early nineties, Thabo assumed responsibility for his brother's widow and children. Practicing a traditional form of "big brotherly love," Thabo took his former sister-in-law as a second wife in a customary levirate marriage.

The relationship between Thabo's two wives struck me as particularly affectionate, close, and collaborative. The former sisters-in-law happily spent much more time with each other than either did with her husband. Thabo owned three modest cabins in their remote, wind-battered village. He occupied the most isolated of the three, an ample, one-room structure, by himself. His co-wives each inhabited the other two cabins, adjacent to each other, along with varying numbers of shared grandchildren and other kin. Had my Zulu translator not been a former neighbor of the Mabuzas, however, I doubt that I would have been let in on a local open secret that vindicated Nobunto's view that polygyny does not prevent philandering. According to my translator, Thabo and his wives had neglected to mention an additional set of children and grandchildren that he had sired with his mistress in a nearby village.

Traditional levirate plural marriages like Thabo's seem destined to disappear if the South African economy and educational system modernize. Not so for the most prevalent variety of informal contemporary polygyny in South Africa, which is a legacy of the brutal system of migrant labor that developed during apartheid. To support their families, the majority of black men in the destitute Bantustands were compelled to seek work in distant gold and diamond mines or in urban factory or construction jobs. The Group Areas Act and Pass Laws prevented their wives, children, or other relatives from migrating with them. Forced to spend most of their working years apart from families whom they could rarely afford to visit, many migrant workers formed informal second marriages and families in the cities and mining towns where they worked. The sex-segregated conditions of the mining towns generated a distinctive institution of same-sex "mine marriages" between some of the adult miners and their "boy-wives."[11]

The racially segregated "homelands" and the Pass Laws of apartheid have come to symbolize the repudiated evils of South Africa's racist past. Disappointingly, however, apartheid's economic legacy of impoverished black migrant labor and the informal dual families it generated remains all too current. *Muvhango,* a popular South African TV "soapie" somewhat analogous to *Big Love,* dramatizes travails, intrigues, and competition between the urban Soweto and the rural branches of a contemporary polygynous family. Globalizing labor conditions are spreading the seedbeds for a variety of dual families among migrant workers across far greater, transnational distances around the world, including in advanced industrial host countries, like the United States and Taiwan.[12]

Finally, post-apartheid ethnographic research has begun to uncover examples of some genuinely distinctive, new practices of queer polygamy that are appearing among South African blacks who live in highly traditional locales. Brian, an informant in a study conducted by anthropologist Graeme Reid of emerging gay spaces in rural South African small towns, had two children with his girlfriend in a port town of northern KZN. At the same time, Brian had maintained clandestine, polyamorous, gay relationships in Ermelo, a rural town near his natal village in neighboring Mpumalanga province. Brian's girlfriend broke up with him in anger when she discovered his homosexual intimacies, but after a few months of missing him, she had a change of heart. Brian and she became lovers again, and he remained involved with his children. Instead of living with them, however, he chose to move back to Ermelo. There, in a polygamous variation of the boy-wife marriages among migrant mine workers, Brian lived openly with Zithembe, his gay male "senior wife," and took additional gay male lovers, referred to as "ladies," whom Zithembe granted him permission to acquire.[13]

Likewise, Sizane, one of Reid's female informants in Mpumalanga, displayed intimate desires that seemed a queer variation of customary traditions of African female husbands. A butch Zulu lesbian, Sizane aspired to emulate Zulu codes of masculinity and patriarchal marriage by paying *lobola* for two wives. Daring to do so within the cultural context of mounting levels of patriarchal and homophobic violence directed especially against black butch lesbians required uncommon confidence and courage.

A Race to Marital Time Shares

In South Africa, one rarely hears public discussion of the jarringly racialized character of legal polygamy and customary marriage, but several legal scholars have labeled this breach of the constitutional commitment to nonracialism its "most embarrassing" feature.[14] Unsurprisingly, it did not take long for a white South African to object to the black racial monopoly on legitimate polygyny. What I do find surprising, however, is the gender of the first person to publicly condemn it as "clear discrimination" against the white minority.[15] Christina Landman, an Afrikaans, self-described feminist professor of theology at the University of South Africa in Pretoria, and a member of the conservative Dutch Reformed Church, garnered a brief international media splash in 1999 when she assailed the injustice of denying white South Africans access to polygyny. White women too need the right to share husbands, Landman argued, if they are to attain and retain marital status. After all, as she pointed out, cultural denigration of single women is not restricted to indigenous African communities. White Afrikaans culture also makes life uncomfortable for women without husbands, and "there are just too few [white] men in the world"[16] to meet the demand.

Cultural insistence on monogamy, Landman reasoned, also forces white women to accept divorces they do not want when their husbands take mistresses. Opening polygyny to whites could help ameliorate these unwelcome effects of gender imbalance. Offering white men the same alternative to sequential monogamy, adultery, and divorce that Walter Luzama and the IPC endorsed could spare many white women the stigma and pain of undesired divorces and spinsterhood. Landman's idiosyncratic feminist twist on this patriarchal logic was to encourage women to take the initiative in the process. She advised divorced white women to "select a married man and go and negotiate with his wife to become part of the family."[17] Landman coined an encomium to polygyny that could serve as a promotional teaser for one of the plot lines on the U.S. cable TV series Big Love: "Timesharing awaits us, ladies," she announced, "and that at a time Viagra was sent for men."[18]

Despite the insouciant flavor of Landman's challenge to the racial restriction on legal polygyny in South Africa, it strikes me as bearing potential constitutional merit. In fact, as someone schooled in the potency of charges of reverse racism in the United States, initially I had trouble understanding the racial logic of the RCMA. Pursuing this topic ranked high on my field research agenda in South Africa in 2007. It served as quite a cross-cultural wake-up call, therefore, to find that none of the Constitutional Court justices I interviewed had even heard of Christina Landman. All conceded that they could imagine the court entertaining a racial challenge to the RCMA. They were "judiciously" circumspect, of course, about expressing their views on the as-yet-untested constitutional questions I posed about customary culture, race, and plural marriage. My dogged questions about this issue did prompt an offhand, somewhat bemused recollection by one justice that in 2006 the court actually had received just such a suit. Two white Christian couples, the justice recalled, had filed an affidavit challenging the constitutionality of the RCMA on grounds of racial and religious discrimination. The justice thought that the court had dismissed the suit without cause on procedural grounds but did not remember the names of the plaintiffs or any details of the case.

Cross-cultural dissonance over racial discourse surfaced again when I set out to pursue this enticing lead. I could find no evidence of media attention to such a suit, and no civil rights lawyers, activists, or academics I queried had even heard of its existence. Luckily, a generous, ingenious law clerk helped me track down the case, and I successfully contacted both of the male plaintiffs, David Witherson and Hendrik Van Heerden.[19] Quite unlike black South African men such as Walter Luzama who register a first civil marriage because they fail to anticipate their future desires for additional brides, both David and Hendrik had made principled decisions not to register their marriages to their senior wives, because they wanted to protect prospective co-wives from having to occupy a secondary status. Hendrik went so far as to wed each of his three wives in separate civil marriage ceremonies at a Home Affairs office, but then to pointedly refuse to file the papers that would officially record any of the unions.

Like Joseph Smith, the nineteenth-century founder of the LDS church in the United States, and like the underground Christian polygamists who are his contemporary heirs, David and Hendrik locate authority for plural marriage in the Old Testament. Complaining that the RCMA clause "which limits its applicability to 'indigenous African people' is discriminatory and infringes [their] constitutional rights," their suit petitioned the court to expand the legal definition of customary marriage to include "customs and usages followed by other groups including groups that regard the Bible and other ancient manuscripts as authoritative in their lives and which form part of the culture of these peoples." The Constitutional Court had declined to grant direct review over the suit, but it did not rule out considering an appeal of the case on its merits if it were resubmitted properly to a lower court first.

Sharp differences between the sexual and marital philosophies of the two white male plaintiffs made me doubt that they would jointly pursue that route. Both men believed their commitment to polygyny was biblically ordained, but they subscribed to markedly incongruent visions of Christian marital intimacy. "We share scriptural understanding of polygyny, but we interpret it differently," summarized David, a fifty-three-year-old management consultant who was raised in the Anglican Church. "I see sex as a very important part of marriage," David explained. "He [Van Heerden] sees it as incidental." David's view could vindicate arguments by slippery slope analysts in the United States, like Stanley Kurtz, that link polygamy to promiscuity. "My interpretation of the word *marriage* is when a man has sexual union with a woman," David elaborated. He viewed (apparently male) orgasm as primarily a spiritual experience, because "male ejaculation projects part of his spirit."

David conceded that an exceptionally strong libido propelled his search for scriptural support for plural marriage. Since adolescence, he had suffered overwhelming sexual cravings and potent fantasies of sexual relations with multiple women simultaneously. A first sexually unsatisfying marriage ultimately failed because he committed an extra-marital transgression after his wife refused to include other women in their marital bed. Traumatized by a painful, expensive divorce in which he lost custody of his two children, he testified to feeling suicidal when a voice spoke to him clearly and led him "to a friend who had a very deep relationship with the Almighty." That experience stirred David to "make a choice to regard the Bible as the law of the Almighty" and to assiduously study the Old and New Testaments.

Reprising the experience of libidinous Joseph Smith a century earlier, David discovered reassuring scriptural references to polygyny. In the process of decoding biblical "passages suggesting that it was pleasing to the Almighty," he too had "a revelation that the Word of God permits a man to have more than one wife." David then tied the knot a second time, with a woman he mistakenly thought understood and shared his sexual needs. But before long, he reported, once again, "sexually I was climbing the wall" and feeling desperate for more bountiful sexual release. Convinced by his diligent exegetical efforts that "casual sex is really not acceptable in the sight of the Almighty," David was no longer willing to commit adultery, and so he divorced again.

This second failed marriage drove David back to scrutinizing the scriptures for a more compatible sexual theology. That was how he arrived at an idiosyncratic, rather New Age version of patriarchal polygyny as the biblical solution to his plight. David agreed with other born-again Christians that the Bible condemns male homosexuality and lesbianism. Careful exegesis of the Holy Word convinced him that it was "an affront and abomination in the sight of the Almighty for a woman to be with more than one man or for a man to be with other men. They'll suffer fire and brimstone." In David's innovative interpretation, however, the Holy Bible permits a husband and his plural, bisexual wives to engage collectively in mutual sexual love.

Fortified with what he believed to be scriptural support for his particular erotic desires, David turned to specialized matchmaking sites on the

Internet to find a compatible libidinous Christian mate. Focusing his selection filters on a woman's heart, soul, and carnality rather than her outward appearance, he soon met and fell in love with "an overweight, not particularly attractive" woman whose sexual passions seemed to match his own. Twice burned, this time David adopted a policy of full and open disclosure about his marital expectations and desires. From the get-go, he revealed his commitment to polygyny and his desire to marry multiple bisexual women who would be sexually involved with each other as well as with him. In addition, in order to preserve his goal of plural marriage, this time David did not enter a legal, civil marriage with his new mate. Instead he drew up "lengthy spiritual legal documents," because "the court of heaven is the ultimate arbiter of what we do in this life."

Perhaps one year later, again through specialized Internet sites, David and his new "spiritual legal" bride recruited a bisexual, Christian woman with a strong sexual drive who was willing to enter a marital trio and share a plural conjugal bed with them. The original understanding, he explained, was that all three parties "should be equally in love and that the women should make love to each other as much as to me." Disappointingly, but perhaps predictably, the triadic erotic honeymoon proved painfully brief. Although the trio spent several nights in bed together, and David made love with both women, the women did not make love with each other. "It turns out that they're not attracted to each other," David conceded with sad resignation. In fact, he acknowledged, "they're not particularly attractive women," and more disappointing, he had concluded that despite their claims, they were not genuinely bisexual either.

Painful jealousy and sexual and domestic incompatibilities quickly surfaced between the two co-wives. Within a matter of weeks, not only were the women refusing to share a bed or even a household with each other, but they were no longer on speaking terms. At considerable financial and emotional cost, David helped to establish his junior wife in a nearby apartment so that he could divide his conjugal time between his estranged wives. He was struggling, perhaps quixotically, to salvage both of his frayed marriages when I interviewed him in July 2007. He found himself "living with parallel monogamy," in his disappointed terms, rather than with the vision of Christian polygamy that had inspired his lawsuit. He still believed that having more than one wife was scripturally legitimate, but he acknowledged having been chastened by what he learned: "It's hugely more difficult to do this in practice than I thought it would be. I really didn't think it would be like this."

Harmonious, Christian, plural married life came much more easily to David's co-plaintiff, Hendrik Van Heerden. A member of the engineering faculty at a Johannesburg technical college, Hendrik, also fifty-three years old but Afrikaans, was raised in the Dutch Reformed Church. He claimed that he began to develop his belief in the religious and moral bases for polygyny when he was a teenager, driven not by sexual urges but because he realized even then that it would lead to "much less debauchery, fornication, child molestation." Hendrik did not attempt to put his theory into practice, however, until much later in life, after his first wife had died in a car crash, and he had spent ten years as a single, celibate parent raising their two children.

When I met Hendrik in 2007, he had three wives whom he had married consecutively over the prior five years and whose ages, counter-intuitively, were forty-nine, fifty-eight, and sixty-eight, respectively. Challenging heterosexual and polygynous gender conventions, as well as my feminist cynicism, Hendrik had married Helen, the youngest of his wives, first, five years before I interviewed the couple. One year later, he took a woman five years older than he as his second wife, and he married his third and oldest wife, a woman fifteen years his senior, less than a year after that.

Hendrik spontaneously confirmed his co-plaintiff's characterization of their differing views on the proper place of sexuality in plural marriage. He lamented that "most men who go into a multiple-wife marriage do it for the wrong reasons" and identified a desire to have sex with several women as the principal error. Hendrik described himself as a man who loved women, but, in contrast to David, for him, "sex is not the priority." Rather, he said, "the point of departure into my marriage is to teach my wives about the scriptures and to teach them to be submissive to the almighty God, the Father." Hendrik believes "that women need to be taught, and they need that covering over them," and he, in turn, loves to meet women's needs for loving, pastoral guidance. His goal is "loving women the right way, and age doesn't matter, outer appearance doesn't matter. What matters is that a woman is a born-again Christian, sincere about wanting to live a scriptural life and wanting to learn, and that she is able to communicate from a basis of mutual love and respect." One aspect of appearance does matter greatly to Hendrik, however. Unlike David, but like Mormon polygamists in the United States, he believes that anti-miscegenation is scriptural. The Seventh Commandment against adultery, in Hendrik's view, does not merely ban extra-marital sex. It likewise prohibits *adulterating* the races through inter-marriage.

Polygyny, the way Hendrik understands and practices it, is "a demanding, scriptural life of responsibility, not for the weak or faint-hearted." Like black IPC patriarch Walter Luzama, Hendrik views polygyny as a committed ethical practice and is appalled by the modern, "civilized" Western world's hypocrisy about fidelity. Mainstream "Western culture incorrectly considers monogamy to be the higher, Christian form of marriage," he lamented, "and yet, fornication is rampant. Most men can't even take care of one woman," he observed with dismay. "They can't even rule over one house, because they don't treat their wives with respect." Establishing trust and loving communication is the critical basis for marital success.

Hendrik professed that he never fights with his wives, forbids himself and them to raise their voices in anger, and makes it his mission to constantly reassure each one of his love: "I always smile at my wives, stay in eye contact with them, cuddle up to them, hold their hands, tell them that I love them, that they're important to me," he elaborated. And indeed, throughout the lengthy interview, Hendrik demonstratively smiled and gazed at, cuddled, held hands with, and exuded affection and support to Helen, his senior wife. He boasted that whenever he brings his wives to social gatherings among born-again Christians who are interested in polygyny, "They all want my wives!"

Unlike his less successful male co-plaintiff, Hendrik had never tried to jointly share a single residence, let alone a single bed, with all of his wives. In fact, one could say that he happily practiced what David had disparagingly termed "parallel monogamy." Hendrik lived with Helen, his "senior" but youngest wife, a divorced, high school history teacher, and with his twenty-one-year-old and her nineteen-year-old son from their respective first marriages. The family's modest single-family house was located, curiously enough, in one of Johannesburg's rare mixed-race residential neighborhoods. Typically, Hendrik spent one night weekly with his second wife, a divorced art teacher and mother of two, who lived in a suburb thirty kilometers away. At least every other week, he tried to make the hundred-kilometer trek to visit his formerly widowed third wife in the large, lavish farmstead she had inherited. Occasionally, Hendrik assembled all of his wives in Johannesburg to enjoy a social evening together with him, perhaps dining at a restaurant or on a movie date.

Helen acknowledged that she and her co-wives sometimes found themselves struggling with feelings of jealousy and competition, just like Nobunto and Lindiwe did. Allocating holidays or access to vacation time alone with Hendrik could prove particularly tricky. Nonetheless, Helen made a incing case that the three women also genuinely liked one another that all felt sufficiently loved by their shared husband and persuaded by his interpretation of scripture to participate in the plural conjugal arrangement with equanimity and goodwill. If Helen had felt any qualms about serving as her husband's co-plaintiff in the suit for white access to legal plural marriage, she kept them well concealed from me. Employing words that echoed Christina Landman's time-sharing proposal, Helen rationalized, "I receive so much love from my husband. So even if I share, I have more than usual women do."

Paradoxes of Polygamy and Modernity

South Africa's experience with plural unions after apartheid can teach us important lessons about polygamy and modernity. The waning popularity of formal polygamy there underscores first how poorly this form of marriage fares in a liberal democracy within a free-market economy. The modern "transformation of intimacy" from bonds forged mainly to serve the religious, economic, and social interests of kin groups to a world of individuals questing for love and passion plants the kiss of death on traditional polygamy. Even in South Africa, where patriarchal polygamy boasts deep historical roots and enjoys legal recognition, this form of marriage and family life is visibly crumbling. If some prominent black men, like current president Jacob Zuma and provincial official Jeri Ngomane, command sufficient resources, stamina, and clout to attract, to sustain, and perhaps to satisfy multiple wives, few of their peers or constituents seem able or eager to follow suit.

All of the traditional African leaders I interviewed heartily endorsed patriarchal polygyny as an African tradition, but not one chose to practice it himself. An NHTL officer, for example, proffered revealing reasons why he personally had taken only one wife. "Tradition doesn't work so well with a monetary system," he allowed, before adding that "women these days are far more educated" and that "the constitution is complicating issues for us." Even the unapologetically patriarchal IPC polygynist Walter Luzama, who lamented that most African men lack sufficient strength and character to choose plural marriage over philandering, also conceded that most women today wouldn't share a husband if they have a better choice: "I don't think it's any woman's wish to have her husband take a second wife."

Increasingly, women in most modern and modernizing societies, including South Africa, believe they do have a better choice, and so do most men. The few maverick white Christian South Africans, like Christina Landman, Mr. and Mrs. Witherson, and Mr. and Mrs. Van Heerden, who seek legal rights to polygyny on racial and religious grounds are spitting into the winds of history. And even *they* desire versions of marital intimacy far closer to the romantic and randy model of plural family life depicted by the decidedly untraditional, fictional Henricksons on *Big Love* than to the atavistic, abuse-prone, patriarchal universe of Warren Jeffs and the FLDS.

Second, if the South African case reminds us that formal polygamy fizzles when societies modernize, it teaches too that this by no means spells the triumph of monogamy. The first epigraph to this chapter conveys the conviction that John Taylor, the third president of the LDS, expressed in 1882 that polygamy is divine. It seems a safe bet to say that most contemporary Americans would judge this view to be misguided at best. However, Taylor came closer to earning his title as a prophet when he boasted that "the United States cannot abolish it. No nation on earth can prevent it, nor all the nations of the earth combined."[20] Although plural marriage appeals to only a fringe of twenty-first-century Christians and secular humanists alike, it has nonetheless proven surprisingly resilient, even within advanced capitalist democracies, including the highly individualistic United States.

De facto forms of plural intimacy and paternity like those that I have surveyed in South Africa also are widespread in North America. A current menu of domestic varietals of polygamy extends far beyond the separatist, sectarian communities of fundamentalist Mormons clustered in Utah, Arizona, Texas, and British Columbia. Indeed, most North American proponents of polygamy today take great pains to distinguish their credos and behaviors from those of the FLDS. Take, for example, the motto "Love, not Force," adopted by TruthBearer.org, a non-Mormon, evangelical Christian pro-polygamy organization.[21] It seems designed to deflect guilt by association with the authoritarian and abusive reputation of fundamentalist Mormons. Or note how Polygamy Day, Inc., which since 2001 has convened an annual conference each August in Old Orchard Beach, Maine, for the small, national movement of polygamy advocates, represents itself: "a nonprofit corporation with the express purpose of promoting public education, awareness, and political action for the cause of de-criminalizing of, and obtaining freedom for, freely consenting, adult, non-abusive marriage-committed polygamy."[22] In the same vein, a matchmaking website for personal ads for polygyny, 2Wives.com, "where Good Pro-Polygamy Families Find More Wives," pointedly reassures prospective clients: "This is only about totally-committed marriage of a husband with 2 wives or more, where all the wives agree 100%."[23] As we have seen, self-designated Christian National Polygamy Advocate Mark Henkel, the founder and leader of TruthBearer.org, predicts wishfully that "freely-consenting, adult, non-abusive, marriage-committed POLYGAMY is the next civil rights battle."[24]

Some of the lopsided marriage-market demographics that undergird the race to time-sharing in South Africa are also expanding potential constituencies for polygyny in the contemporary United States. Despite the anomalous white racist history of homegrown Mormon polygamy, the stunningly skewed "marriageable black male index"[25] of available husbands to wives generates potent incentives for black women to participate in polygyny in the United States, as in South Africa. In June 2008, National Public Radio broadcast interviews with several black Muslim women in Philadelphia who explained their decision to practice polygyny in just these terms. "We're dealing with brothers who are incarcerated," one educated, middle-class woman pointed out, and, "unfortunately, you have the AIDS and HIV crisis, where HIV has struck the African-American community disproportionately to others."[26]

Adrien Katherine Wing, an African American feminist legal scholar, offers rationales for legalizing polygyny similar to those expressed by white South African feminist theologian Christina Landman. Wing views the prevalence of de facto polygamy among African Americans in the United States as a rational response to the dire shortage of marriageable men.[27] Of course, the same social math problem might lead more single black women to consider intimacy with women instead.[28]

Paradoxically, the very globalizing market and media forces that disperse Western individualism, gender and sexual identity politics, and modern transformations of intimacy around the planet also exacerbate the conditions I documented in South Africa that inspire many contemporary varieties of plural marriage. Migrant labor, cultural dislocations, poverty, unemployment, economic inequality, and unequal sex ratios all combine with persistent gender inequality to sustain and spread polygyny and other plural unions in the modern world.

For example, increasing numbers of families from polygynous Islamic cultures have been migrating to countries in North America and Europe whose immigration laws generally exclude polygamous families. This forces migrant men who have more than one wife to choose between sequestering or abandoning their additional wives and children. In March 2007, a fatal fire in a crowded row house in the Bronx, New York, brought this phenomenon into public view when it exposed the secret plural marriage of its owner, Moussa Magassa, an American citizen who was born in Mali. Magassa, a father of five children, perished in the fire, while his two wives, who lived on different floors in the residence, survived.[29]

In addition to religious versions of contemporary polygyny, U.S. cultural soil also sprouts more post-modern and queer species of plural unions than I could readily locate in South Africa. For example, Liberated Christians, a network of non-Mormon Christian sexual radicals, advocates an egalitarian system of polygamy that might pass muster under the South African equality clause. Liberated Christians proudly distinguishes its sex-egalitarian ideology of voluntary polygamy from patriarchal, biblical versions of Christian polygyny. Putting a religious spin on the secular New Age, gender-neutral, free-love ideology of polyamory, the group interprets the New Testament to provide support for plural husbands as well as plural wives.[30]

A host of radical forms of plural union fall loosely under the catch-all term *polyamory,* which the website of the Polyamory Society defines as

> the nonpossessive, honest, responsible and ethical philosophy and practice of loving multiple people simultaneously. Polyamory emphasizes consciously choosing how many partners one wishes to be involved with rather than accepting social norms which dictate loving only one person at a time. Polyamory is an umbrella term which integrates traditional multipartner relationship terms with more evolved egalitarian terms. Polyamory embraces sexual equality and all sexual orientations towards an expanded circle of spousal intimacy and love.[31]

Polyamorists, most of whom literally desire intimacy with many loves, not many wives or husbands, subscribe to a broad spectrum of religious and secular philosophies of intimacy. Polyfidelity, one of the prominent versions, refers to any combination of three or more women and/or men who are committed to a sexually exclusive partnership, such as Franny's duogamous triad of gay uncles. Polyfidelity lovers typically live together, share their lives and resources, and consider themselves married to each other.[32] However, not all polyamorists are sexually exclusive or share homes and nest eggs with their lovers. In fact, some are not even sexually active with all of their intimate partners. And unlike most polygamists (or contemporary same-sex couples), few polyamorists seek the state's seal of approval for their intimate relationships.

Whatever polyamorists' particular patterns, most of them would sign on to the credo of the Unitarian Universalists for Polyamory Awareness (UUPA): "The philosophy and practice of loving or relating intimately to more than one other person at a time with honesty and integrity."[33] The UUPA advocates for "any form of family structure, whether monogamous or multi-partner, which is characterized by free and responsible choice, mutual consent of all involved, and sincere adherence to personal philosophical values."[34] This is a platform spacious enough to encompass Franny's gay uncles as well as the planned three- and four-parent families depicted in chapters 1 and 2. It is a far cry from the patriarchal polygyny of fundamentalist Mormons in the United States or the IPC in South Africa.

Polyamory is also a far cry from the rampant philandering, adultery, and closeted polygamy currently practiced in the United States. A fringe phenomenon that is all too easy to lampoon, principled polyamory is nonetheless an ethical response to the failures of the nation's religiously rooted insistence on the one-size-fits-all regime of monogamous marriage. Polyamorists reject the hypocrisy of imposing on everyone a monolithic set of family and sexual values which winds up driving underground the inevitable, widespread breaches by the Scarlet Lettermen and legions of their less prominent brethren. This shadow world of concealed lapses serves as surefire compost for abuse, hardship, and our chronic political sex scandals whenever they come to light.[35]

Under bigamy statutes in my state of New York, for example, the January 2008 and 2010 weddings of South Africa's President Zuma and the second marriages of Walter Luzama and Marshall Silongo would be Class E felonies, punishable by up to four years in prison. In contrast, adultery is a Class B misdemeanor, with a maximum sentence of three months in jail or probation,[36] and it is a violation, as the tabloid behavior of former mayor of New York City Republican Rudy Giuliani flaunted, that is no longer prosecuted. Although the sex scandal surrounding the exposé of Vito Fossella's secret second family derailed his political career, and he was convicted of drunk driving and sentenced to four days in a Virginia detention center, no charges were filed against him for breaching his monogamous marital vows. Because Fossella and Laura Fay, the mother of his closeted "love child," did not hold themselves out to be a married couple, they did not commit bigamy under New York State law but the much lesser offense of adultery.

Engaging in clandestine plural unions and plural paternity is far less criminal or stigmatized in the United States than openly embracing these practices, as pro-polygamy advocates consistently point out and as hundreds of Eldorado families can readily attest. The state of Utah prosecuted open polygynist Tom Green after he flaunted his family of five wives and more than twenty-five children in appearances on national TV. When the Utah Supreme Court upheld Green's conviction on four counts of bigamy and child rape in 2001, one legal commentator aptly observed, "Green is not being punished for having children with several different women. He is being punished for sticking around."[37] Perhaps it is more accurate to say that he was punished for being open about doing so. After Green served a six-year sentence and was released from prison in 2007, four of his five plural wives (who are mothers of many of his children) still considered themselves willingly married to him. The terms of his parole, however, forbid Green to maintain marital relationships with three of them.[38] It is difficult to understand how this serves the best interests of his children or of the three committed "spiritual wives" he is forbidden to acknowledge. The benefit to society from this prohibition is equally opaque.

A few maverick feminists, including yours truly, would rather encourage more plural husbands, fathers, and lovers to stick around.[39] Closeted co-wives and their children lack essential rights and protections. In 2005, responding to the increased incidence of polygamous immigrant families and to the enduring FLDS communities in their midst, Status of Women Canada (SWC), a governmental organization that advises on policy in the interest of women and gender equality, commissioned a collection of research reports on polygamy. The prominent legal and social science scholars who produced the reports offered competing proposals on how Canadian law should respond to the illegal polygamous marriages within its borders.[40] All of the authors opposed the patriarchal character of Islamic and FLDS forms of polygamy, but they disagreed over how best to assist women in those marriages. While some feminist scholars defended Canadian anti-bigamy statutes, others recommended decriminalizing polygamy and offering recognition to foreign plural marriages among immigrants. Like the South African feminists who supported the RCMA, the Canadians arguing for legal recognition of these plural marriages believe that "women [and, I would add, their children] are most likely to be in need of and most likely to benefit from further recognition."[41] Unrecognized wives, children, and families are unprotected wives, children, and families.

A number of feminist legal scholars in the United States have developed more fundamental challenges to prohibitions on polygamy. Several examine legal traditions of "private ordering" and contract law to develop a legal framework that would decriminalize polygamy and protect the rights of women and children within plural marriages.[42] Adrien Wing's proposed response to the demographic plight of heterosexual African American women who wish to marry, for example, is to revive common law traditions of personal law that could recognize polygynous families like those formed by the Philadelphia black Muslims interviewed on NPR.[43]

A potentially historic test case of the constitutionality of Canadian anti-polygamy laws was filed with the British Columbia Supreme Court in 2009. Likely to reach the national Supreme Court of Canada, it asks whether criminal statutes against polygamy violate protections for freedom of religion in the Canadian Charter of Rights and Freedom.[44] Even in the much more conservative United States, a few mainstream political voices have dared to speak in favor of decriminalizing polygamy. David Zolman, a Republican former Utah state representative, went so far as to advocate issuing a state apology for the raids on Short Creek.[45] Utah Supreme Court Chief Justice Christine Durham's dissenting opinion in the 2006 case *State v. Holm* noted the state's inconsistency in upholding Holm's conviction for bigamy while it did not prosecute unmarried co-habitants.[46] The *Big Love* website hosts a serious forum where members of the program's cast and its audience discuss how it has changed their views of the advantages and disadvantages of plural marriage.[47]

Despite these recent chinks in North America's historically impregnable armor against polygamy, I see scant grounds for the hopeful epigraph to this chapter from the pro-polygamy website predicting that the election of the first African American president in the United States augurs a future out-and-proud polygynous one, like President Jacob Zuma in South Africa. It is not even likely that the election of President Obama has enhanced the prospects for decriminalizing plural unions in the United States. And Mark Henkel's bold claim that the movement to legalize polygamy represents the next great civil rights struggle in U.S. history strikes me as unduly optimistic, if not delusional. After all, despite recent gains for same-sex marriage in New England and Iowa, the prospect of establishing it as a federal constitutional right through congressional legislation or through a gay version of the 1967 *Loving v. Virginia* Supreme Court ruling still appears to lie years ahead. There are no signs that Americans have had a significant change of heart in the past few years from their historical aversion to polygamy. As the final epigraph to this chapter documents, a Gallup Poll conducted in May 2009, "just before we were treated to the saucier details of the lives of South Carolina's Republican governor and Nevada's Republican senator," reported levels of public disapproval nearly identical to those in the 2005 survey—91 percent of Americans judged polygamy morally wrong.[48] Advocates for polygamy would have to amass a monstrous mountain of legal and cultural banana peels to make the slope of human rights principles steep and slick enough for them to slide down.

Nonetheless, for the sake of argument, let's entertain the unlikely event that polygamy advocates will eventually carry this off. Let's imagine that someday this marginal, unpopular constituency will persuade courts, legislatures, and the populace that a democratic society has no more right to dictate the number of spouses its citizens may wed than it does their race, religion, or gender. What consequences would follow for American women, children, families, and society?

The South African experience suggests potential benefits from such an outcome, even for those who oppose plural marriage. By criminalizing the practice, as we saw in chapter 3, the United States drove Mormon polygyny underground, enabling sexual and other abuses to flourish unmonitored. "If you outlaw polygamy," one astute commentator observes, "only outlaws will have polygamy."[49] It is far wiser, I believe, to pursue the South African strategy of legally recognizing polygamy in order to regulate abuses and to nudge its practice toward a gender-equality standard.

Counter-intuitively, moreover, legalizing plural marriages might even lead to fewer rather than more women and children who inhabit them. Strict enforcement of state laws that regulate the age of consent to marry and that criminalize rape, incest, and domestic abuse could undermine the power of ruthless patriarchs like Warren Jeffs who have been allowed to rule over renegade polygamous communities with impunity. Were women genuinely free to consent to enter (and to exit) plural marriages, I strongly doubt that hordes of American women would clamor to share husbands. That is the wager feminists on the South African Law Commission made when they compromised with the demands of patriarchal tribal authorities by recognizing customary marriages while subordinating them to the equality clause.[50] The declining practice of customary marriage in South Africa, even among its most vocal advocates, vindicates this wager.

It seems safe to predict that were plural marriages legal and genuinely consensual in the United States, where polygamy was never part of the cultural mainstream and remains deeply stigmatized, only a small minority of citizens of either gender would choose to enter them. As *New York Times* columnist John Tierney observed after viewing *Big Love*, "After watching the husband on the show struggle to pay for three households and watching his three wives struggle for his attention, the question that comes to mind is not how to keep polygamy illegal. The question is why we bother to ban something that takes so much work these days."[51]

And if modernity erodes the appeal of polygyny to men, modern polyandry is scarcely thinkable. The notion that a contemporary woman would want to have more than one husband at a time serves mainly as the butt of cynical feminist humor. One recent cartoon, for example, depicts a working woman returning home at the end of her workday to find her three unshaven, Joe-six-pack husbands in their boxers and undershirts planted on the sofa watching a ballgame on the tube. Her exasperated gag line: "You mean none of you took out the trash?"

Reportedly, a discussion about plural marriage among South African feminists evoked similar sentiments about polyandry. A lesbian activist in the group asked if there were any lesbians who were in polyamorous relationships who would be willing to volunteer to serve as plaintiffs in a test case to demand equal rights to polygamy under the equality clause of the constitution. When another woman asked her whether polyandry had been recognized, the activist told her that polyandry wasn't legal yet either, but she had concluded that it would be much easier to find lesbians who would be willing to marry several women than to find a woman willing to marry more than one husband. She reported that all of her straight women friends thought she was crazy when she asked them that question. The prospect of coping with more than one husband struck them as punitive rather than liberating.[52]

Western feminists can readily enjoy the humor in this remark and the cartoon, but the South African experience suggests that we too need to temper our knee-jerk ideological hostility to polygamy. The stubborn persistence of fundamentalist Mormon polygyny, despite more than a century of persecution, and the emergence of new kinds of polygamous families in the United States should convince us that some women hunger for intimacies that do not always pass feminist muster. When a culture comes to presume that "love makes a family," love (abetted by lust, religious fervor, cultural traditions, demographic imbalances, economic challenges, and sheer human idiosyncrasies) inevitably will make women who seek or are willing to settle for unions that transgress numerical conventions as well as feminist values.

Feminists must come to terms with the enduring allure to women of diverse religious ideologies and communities, including some that prescribe strong, unequal gender differences in intimacy, parenting, and family life.

Decades of anti-feminist backlash campaigns for family values should have convinced us that a substantial minority of contemporary women continue to desire the domestic order of the "feminine mystique" that so many feminists of my generation rebelled against in the 1960s and 1970s. Polygyny, of course, goes well beyond the feminine mystique, and its appeal to women is even harder for most feminists to fathom or to countenance. I hope that this book will make it a bit easier to do both.

My study of polygyny in South Africa and the United States suggests that it represents an attempt to reconcile men's competing erotic, domestic, and religious passions while offering some modest compensations to the women who love (or are mated to) them. When in 1843, Mormon founder Joseph Smith's potent libido rubbed up against his equally fervent iconoclastic Christian faith, the combustion propelled him to receive his momentous divine "revelation" of "The Principle" of plural marriage.[53] We have seen how similar personal struggles led Walter Luzama from philandering to the polygynous IPC and David Witherson to his idiosyncratic bisexual interpretation of Holy Scriptures. Polygyny, in other words, is a patriarchal bargain offered to and by men who are willing to accept social and economic responsibility for their sexual urges and privileges. Women like Helen Van Heerden, Lindiwe and Nobunto Silongo, Walter Luzama's two wives, Cristina Landman, the Philadelphia black Muslims interviewed on NPR, and many others find this to be the lesser of evils among the, admittedly disappointing, options for intimacy and family life available to too many women in South Africa, North America, and most everywhere else today.

To be sure, a polygynous brew of intimacy is no feminist cup of tea. Yet that does not make it our provenance, or anyone else's, to dictate the beverage of choice for any women but ourselves. The proper mission for feminism and for a democratic society is to upgrade the menu of love potions on offer and to make them available to as many women, and men, as possible.

5

Unhitching the Horse from the Carriage

Love without Marriage among the Mosuo

The primary reason for the emergence of human pair-bonding was to ensure that mothers do not raise children alone. The evolutionary record suggests that men and women developed an unusual way of living together, primarily because the human infant needs a father and the human mother needs a mate.

—David Blankenhorn, *The Future of Marriage,* 2009

Marriage remains the most efficient engine of disenchantment yet invented. There is nothing like uninterrupted cohabitation and grinding responsibility to cast a clear, unforgiving light on the object of desire.

—Caitlin Flanagan, "The Wifely Duty," 2003

IF THERE WERE an international endangered species status for vanishing family forms, I would nominate without delay the Mosuo people of southwest China, whose family system serves as this book's final, least familiar case study. The contemporary world stands to lose a great deal, I believe, if we allow this unique, ancient family system to expire. We would lose a species of happy family life that Tolstoy never contemplated, one that offers creative solutions to intractable contradictions between individual eros and family security that seem particularly pertinent today. The resilient, pre-modern Mosuo family system anticipated by millennia core principles of Giddens's "pure relationship" of late modernity. Recall Giddens's theory that late twentieth-century economic and social conditions "severed [sexuality] from its age-old integration with reproduction, kinship and the generations"[1] and enabled the utopian practice of intimacy that he termed "confluent love" to emerge. He portrayed this as a world where equals can pursue intimacy purely "for its own sake," and intimate

Giddens

Winding mountain switchbacks en route to Lugu Lake.

relationships endure only so long as they "deliver enough satisfactions for each individual to stay within it."[2] Yet the Mosuo people have been practicing intimate relationships that arguably are even "purer" than this for two millennia.[3]

In 1995, I co-taught a graduate seminar on family and kinship, East and West, with the late William G. Skinner, an eminent Sinologist and anthropologist. That was how I first learned of the existence of the Mosuo people, a small ethnic-minority culture in southwest China that, Bill reported to my utter amazement, did not practice marriage. A dozen years were to pass before I finally made a pilgrimage to the magnificent mountain habitat of the Mosuo in order to observe this exotic family system with my own skeptical eyes, ears, and mind.

Thus, in August 2007, I became one of hundreds of thousands of annual visitors who willingly journey seven uncomfortable hours from the nearest city, Lijiang, over jagged, hairpin switchbacks to reach the remote environs of Lugu Lake in Yunnan province. The Chinese state officially recognizes fifty-six ethnic "nationalities," and Yunnan is home to a hefty share of them. Perched high in the Himalayan borderlands of Yunnan and Sichuan provinces near the Tibetan frontier, Lugu Lake is one of the most popular destinations in China's flourishing domestic tourist industry. Promotional materials lure visitors, 90 percent of whom are Chinese nationals, to savor spectacular natural scenery and colorfully costumed members of ethnic-minority cultures. The prime cultural magnets drawing travelers to Lugu Lake, however, are the fabled family and sexual customs of the estimated forty to fifty thousand surviving members of the ancient Mosuo culture who inhabit its surrounding villages.

The Mosuo consider themselves to be an autonomous ethnic group, but the Chinese state officially classifies them as a distinctive subculture of the much larger Naxi nationality.[4] Distinctive, indeed. For the family regime the Mosuo practice is one of the world's oldest, its most flexible and resilient, and arguably its most original. Approximately two millennia ago, Tibeto-Burman ancestors of the contemporary Mosuo devised what appears to be the only family and kinship system in the anthropological or historical record that is not based on marriage.[5] Mosuo family principles directly contradict the three basic contemporary convictions about marriage, parenting, and family life that I identified in the introduction to this book: (1) marriage is a universal institution; (2) the ideal family structure for raising children is an "intact" family consisting of a married heterosexual couple and their biological or adopted children; (3) children generally, and boys especially, need and yearn to know and live with their biological fathers. Perhaps even more provocatively, traditional Mosuo family life also undermines two additional, rarely questioned beliefs about desirable parenting. It challenges, first, the idea that the quality and stability of a couple's marriage profoundly affects their children's welfare and security and, second, the view that parents who indulge in multiple extra-marital sexual liaisons irresponsibly threaten their children's emotional well-being.

Traditional Mosuo family life presents an exception that profoundly questions, rather than proves, all of these rules. Mosuo kinship, in startling contrast with traditional Chinese patriarchy, is primarily matrilineal and matrilocal. "Happiness is defined as the ability to live in harmony with matrilineal kin," explains one of the anthropologists who knows the Mosuo best. "The ultimate meaning of life in this world is to uphold and maintain household harmony."[6] Instead of marrying and sharing family life with one or more spouses, adult Mosuo children remain in extended, multi-generational households with their mother and her blood relatives. Families assign the role of *dabu,* the household head, to whichever adult woman or man they judge most competent to manage their domestic and economic activities. Together, family members own, maintain, and inherit the family property, perform the necessary labor, rear all children born to the women of the household, and care for their aged and dependent members.

Traditional Mosuo family values radically separate sexuality and romance from domesticity, parenting, caretaking, and economic bonds. Sex life is strictly voluntary and nocturnal, while family life is obligatory and diurnal. The cultural attitude toward heterosexual desire is permissive, relaxed, and non-moralistic, so long as individuals observe strict verbal taboos against discussing their erotic activities among relatives or in mixed-gender settings. At the age of thirteen, a girl undergoes an initiation "skirt" ceremony which culminates in giving her a literal sleeping room of her own. In what the Mosuo language terms her "flower chamber," she can freely invite, receive, or rebuff nocturnal visits from any male suitor who chooses to come to call. An analogous "pants" ceremony marks the cultural passage to maturity for boys who turn thirteen, but they do not receive private sleeping quarters. Instead, mature males become eligible to practice *tisese,* which the Chinese misleadingly translate as "walking marriage" (*zouhun*). The Mosuo term, however, literally means that a man "goes back and forth." Men live, eat, and work with their maternal families by day, but after nightfall, they can seek entry into the flower chambers of any women they desire.

Traditionally the primary form of *tisese,* which anthropologist Cai Hua has termed "furtive" or "closed" visiting, entailed no public acknowledgment or obligations between the parties. Under the cover of night, adults were free to enjoy erotic intimacy with as many or as few partners as their hearts and bodies craved. Evidence suggests, however, that the secondary form of *tisese,* termed the "conspicuous" or "open" visit by Cai Hua, is the more widespread practice today, and perhaps always has been.[7] Couples who wish to declare and solidify their love conduct a modest ceremony in which the man's representative presents gifts on his behalf to his lover's kin. After the ceremony, he may openly visit his lover on an indefinite, presumably exclusive basis. It also establishes modest expectations for reciprocal assistance between the pair and sometimes their households. However, whenever a man spends the night with a lover, or *axiao,* whether furtive or open, he is expected to return to his maternal homestead by morning. That is the locus of his domestic life and labor, the site of his primary intimate bonds, his social status, obligations, and security.

Among the many extraordinary features of traditional Mosuo family and kinship, perhaps none is as rare as the equality and autonomy it affords women over their sexual and procreative lives.[8] Mutual desire alone governs romantic and sexual union for women and men alike. Parents and kin do not meddle or concern themselves with the love lives of their daughters (or sons), because mate choice carries almost no implications for the family or society. Under the *tisese* system, men, who must "walk back and forth," exercise slightly more initiative (or depending on one's point of view, bear somewhat more of a burden) than women when it comes to petitioning for sexual and romantic connections. However, Mosuo women can freely refuse any undesired visits, and they can invite desired ones. They do not suffer the nearly universal double standard that regulates women's sexuality elsewhere. Mosuo culture does not venerate female chastity or judge women's sexual behavior differently from men's. Girls and boys alike learn traditional courting songs and receive encouragement to desire, pursue, and enjoy (hetero)sexual lovers.

Likewise, Mosuo women are exceptionally free from reproductive demands, to a degree particularly mind-boggling when compared with both the Confucian and Chinese Communist regimes. Male lovers or in-laws do not pressure women to produce (especially male) heirs or to engage in sexual activity at all if they are not in the mood. Mosuo maternal families do not need or want each daughter to bear as many children as patrilineal peasant families need their daughters-in-law to do. For the economic and social survival of a Mosuo matrilineage, each generation of women must bear at least one daughter and collectively produce a gender mix of children, but no individual woman must procreate. Nor is any woman individually responsible to care for her children, if she does. Lactating sisters traditionally share breast-feeding as well as childrearing tasks. The Mosuo language does not distinguish between a mother and a maternal aunt but employs the same word, *emi*, for both.[9]

Mosuo women's reproductive autonomy has led to distinctive historical fertility patterns compared with women in nearby ethnic groups, and particularly compared with Han women before the revolution. During the twentieth century, Mosuo women gave birth to fewer children overall, spaced their pregnancies further apart, and were more likely to forgo childbearing entirely or to give birth to only one child. The Mosuo also achieved lower mortality rates than their neighbors, until interventions by the Chinese Communists wreaked havoc on their family economy.[10] In fact, traditional Mosuo men enjoy much less control over their parenting prospects than their sisters do. Because men generally do not live with or co-parent their biological offspring, their sexual behavior has no implications for their own parenting careers or family size. Instead, the collective childbearing of their sisters determines men's parental roles. Mosuo men are primary social fathers to their nieces and nephews.

So potently does the typical patrilocal Chinese peasant family need and desire male heirs that it generally considers the birth of a daughter to be at best a "Small Happiness," as the title of Carma Hinton's 1984 documentary film about Chinese gender relations in the revolutionary village Fanshen put it.[11] The Mosuo, in contrast, claim to have no gender preference in their offspring. Western audiences who view a more recent documentary film about Mosuo kinship experience a mind-bending moment along these lines. A Mosuo woman describes the birth of her third child and recounts asking her mother, who had delivered the baby, whether her newborn was a girl or a boy. The new mother claims, perhaps apocryphally, that her mother replied, "I didn't notice."[12]

In fact, the matrilineal character of traditional Mosuo kinship generates at least a modest structural preference for daughters over sons. However, Mosuo culture has also developed mechanisms to cope with the arbitrary effects of infertility or gender imbalance among a family's offspring. Relatives and close friends sometimes exchange or adopt children among themselves when their families need to gain (or to shed) daughters or sons. Yang Erche Namu, an international celebrity Mosuo singer, former fashion model, and entrepreneur, describes how her mother had been offered just such an exchange by a close friend. Because Namu's mother lacked a son, her close friend Dujema offered to trade her youngest boy for infant Namu.[13] Gender-skewed families could also recruit needier relatives or sometimes invite an "open" *axiao* of the missing gender to join their households, so that a genre of de facto, but not contractual, marriage could form within a maternal extended family.

A Society without Fathers or Fatherlessness

Whenever I report that I journeyed to a culture in which adults do not normally marry or live with their lovers, most Western listeners respond with a series of anxious questions about fatherhood: But do the children know who their fathers are? Don't the children want to have fathers? Don't fathers have any responsibility for their children? What happens to the men in the maternal family? What happens to the children (and especially the boys) who grow up without fathers? Questions like these reveal more about contemporary Western family ideology and preoccupations than about Mosuo kinship or concerns, of course. They presuppose that biology determines family bonds, that our contemporary taken-for-granted family relationships are natural and universal, and that what Westerners call "fatherlessness" inherently injures children and societies. It routinely seems to strain credulity when I try to explain that the traditional Mosuo family system does not assign social significance to the role of male genitor, and jaws invariably drop when I quote Namu's claim that people of her mother's generation "did not inquire about their fathers: whatever happened in a woman's room, in the warm light of her own private fire, was a woman's private affair."[14]

All children born to the same Mosuo woman are full siblings, whether or not they share the same genitor. Mosuo culture lacks the Western concept of half- or step-siblings. The woman in the *Tisese* documentary who claimed that her mother had not bothered to notice the gender of her newborn had given birth to three children, and each had a different biological genitor. The woman's first great love had died in an accident soon after her first child was born. She discovered she was pregnant a second time after indulging in a casual, brief liaison with a man she met in an urban center while visiting on family business. She never had contact with that lover again, nor did she inform him of her pregnancy. With her next long-term *axiao,* she had conceived her third and last child. Despite these diverse genetic origins, the three children share the identical family status and identical parents. None is fatherless.

If biological paternity carries no inherent implications for Mosuo kinship, these days it is nonetheless often a matter of common local knowledge. Genetic fathers of children born within open *tisese* relationships typically acknowledge their offspring, give them occasional gifts, and develop avuncular relationships with them, at least for as long as the adult *axiao* relationship with the mother endures. In a sense, one could say that Mosuo kinship rules reverse the social expectations that American culture assigns to fathers and maternal uncles. Likewise, although Mosuo kinship is not rooted in marriage, the culture does not entirely banish marriage. Mosuo kinship has been a flexible system open to pragmatic adaptations that help families to survive. As we have seen, one strategy families have devised to redress gender imbalances allows for exceptions to the cultural rule against couples living together. There are historical precedents for both uxorilocal (residing with the woman's family) and virilocal (residing with the man's family) instances of de facto marriages.

Nonetheless, traditional Mosuo culture does not employ the idiom of marriage to depict such relationships, and the categories of husband and father do not apply. Contemporary Mosuo informants regard *tisese* rather than marriage as their practice "since time immemorial," which according to some scholars extends back earlier than 200 BC.[15] Although there have been substantial changes in Mosuo family practices over time, particularly upheavals since the Communists came to power, *tisese* remains the primary institution for sexual union and reproduction. It now co-exists with secondary forms of contemporary marriage and co-habitation.

Although few Americans, and even few family scholars, seem to have heard of the Mosuo, they have attracted substantial media attention. In fact, the popularity of contemporary ethnic tourism to Lugu Lake is largely a product of the widespread, titillating media treatment that the Mosuo have received both in China and more globally since three provocative books about them were published in the 1980s and 1990s. The books' titles alone sensationalize Mosuo gender and kinship arrangements. *The Remote Country of Women,* a bitingly satirical novel about China's coercive Cultural Revolution, romanticizes Mosuo free sexuality and harmonious mother-centered family life in order to condemn the fanatical repressive authoritarianism of the Maoist regime.[16] *A Society without Fathers or Husbands,* an ethnography published nearly a decade later in French with an introduction by Claude Lévi-Strauss, remains so controversial in the People's Republic of China that it still has not been translated into Chinese.[17] The same year that *A Society without Fathers or Husbands* was published, Mosuo celebrity Namu published the first of a series of uninhibited memoirs that are widely credited with (or blamed for) generating much of the ensuing onslaught of media exposure and domestic tourism.[18]

Recurrent feature stories about the Mosuo have appeared in the popular media in China and abroad ever since in venues ranging from CCTV in China, ABC's *Evening News with Peter Jennings* in the United States, and PBS's *Frontline* to *National Geographic, Time/Asia* magazine, and the *Lonely Planet.*[19] These typically portray the Mosuo as "living fossils" of a lost world, alternately characterizing them as "the last matriarchy" or as a utopian land of peace, harmony, and free love. According to the ABC News version, "Anthropologists say because men here have no power, own no land, and play subservient sexual roles, there is nothing for them to fight about. This makes this culture one of the most harmonious societies on the planet. They have no word for war. There are no murders and no rapes."[20] Or, in *Lonely Planet*'s more succinct summary, "The society's run by women, they don't marry; and taking lovers is encouraged."[21]

Surprisingly, some scholars represent the Mosuo in similar starry-eyed terms. For example, a literary critic's review of *The Remote Country of Women* is more hyperbolic even than the media examples just quoted:

> There is no marriage; women freely take lovers and are primarily respon-
> sible for home and family. The men only have a roof to sleep under if they
> are accepted as lovers by a woman and only so long as she or he desires.
> The Mosuo are not only unabashed in their sexuality, but live powerful
> emotional lives, which, however, almost never erupt into violence because
> they lack a sense of possessiveness.[22]

Romantic and nostalgic depictions of the Mosuo like these foster what anthropologist Louisa Schein calls "internal orientalism" among hundreds of thousands of Asian visitors whom the tourist industry now lures to Lugu Lake annually.[23]

Of course, however, the Mosuo are by no means "living fossils." Although their traditional family system has proven impressively resilient, it is far from static or impervious to history. The Maoist Cultural Revolution followed by capitalist modernization and tourism instigated profound, paradoxical shifts in Mosuo family practices and ideology. Before I discuss these ironic transformations, I want to introduce three contemporary Mosuo families whose elder members lived through them and whom I visited and interviewed during my own ethnic tourist foray in August 2007.

Three Contemporary Mosuo Families

An anthropologist at the Dongba Culture Research Institute in Lijiang arranged for Gezo Ita, a Mosuo woman, to organize and guide my ethnographic tour of her home community.[24] When Gezo was ten years old, her family had sent her from their village near Lugu Lake to attend school in distant Lijiang, where she later married and remained to live and work. I had asked to visit some families who live in Luoshui village, the Mosuo tourist mecca on the shores of Lugu Lake, as well as some in more distant locales not yet on the commercial tourist radar. Gezo accompanied me and my multi-ethnic support entourage on the family visits she had

The author visiting the Dashu household.

coordinated. Our first stop was at the home of the Dashus, the "traditional Mosuo family" she had selected to host us overnight.[25] The Dashus inhabit a working family farm compound situated a twenty-minute drive or an hour's hike beyond Yongning market town, the county seat, and more than an hour's drive from the popular tourist villages on Lugu Lake. At the time of our visit, ten members of four generations of Dashus resided in the family's traditional, large, ancestral Mosuo residence.

The household *dabu*, fifty-four-year-old Jiama, had been her mother's only child and was also the sole member of her generation of Dashus. Most likely this is because Jiama was born in 1953, just a few years before the first team of Communist Chinese People's Liberation Army cadres arrived and used draconian methods to "liberate" the Mosuo from their family, cultural, and property system. Jiama's mother had died long ago, but her aged, hunchback maternal aunt occupied the revered Mosuo status of grandmother, and with it residence in the household's focal "grandmother's room," even though infertility had prevented her from giving birth to any children herself. There were no other surviving members of this

The grandmother of the Dashu family.

oldest generation of Dashus. During our stay, "grandmother" participated in lighter household chores—fetching kindling from the courtyard for the eternally lit hearth, emptying plastic wash basins used for morning tooth brushing, feeding the chickens and pigs, and gesturing enthusiastically to cajole guests like me to sample the fried bread and oil tea that the family had prepared specially for our visit.

Fortunately for the once-endangered Dashu lineage, Jiama had proved much more fecund than had her mother or aunt. For more than three decades, she had sustained an exceptionally long-lasting, exclusive walking marriage with a man with whom she conceived seven living children. At the time of my visit in August 2007, her four daughters and three sons ranged in age from nineteen to thirty-eight. Three of the daughters but only the youngest son still lived at home. Jiama's oldest daughter had suffered a severe head injury when she was a small child, and she was left both deaf and mute. During our stay, she performed most of the visible indoor domestic chores of food preparation, cleaning, and serving. Her two resident sisters, both of them mothers, made only brief appearances in the central grandmother's room or the public courtyard during our stay.

Jiama's youngest child, who is bilingual in Mosuo and Chinese, was planning to go to a provincial university the following year. I observed this affectionate, engaged young uncle reading to his younger nieces and nephew, drilling them on Chinese words, and patiently looping himself in rope for the endless rounds of Chinese jump rope his nieces loved to play. Close upon the heels of our arrival at the Dashu residence, Jiama's twenty-nine-year-old son arrived home for a visit from distant Lijiang, where, I was told, he and his wife lived and worked in "the tourist industry." Accompanying this son home for the visit were two women friends and colleagues, one Han Chinese, the other a Turkish-Swede who, like me, spoke neither Mosuo nor Mandarin. Jiama's other two adult children also live and work elsewhere, one of them reportedly also in a "modern" marriage with children.

Three members of the fourth, youngest generation of Dashus were home during my visit, each born to a different mother. Jiama's ten-year-old grandson was her second daughter's son. However, I discovered that only one of the two avid Chinese jump ropers actually was a full-fledged

The author with the fourth generation of the Dashu family.

member of the Dashu lineage and homestead—Jiama's third daughter's seven-year-old girl. It turned out that the girl's five-year-old playmate was not a Dashu, because she was the daughter of Jiama's married son who had brought his women friends home with him from Lijiang. He had arrived laden with new Western clothing and toys for his daughter, who was the primary reason for his visit. The little girl no longer lived with either of her genetic parents. She was spending the summer in this, her father's household, in part because it offered her companionable playmates. During the school year, however, she would return to her maternal grandmother's household, located closer to her school in Yongning. One year earlier, her parents had moved together to distant Lijiang to work in the tourist industry, and since then they had been taking turns visiting their daughter as often as they could.

The second "traditional Mosuo family" that Gezo arranged for me to visit lived in an even larger family farm compound than the Dashus did and even further off the trodden tourist trail. Nonetheless, this family proved to be even less traditional than the Dashu lineage. Ayi, the second family's *dabu*, was once again a woman in her fifties and the only household member of her generation. Ayi headed a three-generation family composed simply of her own mother, herself, and four of her six adult children. When I inquired about grandchildren, she told me that so far only her oldest son had any offspring, and thus her first grandchild lived with his mother's extended family. However, Ayi felt optimistic that soon her matriline would have a grandchild of its own, because, she said, one of her daughters had recently married.

In fact, when our party had entered the courtyard, my travel companion and unofficial translator Ron Cho had pointed out that a large Chinese "red double happiness" wedding sign was prominently displayed on one of the windows. We learned that the "newlywed" couple it blessed were not legally married and did not live together but had conducted the ceremony for an open walking marriage. Ayi's third daughter was co-habiting with her husband elsewhere in an urban "modern marriage." One of Ayi's three sons, in contrast, lived in a Buddhist lamasery, where he was studying to become a lama. He had come home for the weekend with his teacher, and throughout our two-hour visit, they were chanting in the family's elaborately decorated worship room. One other daughter and Ayi's other two sons still lived at home, and none of these had a publicly recognized mate.

Ayi, also like Jiama, had been in an exclusive walking marriage for several decades, and all of her children shared the same father. What's more,

The Walking Marriage Bridge over the Sea of Grass.

Ayi and her children regarded her longtime *axiao* as her husband and their father, and they were grateful to him for how much help he had provided them during very difficult times. When their father's own mother died, therefore, the adult children had invited him to move into their matrilineal home. Reportedly, Ayi's long-term mate spent most nights and days living and working with Ayi and her family, but he also spent a couple of nights each week in his own maternal home, now headed by one of his sisters. In addition, he often accepted overnight hospitality from a married daughter and her husband who lived in a town where he participated in occasional construction work.

On our journey from these two more remote Mosuo families to visit Luoshui, the famed, affluent tourist mecca on Lugu Lake, we made several detours to inspect aspiring competitors that were also vying for the ethnic tourist trade, including a smaller lakeside village and the controversial new, upscale cultural "palace" guesthouse that celebrity Namu had built. We also hiked across a lengthy, beautiful new "Walking Marriage Bridge" over a marshy "Sea of Grass," which, according to the tourist signage at its entrance, had been built to facilitate *tisese* between lovers in Mosuo villages on the rapidly developing Sichuan side of the lake.

In Luoshui, Gezo had set up a third formal home visit and interview for me with one of the seventy-two official Mosuo families who own and operate the three popular ethnic-tourist commercial activities in the village —trough-boat rides, donkey rides, and nightly courtship song and dance performances. Like most Luoshui property owners, this family had converted their ancestral home into as large a hotel as the site and village regulations would accommodate. Gezo was eager for me to see the homestead's four-hundred-year-old grandmother's room and to introduce me to Halba, a man of considerable intelligence, cultural sophistication, and political savvy who was the senior uncle of the household. She warned me, however, not to embarrass him (or her) by asking any sensitive questions about his personal life, because, she said, he was a childless bachelor, a concept that was alien to traditional Mosuo culture.

Gezo's enthusiasm about this lakeside house and its thoughtful, articulate senior male proved amply justified. I had been duly impressed with the form, space, and traditional decor of the first two Mosuo domiciles I had visited, but this Luoshui homestead was on a decidedly grander scale. Grandmother's sleeping alcove was elaborately carved and carpeted, the requisite "female" and "male" supporting pillars were taller and thicker, and a richer array of antique Buddhist ceremonial objects adorned the center altar behind the hearth, although incongruously they shared the honor with a modern fax machine.

It was Halba, the astute, articulate senior uncle, however, who made my visit to this family so enlightening and memorable. He was not the family *dabu* but unquestionably its chief moral authority and spokesperson. In fact, I only met the surprisingly young *dabu*, who was one of Halba's nieces, as we were about to leave the premises. Gezo introduced the niece to me as the *dabu* but later quipped that while the young woman was the *dabu* of the household, Halba was the director.

After Halba welcomed us, he propped his somewhat senile eighty-four-year-old mother on the honorific senior woman's cushion to the immediate left of the hearth, where she nodded in and out of consciousness during our stay. He then assumed the senior male's perch on the right and briefly outlined the four generations in his family. Like Jiama and Ayi, Halba is in his mid-fifties. Unlike them, however, he was not an only child and was not the only member of his generation residing in the family. Halba had four sisters, who collectively had given birth to seven children. I met only one of his sisters and one niece—the young woman who had returned after university to become *dabu* (and to run the family hotel). Most of the rest of Halba's nieces and nephews were away at university or living and working elsewhere. Thanks to Luoshui's affluence, all seventy-two of its official Mosuo families could afford to send all of their children to university and no longer needed their labor at home. I mistakenly presumed that the teenage girl who bustled around the kitchen, served us tea, kept the kettle boiling, and ministered to Halba's mother was also a niece. Later I learned that she was a hired domestic worker, an ethnic Pumi recruited from a poorer nearby village that had not shared in the tourist industry bounty.

Although Gezo had warned me not to raise the subject, Halba volunteered how fortunate he felt to have such wonderful, loving nieces and nephews, because he himself had not married and had not had any children of his own. Thanks to his sisters, however, he was now blessed with young grandchildren, the emergent fourth generation of his family. His niece, the *dabu*, was toting one of these newest family members on her hip when we crossed paths with her in the courtyard. When I asked if the toddler was her only child, she told me that in fact he was not hers but was the son of one of her sister's. She hoped to have children someday, she added, "but I'm not married yet."

Conquerors, Communists, and Marriage Politics

As even this skeletal sketch of three families indicates, contemporary Mosuo culture has incorporated some of the rhetoric of marriage as well as occasional forms of marital relationships. Over the centuries, waves of first imperial and then Maoist conquerors actively intervened in Mosuo kinship practices. Mosuo sexual, gender, and family values had mystified and offended ruling imperial Chinese and Communist sensibilities at least as much as they challenge contemporary Western convictions about proper family life. Mongol, Confucian, and Communist invaders were nonplussed when they encountered the absence of marriage and the presence of maternal domestic units in Mosuo communities, and they applied varying degrees of coercion to correct both affronts.

When Kublai Khan founded the Yuan Dynasty in the thirteenth century, his forces subjugated the indigenous cultures of southwest China and incorporated their native chieftain system into the state's centralized bureaucracy. In order for Mosuo chieftains to maintain inheritance of their royal authority, they began to adopt patrilocal marriage for the ruling families, while commoners, serfs, and even other members of the elite continued the *tisese* system.[26] According to Shih, the *tisese* system began to include exclusive pairing at that point, that is, to incorporate the kinds of monogamous walking marriages that Jiama, Ayi, and other members of the families I described seem to favor. Shih claims that the Ch'ing Dynasty (1644–1911) institutionalized these two modifications of traditional Mosuo kinship patterns.[27] The Ch'ing imposed on the chieftains an inheritance system of patrilineal primogeniture (the eldest son receives the property). This led the royal families to shift from a maternal family residence to a patrilocal marriage norm. Marriage never became the norm among commoners, however, or even among members of the elite who were not chieftains. Nonetheless, walking marriage, or what Cai Hua has termed the "conspicuous" visiting relationship, developed into a secondary institution of sexual union at that time.

Over the centuries Chinese imperial policies modified the Mosuo's exclusively mother-centered and non-marital traditional culture. Far and away the most dramatic and disruptive interventions in Mosuo family and society began in the late 1950s and early 1960s, when Chinese People's Liberation Army cadres made their way to Lugu Lake. Close on their heels, the Chinese Communist Party sent research teams of Marxist anthropologists who had been schooled in the evolutionary stage theory of family and kinship that Marx's comrade and benefactor Friedrich Engels had derived from the work of nineteenth-century anthropologist Lewis Henry Morgan.[28] These Communist anthropologists conducted extensive fieldwork among the Mosuo and published the first, portentous ethnographies about their kinship and culture. They generated descriptions of Mosuo gender, sexual, and family practices that now lure hordes of titillated tourists. At first, however, their depictions provided targets for ruthless Maoist efforts at "modernization."

Viewing Mosuo maternal family residence and *tisese* through Marxist evolutionary spectacles, the researchers believed they were observing forms of primitive matriarchy and group marriage amid a culture that had failed to evolve. A paradigmatic Chinese ethnographer of the period marveled, "They are like a colorful historical museum of the evolution of families in which one finds living fossils of ancient marriage formations and family structures."[29] Similarly, an early state-produced documentary film portrayed what it imagined to be the primitive group-marriage system of the Mosuo as evidence of their oppression prior to Communist liberation.[30] Ranking high among several supremely ironic (and painful) chapters of Chinese Communist family history was the ensuing set of Maoist campaigns to "liberate" the Mosuo from their kinship regime by helping them to "evolve" from their primitive sexual and household relations into a modern, male-headed, nuclear family system. Namu sarcastically recalls the Maoists' relentless attempts "to reeducate the people—because the Moso shared everything, including their lovers, which amounted to a form of primitive communism that was a health hazard and a blight on the face of modern China."[31]

Two decades of increasingly coercive waves of this "liberation, Maoist style," which bears some resemblance to the attempts by the U.S. federal government to "liberate" Mormon women and children from polygamy, began in 1958. Communist cadres and Red Guards staged vigorous campaigns to eradicate *tisese* and usher Mosuo villagers into modern marriages. They came repeatedly, in Namu's words, "to harangue the people there on the dangers of sexual freedom and the benefits of monogamous marriage."[32] Illustratively, a Communist Party cadre in Bai Hua's scathing fictional parody of the Cultural Revolution exhorts Mosuo villagers, "We want you to live a decent, monogamous, legitimate life. What kind of life are you leading now? Only cavemen living ten thousand years ago had lives like yours, so chaotic that a child knows his mother but not his father. This is the residue of group marriage. . . . Aren't you ashamed of yourselves?" Two of the novel's protagonists, Comrades Zhang Chunqiao and Yao Wenyuan, instruct local officials on "how to accomplish [their] great historical mission": "In the shortest possible time, by force or by persuasion, you must drag our Mosuo kinsmen out of the stone age and into modern life with the rest of us!"[33]

Access to party membership and political status served as potent means of persuasion. Just as the Ch'ing Dynasty made marriage necessary for chieftains to bequeath royal status to their descendants, under Communism, marriage became de rigueur for anyone seeking to establish political correctness and status. The inverted class hierarchy of revolutionary Maoist ideology led peasants to fear intimacy with landlords and "rightists," and so the universe of potential mates diminished, and the formerly democratic practice of *tisese* became much more class conscious and stratified.[34]

When the People's Liberation Army first arrived in Ninglang County in 1956, between 10 and 14 percent of Mosuo couples were formally married.[35] The first marriage campaign during the Great Leap Forward of collectivization in 1958 marginally increased the proportion of couples who were living jointly (whether married or not) to approximately 20 percent in 1960.[36] A more aggressive campaign during the Cultural Revolution in the 1960s convinced perhaps half of Mosuo partnered couples to get married. However, once again, a few months after the campaign ended, two-thirds of the newlywed pairs divorced and returned to their maternal homes.[37]

When persuasion proved insufficient to propel the Mosuo's sexual and domestic "evolution," the Communists turned to force. The early sporadic campaigns had been organized at the county level, but after they failed, the provincial government stepped in to wage the draconian "One Husband, One Wife" campaign of 1975. The Party made marriage compulsory for every adult who had a partner and posted nighttime sentries in village streets to ambush men en route to visit their lovers. Zealous cadres dragged visiting couples out of their beds and exposed them naked to their relatives. Officials forced the Mosuo to build houses for married couples to inhabit jointly. They withheld grain and cloth rations from children whose mothers refused to reveal the names of their biological fathers as well as from men who were caught attempting a night visit.[38]

Coercion proved more effective than exhortation. This time, virtually all couples married, and the vast majority remained so at the time of Mao's death in 1976.[39] Through meticulous fieldwork in the 1980s, anthropologist Shih Chuan-kang identified 424 couples in the Yongning area who had been forced into registered marriages.[40] Jiama Dashu and her lover would have been among these, as were three of Halba's four sisters and their lovers. Jiama reported that she managed to tolerate living with her husband's family in her forced marriage for only three months before she quietly moved back to the maternal home where she is now the *dabu.* Ayi told me that she had been spared a forced marriage because she was an only child who had already had a child. However, she knew many people who were forced to marry, and she claimed that most of those marriages quickly fell apart. Halba's family had depended heavily upon the labor of his sisters and was short of men. Consequently, when cadres compelled three of his sisters to marry their lovers, Halba's family invited the men to move in with them.

Mosuo adults who lived through the marriage campaigns recount endless stories of domestic disharmony and even violence unleashed by this coerced co-habitation, especially when women were forced to move in with their husbands' families or to live with their husbands and children in modern nuclear households. This Maoist modernization compelled Mosuo couples suddenly to merge the domains of romance and eros with economics and domesticity, domains that their culture had always deemed incommensurable. Forced family evolution also plunged the Mosuo into a challenging crash course on a category of kin quite novel to them — in-laws. The Mosuo language did not contain a word for this relationship.[41]

Unsurprisingly, therefore, the Mosuo who survived these campaigns "describe the rupture in family arrangements that occurred during this time as the most painful effect of cultural policies during the Mao years."[42] Halba, for example, reported that most of the forced marriages that took place in Luoshui village ultimately failed, and many extended Mosuo families broke up during the Cultural Revolution. According to Halba, prior to Liberation, only seventeen large, extended maternal-lineage households inhabited Luoshui. The Cultural Revolution wreaked so much havoc on family life that these households repeatedly divided. By the time Mao died in 1976, the initial seventeen families had fractured into seventy-two smaller ones. Although Halba's family also had suffered considerable conflict after his sisters were forced to marry and their husbands moved into the household, his family stoically resisted the urge to separate. They uncomfortably endured the unwelcome marriages in their midst for what turned out to be several years, until Deng Xiao Ping's regime came to power and reversed the Maoist assimilation agenda toward ethnic-minority cultures.

In 1981, the national minorities received official permission to resume their traditional customs. Halba told me that as soon as the reform policies were announced, Luoshui families held a village meeting and collectively agreed to return to the traditional *tisese* system. At that point, Halba's three imposed brothers-in-law departed the household and returned to their maternal domiciles. The former conjugal couples converted their Maoist modern marriages back into walking marriages, which were still going strong at the time of my visit. Research indicates that this was a widespread pattern throughout Ninglang County. Most of the conscripted Mosuo spouses moved back to their maternal homes. Recall that two-thirds of Mosuo couples still were married when Mao died in 1976. In 1983, however, a mere two years after the new policies were implemented, the marriage rate dropped and stabilized at 32 percent. This brought the Mosuo marriage rate below what it had been before the 1975 One Husband, One Wife campaign and only 10 percent above what it had been in 1960, several years before the Cultural Revolution.[43]

Novelist Bai Hua depicts the revival of Mosuo *tisese* in the characteristically romantic terms of "internal orientalism": "The Mosuo were a simple people. They soon consigned the second political encroachment of the civilized world to oblivion, as if they were forgetting two invasions by mammoths or hordes of elephants. They healed instantly. No sooner had the engines of the departing work team started snorting than the axiao embraced each other."[44] The reality, of course, was more complex. Although one cannot fail to be impressed with how rapidly the Mosuo dispensed with the marital forms of Maoist modernization, they did not develop social amnesia or emerge unaffected from two decades of this crude social engineering. Not only had most Mosuo families suffered and then splintered. The years of Maoist interventions also introduced some lasting ideological changes in Mosuo family values, discourses, and practices that I will return to later.

Performing Kinship for Extra-marital Tourism

The People's Republic of China's decision to stop forcibly modernizing the traditional cultures of ethnic minorities coincided, paradoxically again, with the Communist nation's startling shift from socialist class struggle to the Four Modernizations economic development strategy in 1978. At the same time that the Chinese Communist Party adopted its momentous turn toward the global capitalist market economy, it granted formal recognition and state support to preserving its distinctive ethnic-minority cultures. This unlikely conjuncture allowed the Mosuo to revive their maternal families and the practice of tisese, but it also unleashed forces that continue to reshape and threaten the kinship and cultural system that the new policies sought to preserve.

Around the time that Chinese policy began to embrace ethnic diversity in the early 1980s, ethnographies based on the earlier research reports about the Mosuo were published, and state TV produced documentaries that featured their provocative sexual and family system. This ignited the Chinese public's appetite for ethnic tourism to Lugu Lake just when private enterprise was developing a domestic tourist industry. And so it happened that the very customs and practices that the Maoists had tried to eradicate came to be celebrated as sources of Mosuo cultural and economic value. Savvy Luoshui villagers seized the moment. Although the population of the well-situated lakeside village included almost as many ethnic Pumi as Mosuo, they joined to capitalize on Mosuo ethnic allure.[45] During the post–Cultural Revolution meeting that Halba described to me when representatives of the then seventy-two resident families agreed

A scenic view of Lugu Lake. Reprinted by permission of Jason Huang, http://www.flickr.com/photos/mcwolf.

to resume the Mosuo *tisese* sexual system, they also decided to freeze the number of official Mosuo maternal households in Luoshui at that number. In a self-conscious attempt to prevent jealousy, inequality, and community schisms that they feared would arise were families to compete for the burgeoning tourist trade, the village established a cooperative to operate and share the profits from its three commercial tourist activities—the boat and mule rides and the evening folk song and dance performances. Each family must contribute one worker to these activities, and the families divide the profits equally. As a further self-protective measure, the cooperative agreed never to sell Luoshui houses to outsiders.

Ironically again, the period of Maoist collectivization worked to privatize Mosuo families by coercing intimate couples into a form of state-arranged marriage, but the turn to unbridled market capitalism led villagers of varied ethnic backgrounds to collectivize earnings they gain from performing the Mosuo's non-marital brand of ethnic kinship. Capitalizing on fascination with traditional Mosuo family and sexual practices among first mainstream Chinese and later a global clientele, Luoshui rapidly made itself the premier ethnic tourist destination in China. Lugu Lake officially

A Mosuo woman in traditional dress posing with a tourist. Reprinted by permission of Mingjie Feng, http://www.flickr.com/photos/luckywater/.

opened to domestic tourism in 1990 and to foreign travelers two years later. Tourism really took off in the mid-1990s, and by 2004 over two hundred thousand visitors annually, 90 percent of whom were Han Chinese, were making the long trek to Lugu Lake.[46] My driver, Mr. Li, claimed that five hundred thousand tourists had visited in 2006. More than 90 percent of this trade includes a visit to Luoshui village, which has become astonishingly affluent as a result. Once among the poorest Yunnan peasant villages, Luoshui is reputed to have become a community of millionaire hoteliers and merchants (and their much less affluent employees). There were more than thirty-five hundred guest accommodations in tiny Luoshui in 2005, and an increasing numbers of these were in four-star hotels.

As the title of a *Time/Asia* magazine feature story in 2002 put it, "The Mosuo, a small matrilineal tribe in central China, are preserving their traditions by exploiting them."[47] Feminist anthropologist Eileen Walsh illustrates how local and external entrepreneurs profitably harvest three,

promotion
exotic
appeal
(v)
misrep
of
tisese

somewhat contradictory, seeds of the Mosuo's exotic appeal, all of which center around women. The most potent and problematic lure is the Mosuo reputation for free love. Misrepresentations of *tisese* as sanctioned promiscuity disseminated in the books by Bai Hua, Namu, and Cai Hua and in the popular media attract numerous wishful male sex tourists to Lugu Lake. "Within the touristic frame and imagination," Walsh suggests, "the multiple ways of imagining Mosuo territory, as a land of women and a land of sex, blur into a land of women for sex."[48] Along with the tourist trade, a red-light district quickly developed on the outskirts of Luoshui, where at least a dozen establishments employ female sex workers of diverse ethnic and geographic origins who dress as Mosuo women to service male tourists. An exposé of the sex industry in 2004 generated campaigns to eradicate it, but after several years, sex commerce began to reappear.[49]

There is no evidence that men also perform sex work in Lugu Lake, but the Mosuo reputation for free love does attract some Han women, who seek romantic refuge from their more patriarchal and puritanical Chinese sexual culture.[50] Widespread publicity about Helen Xu, a rare Han woman tourist who fell in love with a Mosuo man and married and settled in Luoshui with him, stoked this less prevalent brand of romance tourism. Walsh claims that most local men happily accommodate female tourists who wish to experiment with *tisese*, much to the distress of local Mosuo women. During a hired boat ride on the lake, I asked the three brothers who took turns rowing and napping about their own experiences with women tourists. They recounted receiving frequent flirtatious overtures, but only one of the three acknowledged, rather reluctantly, that he had ever acquiesced. There was no point in doing so, they claimed, because such romances could not last. Because outsiders cannot purchase local property, and they lack a local family residence, they cannot integrate into Mosuo family life unless they secure an invitation to join a lover's household. Such an unlikely circumstance also violates the basic principles of *tisese* that attract tourists to begin with. I interviewed a twenty-five-year-old Han man from Guangdong who had come to Luoshui six months earlier to work on a local education project for the children of migrant workers. He told me that he and other Han men he knows would love to enter a Mosuo walking marriage but that this was virtually impossible because they had no families to live with. As a result, outsiders rarely attain access to anything beyond an episode or two of furtive *tisese*.

The seductive sex appeal of the Mosuo collides somewhat with two other ethnic images marketed to tourists. Popular depictions of the Mosuo as matriarchal attract a smaller clientele of feminist tourists, including scholars like me who are veterans of feminist debates about the universality of patriarchy. Aware that many Western feminists hope to find households of cooperative sisters led by wise, respected mothers, some Luoshui families perform the desired script. Walsh observed a visit by two Australian feminist tourists to the family of one of her Mosuo friends who feigned a loving sister relationship with a cousin from a poorer village. In reality, the cousin worked for her wealthier Luoshui relatives, whom she resented and regarded as "not Mosuo anymore."[51]

If the Mosuo's matriarchal image strikes the fancy of a limited feminist tourist market, it overlaps with a third ethnic image that has far broader allure. Romantic notions of a lost primitive world intensify rampant nostalgia among mainstream Chinese members of the one-child family era who yearn for the imagined harmony of the large extended families of yore. Walsh suggests that the Mosuo self-consciously cater to these desires by performing family harmony for tourists. Indeed, the Mosuo I interviewed uniformly claimed that their families were more harmonious than families based on marriage, because it is easier for adult children to get along with the relatives they grew up with than to have to adapt to life with spouses and in-laws. Perhaps I was too readily taken in by the theatrical skills of the families I visited, but from what I observed, such claims seemed to have merit.

Marriage Markets

Many Mosuo themselves have begun to worry about how long they will be able to sustain their unique family culture. The *tisese* system revived impressively after the Cultural Revolution but, as we have seen, not without alterations. Notions of marriage, husbands, and fathers that used to be marginal have gained greater cultural currency and consequence. Current Mosuo family life mixes elements of traditional *tisese* with some of modern marriage.

On the one hand, the tourist industry coyly and profitably markets *tisese* as a free-love regime. After we returned to Lijiang from Lugu Lake, Ron Cho and I attended an extravagant ethnic-minority spectacle in the city's massive new Cultural Center Performance Hall, whose thousands of seats were quickly filled by occupants of a steady stream of tour buses. The show portrayed a sampling of China's ethnic-minority cultures through

Las Vegas–style song and dance renditions of their traditional customs. Predictably, the modern dance choreography to depict the Mosuo pantomimed night visiting. First, three enthusiastic male suitors climbed the imaginary walls to the flower chambers of three beautiful Mosuo maidens, who welcomed them with kisses. Each man hung his hat outside his maiden's window to signal that the room and its resident were occupied. Next, the delighted audience laughed on cue when the tardy ascent of a disappointed fourth suitor was greeted by a competitor's cap.

Despite the apparent effectiveness of the popular marketing strategy that features the titillations of *tisese*, all the Mosuo I met were quick to distance their culture from the taint of promiscuity. Contemporary locals consistently downplay notions of sexual freedom. Instead they stress a norm of long-term walking marriages like Jiama's and Ayi's. Both the title and the author of the massive ethnography about their culture, *A Society without Husbands or Fathers,* elicit widespread hostility from contemporary Mosuo. The Mosuo I met insist that Cai Hua exaggerated and distorted the amount and the permissiveness of sexuality in their culture. Contrary to Cai Hua's claims, they now routinely employ the vocabulary of marriage and paternity.

The Mosuo now seem to endorse a norm of long-term, monogamous, visiting marriages.[52] Whatever the empirical reality of their contemporary practices, it is significant that the Mosuo reject the very image of their sexuality that the government and private tourist industry so successfully exploit. I found no one willing to acknowledge having personally engaged in multiple, casual, furtive visits, and most were loathe even to concede that others indulged in these. Just to elicit the concession that not every Mosuo enters a permanent walking marriage with her or his first lover or that not all such "marriages" endure permanently, demanded persistent, skeptical questioning on my part. This represents a notable change in norms from most of the earlier descriptions of *tisese* by anthropologists, journalists, and biographers. Mosuo ideology, and perhaps behavior as well, seems to have shifted toward more committed, stable monogamous coupling.[53]

Contemporary Mosuo apply the term *marriage* broadly to both long-term visiting couples and registered, co-habiting ones. Recall the "Walking Marriage Bridge" sign mounted over the Sea of Grass and the red double happiness symbol that Ayi displayed to honor her daughter's newly recognized visiting relationship. Similarly, whenever I asked a particular young woman, like Halba's niece-*dabu* or a university-educated docent at the Luoshui cultural museum, whether she had children, I received a standard response: "No, I'm not married yet." Mosuo women today seem to routinely use the term *husband* to refer to *axiaos* who visit openly and regularly, and typically these men seem to become identified, engaged fathers when children are born. These days, when you see a Mosuo man who is caring for a child, it is not easy to guess whether he is the child's uncle or genitor. While I was interviewing a forty-year-old café proprietor in Luoshui about his own walking marriage of fifteen years, one of two sons from that relationship draped himself affectionately around his father's shoulders. This surprised me less than it might have before I had lodged with the Dashu family and observed the close ties that Jiama's youngest granddaughter enjoyed not only with her genetic father but with her father's maternal family as well.

Moreover, many of the rising numbers of younger Mosuo who go to university and move to cities for work, like my guide Gezo, wind up entering the modern, registered, co-habiting marriages that the Maoists largely failed to impose. During the long car ride back from Lugo Lake to Lijiang, I stumbled onto the genealogy of one such modern marriage laden with more ironies than a Noel Coward could conjure. I had learned that my driver, Mr. Li, was a friend of the married son of Jiama's I had met, and I was asking about the sort of work that the latter did in the tourist industry. That was how I heard about Dongba Valley Cultural Village, one of the newest of the ethnic museums that the state and private enterprise had begun to establish in locations more convenient for tourists than Lugu Lake.[54] My driver explained that Jiama's son, his "wife," and one of his nieces live and work in a privately owned "authentic minority culture valley" that opened outside of Lijiang in 2006. They had been hired to literally perform Mosuo culture as the sort of living fossils of ancient family life in a "colorful historical museum of the evolution of the family" that the Marxist anthropologists had mistakenly imagined the Mosuo to represent decades ago.

I discovered that Dongba Valley Cultural Village hires members from several Chinese ethnic-minority groups to inhabit "traditional" houses and serve as living displays of their respective cultures, almost as if Old Sturbridge Village in Massachusetts or Colonial Williamsburg, Virginia, were populated by time-capsule transplanted colonial settlers. Mr. Li explained that Jiama's son, his wife, his niece, and three unrelated young women earn their livelihoods by residing together and enacting a living diorama of putative Mosuo family life. Fortuitously for me, just as Mr. Li was describing Dongba Valley, Jiama's son pulled his car up behind and signaled for us to stop. He needed help with a dangling license plate. That gave me an opportunity to inquire further about family and work life at Dongba Valley and to make a remarkable discovery.

I learned that before Dongba Valley had opened one year earlier, Jiama's son and his wife had had a traditional Mosuo walking marriage. He had lived and worked in his mother Jiama's household, while his "wife" and her young daughter resided twenty miles away in their own matrilineal homestead. The opportunity to work at distant Dongba Valley precipitated a dramatic family change. In order to display "authentic" Mosuo life for pay, the couple had to abandon their authentic walking marriage along with their young daughter, their maternal households, and their native Mosuo communities. They became instead a co-habiting couple who lived and worked together very far from their Mosuo homes.

Further ironies emerged. I learned too that Jiama herself had applied to live and work as the *dabu* in the living museum's Mosuo household, but the proprietors had rejected her because she does not speak Chinese. Jiama only speaks her traditional Mosuo language, and so she would not be able to explain her "authentic" culture to the Valley's primarily Han visitors. Instead, the museum manager had assigned the paid "matriarchal" role to the wife of Jiama's son, until skeptical tourists astutely objected that she was not old enough to be her husband's mother! The museum then abandoned the theatrical kinship charade and scaled back the live displays by its employees to having them don traditional costumes and perform domestic activities and songs and dances. Moreover, even though Dongba Valley employs parents of young children, like Jiama's son and his wife, no children reside in the ethnic display houses. I asked Mr. Li, who ferries many tourists to Dongba Valley, what they think when they find no children living in these supposedly authentic families. His witty, bemused reply: "Most tourists aren't anthropologists."

Back in Luoshui, tourism is also inducing subterfuges and changes in Mosuo kinship. I belatedly learned that only 40 percent or so of the members of the seventy-two official Mosuo families actually are ethnically Mosuo. Another 40 percent or so are Pumi, and perhaps 12 percent are Han.[55] Like me, tourists presume that almost everyone who lives in Luoshui is Mosuo, and members of other ethnic backgrounds who interact with tourists reinforce our mistake by dressing in Mosuo costumes and deploying locutions like "we Mosuo."[56] Affluent Mosuo families, like Halba's, hire workers from other ethnic groups to perform domestic and service work. Even some of the official cultural performers are not actually Mosuo.

For example, Jama, a twenty-six-year-old Pumi woman who was featured in the *Time/Asia* story, rows a boat for tourists while dressed in Mosuo garb.

What is more, the high cultural status of Mosuo women that is part of their appeal to tourists risks becoming a victim of entrepreneurial success. Mothers have become more reluctant to school their daughters than their sons for fear of losing them to the cities or to marriage.[57] Anthropologist Walsh found that because tourists regard women as the essence of Mosuo family and ethnicity, men have begun to find it embarrassing to be seen doing household labor, and many prefer to identify with national rather than ethnic culture. Luoshui women complained to her that men were becoming lazy and spoiled and that affluence led many to drink and gamble. Some women claimed resentfully that most local men were being intimate with outside women visitors and sex workers and that it had become harder for a Mosuo woman to find and keep a boyfriend.[58]

Some of the state's affirmative-action benefits for ethnic minorities also undermine the distinctive Mosuo culture and family system that the state seeks to sustain. In contrast with most of China, schooling is free through the ninth grade in Yongning, and affluence enables all qualified Luoshui children to afford university education. Studying in ethnically mixed schools in which the instructional language is Mandarin introduces Mosuo children to Han culture along with global concepts of modernity and family. To sustain ethnic minorities, the government had exempted them from the one-child family policy and allowed them more liberal birth quotas, depending on local demographic and economic conditions. Mosuo women had been allowed to have three children each, but increasingly, the state has begun restricting ethnic minority groups to a two-child policy.[59] Given the small remaining numbers of Mosuo and their traditionally low fertility rates, they may not be able to reproduce the traditional extended households that attract tourists.

Fully aware of these threats to their family and culture, the Luoshui collective of official families has taken some protective measures. In order to dissuade their youth from entering modern marriages, it does not allow couples to establish new households in the village, and it restricts participation in the tourist jobs to the seventy-two member families. Halba claimed that the cooperative's principle of economic distribution also tries to preserve the walking marriage system. It divides collective profits equally among the families, irrespective of their size, to discourage smaller families from adding a spouse in order to qualify for a greater share of earnings. However, I suspect that this policy could have perverse effects. If each family only needs to supply one worker to the collective, larger families can choose to expand their sources of income by dispersing some members to work elsewhere, just like Jiama's son, daughter-in-law, and niece are doing in Dongba Valley.

Halba soberly regarded the village policies as stopgap measures that might help to retard but cannot prevent the ultimate erosion of the Mosuo family system. Today, thirteen-year-old Luoshui boys as well as girls have come to expect rooms of their own, and families with sufficient space allocate individual bedrooms even to younger children. Traditional customs, like signaling a nocturnal visit with animal calls or songs, have succumbed to technology, as would-be lovers send text messages from their ubiquitous cell phones. Families in Luoshui all had become much more affluent, but Halba does not think they were happier than before. He rues the "declining morals" he perceives in a generation that has been educated in Han schools and exposed to TV, university education, and materialism. Perhaps the Mosuo family system can survive in remote areas, Halba hopes, but he doubts that it can withstand the impact of wealth on Luoshui and the expanding number of tourist-oriented villages. The forty-year-old café owner I interviewed shared the perception that affluence and tourism are eroding traditional Mosuo families. He noted that many of the youth sent to universities wind up intermarrying with Han and staying in cities, as Gezo has done. Like Halba, he pins his hopes for the survival of Mosuo kinship on more remote areas, where he anticipates it might last "at least for another seventy to eighty years."

On the other hand, the café owner pointed out that some local ethnic Pumi have begun to adopt the practice of walking marriage, raising the possibility that Mosuo family practices might spread to other cultural groups. A Pumi woman who runs a stall in the popular outdoor evening barbeque market told me that her mother participates in a walking marriage with a Mosuo man. The *Time/Asia* feature story on the Mosuo also reported that walking marriage is spreading rapidly among the Pumi near Luoshui. Jama, the twenty-six-year-old who rows tourist boats while attired in Mosuo garb, had adopted Mosuo family values as well. She said that she chose a walking marriage rather than marrying her boyfriend, the biological father of her young daughter, because "if I decide my boyfriend isn't worth it, we'll split up, so we don't fight like married couples do." However, only those who have cooperative residential families nearby can make such a choice, and rapid development is likely to diminish the local ranks of families like these.

The greatest dangers of tourism for Mosuo culture, however, may be indirect. Halba has traveled widely throughout China, partly to investigate the impact of tourism on communities elsewhere. He came away from his journeys preoccupied with the environmental dangers of development. The biggest looming threat to Lugu Lake is a state plan to build an airport on the Sichuan side of the lake. Initial development plans located the airport directly in the exquisite Sea of Grass, but concerted local opposition to such environmental damage convinced authorities to site it a bit further from the lake. Halba took understandable comfort from this hard-won concession, but the airport nonetheless will unleash unavoidable destructive effects on Mosuo cultural life as well as on the environment, effects that strike me as fierce. Considering how staggering the growth of tourism has been even while Lugu Lake remains relatively inaccessible, direct access to the region by air will geometrically expand the number of visitors and change their character. The newly paved road and massive five-star hotel that were under construction on the Sichuan side of the lake foreshadow the dramatic changes they invite.

Endangered Kinship

In my view, Mosuo *tisese* represents a stunning pre-modern version of the "pure relationship," and a version that was arguably "purer" and more egalitarian than what Giddens envisioned. *Tisese,* as we have seen, separates sexuality and romantic love from kinship, reproduction, and parenting, and it does so more radically, I believe, than the late-modern transformation of intimacy that Giddens endorsed. It also enables more gender equality in the realm of heterosexual intimacy than feminists anywhere have yet achieved. Traditional Mosuo sexual unions are governed almost exclusively by mutual desire and affection, unencumbered by other responsibilities. Lovers do not share homes, money, childrearing, daily labor, or relatives. Because an individual's choice of mate carries next to no implications for his or her family's income, labor, security, or status, families need not intervene, approve, or even know about it. Lovers may freely pursue exclusive or multiple relationships that are enduring or short-lived and that cross class, age, religious, and ethnic boundaries, as they prefer.

Giddens has been rightly taken to task for ignoring the implications of his idealized vision of the pure relationship for parenting, kinship, dependency, and caretaking. Feminist legal theorist Martha Fineman, on the

other hand, places caretaking front and center in her search for legal strategies to redefine family in ways that avoid the "tragedies" that are inherent
in what she terms the "sexual family."[60] Fineman employs that jarring concept to designate a family system centered around an adult sexual pairing,
precisely opposite, one might say, to what Giddens meant by "plastic sexuality." The "tragic" flaw in this modern family structure is the way it hitches
family security, property, and especially the welfare of women and children
to the vagaries of Cupid's antics. Most of the seismic upheavals and divisive controversies in modern Western family life over the past half century
radiate from this fault line. Internal contradictions between the horse and
the carriage of modern family life are the primary source of those pitched
battles over "the divorce revolution," unwed childbearing, "fatherlessness,"
abortion, day care, the "second shift," same-sex marriage, lesbian and gay
parenthood, and of the ever-expanding ranks of Scarlet Lettermen.

Most pre-modern societies opted for patriarchal control of women's
sexuality and procreation in order to manage inescapable conflicts between individual eros and collective (particularly male) family interests.
The ingenious Mosuo, in contrast, devised what I consider to be a brilliant,
time-tested alternative both to patriarchy and to the modern sexual family. Mosuo *tisese* boldly exceeds Fineman's proposal to make the mother-
child dyad the central unit of family law. It radically frees family fortunes
from the capriciousness of sexual love by eliminating marriage altogether.
"Women and men should not marry," as Namu explained the Mosuo perspective, "for love is like the seasons—it comes and goes."[61]

With the surgical stroke of excising marriage, Mosuo kinship circum-
vented a plethora of Fineman's "twentieth-century tragedies." A society
without marriage is one without divorce and with no spinsters or bachelors, widows or widowers, or unmarried, solitary individuals of any sort.
Nobody's social status or fate hinges on the success or failure of their love
life or marriage, whether chosen or arranged. Although Halba does not
have a "wife" or biological children, he is embedded in an intergenerational
family. He spoke convincingly of his love for his nieces and nephews and
his gratitude for the love and support they provide him in return. Likewise,
Jiama's deaf and mute adult daughter fully participates in an integrated,
stable, and productive family life. In a family system without marriage,
no children are illegitimate, "fatherless," or "motherless," and few are orphaned. No marriage or divorce means no remarriage as well, and thus no
wicked step-mothers, step-sisters, or Cinderellas. Rarely need anyone become a single parent, and even biological only-children, like Jiama's three

grandchildren, can grow up with siblings and playmates in their households. It seems likely that this helps to explain how the Mosuo achieved lower fertility and lower mortality rates than their neighbors long before they experienced the modern economic developments that typically propel that demographic transition.

Eliminating institutionalized marriages profoundly alters sexual meanings and consequences, and in the case of the traditional Mosuo, this brings striking benefits for women. Lacking concepts of premarital or extra-marital sex, Mosuo culture does not fetishize female virginity and chastity or judge women and men by a double standard of sexual behavior that sorts women into Madonnas or whores. For this reason, most outsiders presume that *tisese* implies widespread promiscuity, an impression that was reinforced by Cai Hua's controversial ethnography and Namu's salacious memoirs and that the tourist industry is happy to leave unchallenged. To be sure, most scholarship supports the view that traditionally Mosuo women and men alike have felt free to engage in sexual intimacy with a variety of partners, if they so desire, without fearing social disapproval.[62] Less often noticed, however, is the fact that *tisese* also grants equal respect not only to those who practice monogamy but to the sexually chaste as well. Counter to popular titillating representations of the Mosuo, they seem to have sustained significant rates of chastity, a second factor that has contributed to their lower fertility rates.[63]

It is impossible to determine how durable most open, visiting unions were in pre-revolutionary China. On the one hand, many features of walking marriages can sustain romance, passion, and affection longer than most legal marriages seem to do. Couples who do not share residences, finances, parenting, relatives, or other obligations bypass most of the primary triggers of conjugal conflict. They do not need to adapt to the often incompatible preferences, habits, and quirks of an individual (of a different gender) who was socialized in another mother's household. They do not struggle over how many (if any) children to have, how to reward and discipline them, who does the dishes or takes out the trash, what church (if any) to attend, how much money or time to spend on what, where, when, or with whom. All of the Mosuo I interviewed claimed that walking marriages last longer than other marriages because they generate so few sources of conflict.

On the other hand, traditional Mosuo couples experience few social or economic incentives or pressure to sustain unsatisfying relationships or to be sexually exclusive. Mosuo country promises scant profits to a couples-counseling industry. If and when lust, love, or affection wanes, "like the seasons," little countervailing social or economic glue or public rituals or investments work to sustain anyone's commitment to maintain a flagging union. What's more, the fact of lifelong family security and the tolerant sexual norms of *tisese* make it easy for a disaffected lover to stray or to just walk away. Predictably, therefore, the question of how the Mosuo manage sexual jealousy, a theme central to the plot of *The Remote Country of Women*, preoccupies many outsiders, just as is true with polygamy. Cultural norms seem to operate to suppress sexual possessiveness, as Namu explains: "Although we feel such passions, we must repress jealousy and envy, and we must always be prepared to ignore our differences for the sake of maintaining harmony. All this possibly sounds utopian, but it is absolutely true. In Moso eyes, no one is more ridiculous than a jealous lover, and short of committing a crime such as stealing, nothing is more dishonorable than a loud argument or a lack of generosity."[64]

If Mosuo culture discourages displays of jealousy and anger, it does not seem to promote promiscuity or to honor fickleness. Small-scale societies exert potent indirect influences on behavior through gossip and reputation. The docent at the Mosuo cultural museum claimed that individuals earn bad reputations if their romantic behavior appears too licentious or selfish and that companionship, loyalty, and affection cement walking marriages as much as eros does. Although I was surprised to learn that both Jiama and Ayi have sustained their walking marriages over the course of several politically and economically turbulent decades, neither woman considered this noteworthy.

In the end, however, asking whether Mosuo walking marriages typically dissolve sooner or later than legal modern marriages is an ethnocentric sociological question, one that assumes a particularly obsessional public status in the United States. Traditional Mosuo culture grants individuals autonomy over such matters of the heart and the hormones, because it makes their consequences socially irrelevant. What matter are the durability, stability, and harmony of the maternal family household. More meaningful, in my sociological view, is the durability of this pre-modern family system itself and the trenchantly simple way it reconciles the contradictory goals of individual eros and family security. Mosuo *tisese* and the maternal extended family combine the democratic and libertarian features of Giddens's concept of the pure relationship with broader social needs for family stability and solidarity. Coming close to having their cake and eating it too, the Mosuo enjoy "plastic sexuality" and gender equality freed from the demands of reproduction, kinship, or economy.

Mosuo freedom from pressure to find a spouse contrasts vividly with the unhappy circumstances of many contemporary Chinese as well as Westerners. The historical patriarchal preference for sons and the one-child family policy in China have shrunk the ranks of girls born and raised there (ironically, to the benefit of many single women, including lesbians, in the United States, who adopt unwanted Chinese daughters). The marriage prospects of low-income Chinese men also have shrunk as a result. At the same time, many highly educated, professional women on both sides of the Pacific Ocean anxiously confront a shortage of husbands who they consider to be suitable spouses.[65] In the United States, a vigorous marriage-promotion movement censors premarital sex and stigmatizes single parents, worsening the plight of women across the class spectrum, but disproportionately African American women, who face a dearth of marriageable suitors. Children, and especially daughters, born to unmarried women are a "big happiness" for their Mosuo families, but they can incur discrimination and financial duress for single American and Han Chinese women.

The Mosuo I interviewed were unable, or perhaps just unwilling, to identify any downsides to *tisese* or their family system. I repeatedly asked about disadvantages and difficulties, but to no avail. Everyone emphasized how much more harmonious their families are than what they observe among the Han and other marriage-based cultures around them. No doubt this sunny narrative reflects some rays of entrepreneurial ethnic self-interest. It helps to sustain the remunerative cultural image that lures visitors like me to Lugu Lake. Likely too, it reflects cultural taboos against public discussions of intimacy and a cultural propensity to suppress controversy and conflict. Locals denied the existence of sex workers in Lugu Lake, and they claimed that Mosuo culture never included homosexuality and that HIV was strictly an outsider problem. Only through persistent prodding could I elicit the most minimal concessions about the existence of sex and romance tourism. Well, yes, some outside sex workers had operated near Luoshui in 1999, Gezo reluctantly acknowledged, but she immediately reassured me that they were quickly driven away. Likewise, Mosuo men and women insisted that although tourists flirt and sometimes attempt to seduce them, locals do not cooperate, because they know that such relationships will fail.

A more individualistic, modern Western perspective would chafe at the level of conformity to family and social norms that Mosuo kinship demands. It is difficult for most mobile, modern Westerners to imagine residing permanently with natal kin. Practicing *tisese* within the context of verbal taboos over sexuality and cultural denials of HIV and homosexuality should place the Mosuo at high risk of HIV and other sexually transmitted diseases. Indeed, early twentieth-century opium traders introduced into Mosuo society sexually transmitted diseases that further depressed Mosuo fertility until effective treatments overcame the crisis.[66] One wonders too about genetic risks posed by the opportunities that *tisese* provides for genetic half-siblings to inadvertently engage in incestuous sexual intimacy. Finally, it seems possible to me that practicing the pure relationship, Mosuo style, might prove exceptionally challenging to anyone considered physically unattractive, because just like gay cruising culture, it elevates the realm of individual desire above all else. Factors like status, character, achievement, competence, money, family connections, and to some extent even personality might lose some of their compensatory power to attract a mate.

In the end, however, the fate of Mosuo *tisese* and family life will not depend on this sort of cost-benefit analysis of their merits and pitfalls. Somewhat poignantly, the very factor that dooms durable relationships between the Mosuo and outsiders now threatens the survival of the Mosuo kinship system itself. To reconcile the pure relationship with family stability, *tisese* depends upon a high degree of geographic immobility, and perhaps on social and economic stability as well. Cultural conformity also is crucial to sustain intergenerational, extended families. Inherent Mosuo family conflicts over whether or when to divide households due to size and discord seem certain to increase under the centrifugal and individualizing pressures of market capitalism. The ultimate paradox is that after having been rescued from Maoist repression by market reforms that attracted lucrative ethnic tourism to Lugu Lake, Mosuo *tisese* and maternal families may fall victim to the sources of their success. Sadly, our world risks losing its most successful, egalitarian, and enduring species of non-marital kinship just when the viability of modern marriage seems in gravest doubt.

Conclusion

Forsaking No Others

Try, try, try and separate them, it's an illusion
Try, try, try and you will only come to this conclusion:
Love and marriage, love and marriage,
go together like the horse and carriage
Dad was told by mother, you can't have one without the other.

READERS WHO HAVE accompanied me to this point on our family odyssey should have come to a very different conclusion about the inseparability of love and marriage. You should be well prepared by now not to fall for this trick question:

Q: Which of the following famous (and infamous) people grew up in a family with their two married biological parents? Adolph Hitler, Alan Greenspan, Barack Obama, Barbra Streisand, Benito Mussolini, the Dalai Lama, Francisco Franco, George Washington, Joseph Stalin, Julia Roberts, Lance Armstrong, Michael Phelps, Mother Teresa, Nelson Mandela, Oprah Winfrey.

A: Hitler, Stalin, Franco, and Mussolini.

Transparently tongue-in-cheek, my rhetorical tactic pokes fun at the dogma about the superiority of a family composed of a married mom and dad and their biological offspring. Placing it on the heels of the chapter about the non-marrying Mosuo, however, I did not expect many readers would still presume that this is the gold standard family for raising healthy children.

After all, at the same time that American idol Frank Sinatra was popularizing those corny lyrics, he was helping to keep legions of Hollywood and Beltway gossip columnists gainfully employed with his own tabloid escapades of (illicit) love and (four) marriages.[1] Sinatra's transgressive history of intimacy and the transnational case studies of family life that I have presented in this book lead to a conclusion nearly opposite from the one he crooned. Love and marriage do not often sit comfortably together, at least not for very long. In fact, a family system that insists on hitching eros to domesticity through monogamous marriage is a recipe not for stability but for high rates of adultery and divorce, just as defenders of polygamy delight in pointing out.

Now that we have completed our far-flung family visits, it is time to unpack our bags and inspect their rumpled contents to decide which garments are worn out, which held up well, and whether anything needs some alterations. I hope in the remaining pages to convince readers that the most crucial item to discard is the ideology of the normal family itself, because like the traditional Western marriage vows, it encourages us to forsake too many others, inflicting serious harms on vast numbers of citizens, children, and families and on the societies where it holds sway. Both empirically and theoretically, claims about the superiority of the married-couple-with-children family have proven irreparably flawed. The unwarranted, bipartisan public legitimacy that the normal family dogma enjoys in the United States is a product not of research but politics.

Family Diversity Is Normal

Ethnographic portraits in this book drawn from my research among gay men in Los Angeles, polygynous families in South Africa, and maternal extended families who raise children "without husbands or fathers" near China's Lugu Lake attest to the irrepressible variety of intimacy and kinship in the modern, as well as the pre-modern, world. Recall, though, that during the Cold War era, leading American sociologists, such as William Goode, predicted that modernization would disperse the Western brand of nuclear family across the globe. He envisioned the global triumph of the love-match marriage and believed it would raise the status of women wherever it took hold.[2] Several decades later, in the wake of the sexual revolution, feminism, and gay liberation, British sociologist Anthony Giddens pronounced that intimacy was being liberated from the dictates of biology, reproduction, and kinship and becoming a realm of pure relationships that individuals enter (and exit) strictly for our mutual satisfaction.[3] Both of these optimistic theories about the fate of family life under modernity, along with their more pessimistic cousins that bemoan its decline,[4] have turned out to be as myopic as has the related, popular twentieth-century thesis about the inevitable march of secularism.

To be sure, processes of "modernization" that now plug most cultures of the world into interlocking economic, technological, and communications circuits do disrupt local practices of eros and domesticity. Hollywood, the World Wide Web, international finance, commerce, travel, research and education, non-governmental organizations that promote human rights, public health, and economic development projects, Christian missionaries, and multi-directional waves of migration constantly transmit images of Western love, marriage, and family values all over the planet. Often, as the family-modernization thesis promised, these forces undermine fundamental features of traditional family systems, including, as we have seen, formal polygamy in South Africa and maternal extended-family households among the Mosuo.

Modernization theorists, likewise, can point to campaigns and advances for sexual rights on every continent. Gay parents are an out, proud, and *legal* fact of everyday life not only in Los Angeles and Johannesburg or in Canada and much of Europe but also in Uruguay, which legalized gay adoption rights in 2009, long before the United States or France seem apt to do so. Same-sex marriage is now the law of the land even in unlikely nations, like South Africa and Catholic Spain, Portugal, and most recently Argentina and Mexico City. In 2009, India's Supreme Court struck down sodomy laws, and in 2010, Nepal invited same-sex couples to celebrate their nuptials on the world's highest peak.

At the same time, however, living in a post-9/11 world should convince us that globalizing forces also have generated some unexpected and paradoxical family transformations. Anger against Western dominance helps to fuel a resurgence of religious fundamentalisms in many societies that passionately reject Western brands of love, marriage, and family values. Instead of promoting gender equality and sexual rights, these sentiments help to galvanize severe patriarchal regimes, like the Taliban, and to breed homophobic repression in some cultures that had tacitly tolerated homoerotic relationships prior to Western contact.[5] We saw how, even in post-apartheid South Africa, despite its sweeping constitutional guarantee of protection against discrimination on grounds of sexual orientation, politicians and traditional leaders exploit the erroneous belief that homosexuality is un-African. Some anti-colonialist African proponents of polygamy were willing to enter an "unholy alliance" with Western, Christian family-values crusaders, including James Dobson, to campaign against same-sex marriage.

Contrary to modernization theories, transformations of intimacy and kinship do not travel along a one-way street that conveys traffic solely from the West to the rest. The Internet and transnational cultural exchanges and migration flows shape family practices in Western societies as well. For example, they enable global access to a cross-cultural market for arranged, binational, and plural marriages, for transnational adoptions, and for mail-order brides. We have witnessed the renewed appeal under modernity of some traditional forms of family life, such as informal varieties of polygamy in the United States, as well as in South Africa. We saw too how in China, first the Maoist revolution and then the turn to the global market produced paradoxical disruptions of desire and domesticity among the Mosuo. The culture that originated the "purest" intimate relationships in history may well have been the *pre-modern* Mosuo. Few, if any, modern cultures rival the radicalism of the Mosuo's traditional practice of *tisese* or offer women as much sexual autonomy and parity as theirs does. Counterintuitively, modern market forces rescued *tisese* and Mosuo maternal extended families from Chinese Communist efforts to "modernize" them into oblivion. Now, however, those same market forces are eroding traditional Mosuo intimate practices. Ironically, the market is nudging the culture *away* from the pure relationship toward more conventional "modern" marriages and families.

In short, modernity has not produced a monolithic planetary transformation of intimacy through the global triumph, or imposition, of Western family values. Not even at home. We have seen that instead of disappearing, polygamy has diversified even in North America. At the same time, multitudes of gay men (and lesbians and transgendered people) who formerly were sexual and family outlaws have been cruising to familyland, desperately seeking access to marriage and parenthood while they are reshaping both. The normal family is not normal. Family diversity has always been normal, and it is here to stay.

We Are All Negro Families Now

If the normal married-couple family that was so taken for granted in my youth no longer describes the intimate lives of even many of the most conservative Christian Republicans in the United States, and if family diversity is both the historical norm and its irreversible current course, why does the ideology of the normal family remain so potent? Why haven't our beliefs about happy and unhappy families morphed along with our behaviors? In part, this is because of the ways in which the personal became so politicized during the last half century. Since the 1960s, every time the U.S. Census Bureau released new data that indicated slippage from Ozzie-and-Harriet ideals, it provoked fractious finger-pointing over the social culprits and casualties of family changes. From soaring rates of single mothers (first among black women, later among whites), the "divorce revolution," "deadbeat dads," working moms, day care, the "mommy track," and the "second shift" to dwindling percentages of couples who exchange vows and rings and to the mounting masses who live alone, with their lovers, roommates, or "child-free," or most controversially during the past decade, to the escalating ranks of lesbian and gay couples and parents insistently demanding equal rights—moralistic clashes over personal life offer tempting wedge issues to politicians hungry for motivated voters. They have become routine features of the political landscape.

With rearview vision, I would anoint the late senator Daniel Patrick Moynihan the great granddaddy of the modern politics of family values. His 1965 report, *The Negro Family: The Case for National Action,* written for the Johnson's administration's War on Poverty, branded the burgeoning number of black single-mother families a matriarchal "tangle of pathology" and blamed it for a host of social ills.[6] Penned (when writers still used pens) in a turbulent decade of racial combat and cultural upheaval, those were fighting words. Black leaders promptly condemned what came to be called *The Moynihan Report* as racist, and a reborn feminist movement soon pilloried it for sexism as well.[7] During the sixties, Western family verities began to take it on the chin from all sides. *The Feminine Mystique,* Betty Friedan's incendiary critique of the gender conventions of the *Father Knows Best* family of my youth, had been published just one year earlier. Grassroots movements for women's and gay liberation were about to explode. And, of course, those were the years when the Age of Aquarius dawned, thanks in part to the Pill—a counter-cultural youth rebellion swept up in sex, drugs, and rock 'n' roll. To criticize waning rates of marriage and waxing rates of fatherlessness, particularly among black victims of searing racism, sexism, and poverty, as Moynihan had done, seemed politically tone deaf, if not unforgivably retrograde, then.

Well, that was then. Since the late 1970s, Moynihan's diagnosis of black family failures has enjoyed a stunning reversal of fortune. Its shift in cultural stature from inflammatory to mainstream common sense, among even leading black scholars and politicians in the United States, including President Obama, serves as a handy litmus test of the gains that pro-marriage ideology has been scoring ever since.[8] Moynihan's analysis of black family disarray proved to be a harbinger of the culture wars over mainstream family values that were about to erupt, not to speak of offering an object lesson in the perverse Law of Unintended Consequences. For *The Negro Family*, despite its liberal origins in the Great Society and its commitment to the War on Poverty, anticipated arguments that later became pivotal to the startling ascent of the religious New Right and the ultimate dismantling of the U.S. welfare state.

When Moynihan tolled the alarm bells for black fatherless families in 1965, 22 percent of black children were born to unwed women (and girls).[9] By the early 1980s, the percentage of unmarried white mothers broached that level, and what Moynihan had bemoaned as the pathology of an underclass took on the stature of a national catastrophe for his intellectual heirs.[10] Welding the links that he had drawn between marriage, morality, and social pathology into an ironclad Christian gospel, the New Right propelled the Reagan revolution and ushered in nearly three decades of conservative Republican dominance.

Since the late 1970s, New Right culture warriors have battled, with startling success, to rescue 1950s, *Father Knows Best* family *ideals* (behavior is quite another matter, of course) from ravages of what they construe to have been the narcissistic, irresponsible, Aquarian culture of the sixties and seventies. They scuttled President Carter's attempt to convene a national White House Conference on the Family in 1979. Furious battles over the legitimate definition of family broke out when the administration appointed Patsy Fleming, a divorced, black, single mother of three, as executive secretary.[11] The planned national event fractured into three contentious regional conferences on *families*. Waving the banner of family values, the New Right also seized defeat of the Equal Rights Amendment from the jaws of a feminist near-victory.[12] Conservative family values composed a core platform of the Moral Majority, which was a key constituency behind Reagan's presidential landslide in 1980, and of the Contract with America that Newt Gingrich designed to engineer the triumphant Republican congressional takeover in 1994.[13]

The New Right wielded religious and cultural authority to support its brand of family values. Armed with Holy Scriptures, Moral Majority's founder, the late Jerry Falwell, and James Dobson, of Focus on the Family, crusaded against abortion, premarital sex, infidelity, divorce, and homosexuality.[14] In one of the more surreal episodes in the U.S. family wars, 1992 Republican vice presidential candidate Dan Quayle lambasted the unwed pregnancy of a fictional TV sitcom anchorwoman, Murphy Brown. As if summoning the ghost of fifties film star Ingrid Bergman, Quayle railed against Hollywood and the popular-culture industry for undermining family values by glamorizing single motherhood.[15]

In the early 1990s, however, Moynihan's views of family pathology attracted new political converts. They too appealed to social science to give heft to their arguments. A centrist, secular marriage-promotion campaign emerged that replenished the right-wing, religious troops doing battle to resist the winds of family change. In the early 1990s, Senator Moynihan himself repeatedly reprised his old argument. A 1994 campaign fundraising letter of his, for example, reprinted famous lines from his 1965 report and lamented that they had come to describe the sorry state of American family life as a whole:

> From the wild Irish slums of the 19th-century Eastern seaboard to the riot-torn suburbs of Los Angeles, there is one unmistakable lesson in American history: a community that allows a large number of young men to grow up in broken families, dominated by women, never acquiring any stable relationship to male authority, never acquiring any set of rational expectations about the future—that community asks for and gets chaos. Crime, violence, unrest, unrestrained lashing out at the whole social structure—that is not only to be expected; it is very near to inevitable.[16]

The contemporary secular marriage movement owes Moynihan a direct intellectual debt. It too blames most social problems on marital decline and the spread of fatherlessness. It too brandishes social science research rather than scriptures or cultural tradition as authority. The opening lines of *Fatherless America,* by David Blankenhorn, founder of the Institute for American Values and a leading figure in this campaign, typify the genre: "Fatherlessness is the most harmful demographic trend of this generation. It is the leading cause of declining child well-being in our society. It is also the engine driving our most urgent social problems from crime to adolescent pregnancy to child sexual abuse to domestic violence against women."[17] Despite its self-description, the secular "Marriage Movement" is not a grassroots social movement. It is an ideological campaign coordinated by public intellectuals like Blankenhorn, Maggie Gallagher, and David Pope-noe, who have set up independent think tanks and councils, like the Institute for American Values, the Institute for Marriage and Public Policy, and the National Marriage Project.[18] With financial backing from private foundations and intellectual support from a smattering of sympathetic social scientists, they pursue a form of cultural politics that they inappropriately liken to the anti-smoking campaign.[19] Of course, when anti-smoking forces warn that inhaling tobacco laced with nicotine risks lethal effects on our lungs and lives, they are accurately reporting an overwhelming scientific consensus based on published, peer-reviewed research evidence. Marriage-promotion advocates, in contrast, dispense a steady stream of what I have described as "virtual social science" that touts the benefits of heterosexual marriage for adults, children, and society and warns that dire social consequences attend its decline.[20]

Whether or not the secular marriage campaign has nudged many repentant, confirmed bachelors and bachelorettes down the aisle or stemmed the stampede of feckless spouses to the divorce courts is impossible to say, but there's no denying the campaign's potent influence on U.S. political rhetoric and public policy. What had been the credo of a right-wing religious minority became bipartisan mainstream orthodoxy during Clinton's presidency. In 1992, Murphy Brown seemed to have won her prime-time debate with Dan Quayle, and successful Democratic candidate Clinton defended pluralist family values. However, less than a year after Clinton took office, even the liberal wing of the mainstream media reversed course on family values. Early in 1993, for example, the *Atlantic Monthly* published a wildly popular cover story, "Dan Quayle Was Right," by Barbara Dafoe Whitehead, who was then Blankenhorn's co-director at the Institute for American Values.[21] Clinton speedily caught the new current: "Remember the Dan Quayle speech?" he soon mused in a *Newsweek* interview. "There were a lot of very good things in that speech. . . . Would we be a better-off society if babies were born to married couples? You bet we would."[22]

With unsettling haste, and considerable political irony, the only Democrat to occupy the White House between 1981 and 2009 (and the son of a divorced mother, to boot) was the one who signed into law two weighty, and in my view wrongheaded, public policies rooted in marriage-promotion ideology—the 1996 Personal Responsibility and Work Opportunity Reconciliation Act (popularly known as the Welfare Reform Act) and the Defense of Marriage Act (DOMA). The former, more consequential of these, opens with a textbook illustration of virtual social science. "The Congress makes the following *findings* [my emphasis]," the act's preamble begins, and then it proceeds to itemize them:

(1) Marriage is the foundation of a successful society.
(2) Marriage is an essential institution of a successful society which promotes the interests of children.
(3) Promotion of responsible fatherhood and motherhood is integral to successful child rearing and the well-being of children. . . .
(7) The negative consequences of an out-of-wedlock birth on the mother, the child, the family and society are *well documented* as follows . . .

And what follows is a list of misleading correlations, including claims that out-of-wedlock children are more likely to suffer child abuse, low cognitive attainment, lower educational aspirations, and so on.[23]

The 1996 Welfare Reform Act poured the political concrete for a profound shift in the priorities of national poverty policy from promoting welfare to promoting marriage. In another poignant irony, Moynihan proved to be the most prominent and eloquent senator to oppose the law in the end. He denounced the decision to drop children born to unmarried women from "federal life-support" as the most "regressive and brutal act of social policy since Reconstruction."[24] The entire edifice of the subsequent Bush administration's faith-based Federal Marriage Initiative rested on this foundation.

A second, competing marriage movement also congealed in the 1990s, of course—the international drive to legalize same-sex marriage. A favorable ruling by the Hawaiian Supreme Court in 1993 aroused national hopes and fears that the island state would be the first to make same-sex marriage legal. The issue swiftly became the central focus of the gay rights movement, and opposing it began to usurp abortion as the favorite wedge issue for New Right cultural warriors. Almost overnight, presidential candidates felt politically obliged to oppose gay marriage. That explains why during President Clinton's reelection campaign in 1996, he signed into law the Orwellian-named Defense of Marriage Act, which passed with overwhelming bipartisan support.[25] DOMA authorized states to refuse to recognize, let alone to defend, the marriages of same-sex couples who wed in states where it was legal. There were no such states then. But of course, that was then. As of this writing, there are five, and most recently, the nation's capital city, Washington, D.C., and of course the high-visibility, high-stakes court battle over Prop 8 under way in California as this book goes to press that is designed to reach the U.S. Supreme Court.

The presidential victory of Barack Obama in 2008 seemed to signify a generational shift in American politics that would spell the end of cultural combat between loyalists of white-bread fifties values and the aging Aquarian remnants of the rebellious sixties and seventies. Although Obama hewed to the obligatory, bipartisan line that marriage is for a woman and a man, he made a daring campaign promise to work to repeal DOMA (as well as the "Don't Ask, Don't Tell" military policy). With the electorate facing economic meltdown and military quagmire, for the first time since 1980, the politics of family values failed to influence the outcome of a national election in the United States. Despite Obama's stance against DOMA, he won even in two big states, California and Florida, whose voters passed ballot measures against same-sex marriage on the same day.

Nonetheless, President Obama himself seems to subscribe to core principles of marriage-promotion ideology. It is refreshing and to his considerable credit that Obama appears actually to practice the family values of commitment to monogamous marriage and responsible fatherhood that he preaches, unlike so many of the prominent Republican Scarlet Lettermen who were the main architects and advocates of the political ideology. However, Obama too has bought into the inaccurate, virtual social science claims that marriage-promotion advocates disseminate. In fact, Moynihan, Blankenhorn, or even the author of Dan Quayle's Murphy Brown speech could have written lines from the major Father's Day sermon that candidate Obama delivered to a black church in Chicago during his 2008 presidential campaign:

> Of all the rocks upon which we build our lives, we are reminded today that family is the most important. And we are called to recognize and honor how critical every father is to that foundation. They are teachers and coaches. They are mentors and role models. They are examples of success and the men who constantly push us toward it. We know the statistics — that children who grow up without a father are five times more likely to live in poverty and commit crime; nine times more likely to drop out of schools and twenty times more likely to end up in prison. They are more likely to have behavioral problems, or run away from home, or become teenage parents themselves.[26]

President Obama reprised this theme the following year on his first Father's Day in office in June 2009.[27] One could be forgiven for expecting that having grown up with a single mother who divorced twice during his childhood, Obama's own stupendous achievements would have served as sufficient rebuke to this doomsday message about the critical need for fathers to achieve successful child outcomes. At the very least, it should have aroused the president's skeptical curiosity about the source and validity of that litany of alarming statistics that he asserted "we know." Instead, the ideological claims of the marriage-promotion campaign seem to have trumped both President Obama's life experience and his propensity for critical reflection. Like a preponderance of contemporary citizens, policymakers, and even some scholars, the president appears to have been persuaded that research supports the main popular beliefs about love, marriage, and family values that this book has sought to dispel. I can think of no more unsettling testimony than this to the unwarranted ideological success of the marriage-promotion campaign whose lineage dates back to the publication of Moynihan's *The Negro Family* in 1965.

Untying the Knot

This book has disputed core principles of the two competing contemporary marriage movements. Despite their political antagonism, the campaigns share more values than their supporters might like to admit. They both idealize monogamous marriage and fail to question the weighty privileges that married couples receive compared with other ways of living and loving. Both marriage campaigns abjure polygamy. And both movements anoint their values with the authority of social science research, one hoping to restore the battered institution to its former glory, the other struggling to refurbish it by making it a bit roomier and au courant. In this book, I have drawn on my personal social science research (and my own limited authority) to undermine these shared premises and to challenge opposing arguments advanced by the two campaigns.

The cross-cultural stories of intimacy I have conveyed show that, contrary to the doctrinal principles of the heterosexual marriage-promotion crusade, (1) marriage is *not* a universal or necessary institution; (2) fatherlessness is the wrong diagnosis for what ails our children and communities; and (3) promoting marriage cannot cure our social maladies. I have presented evidence too that, contrary to Marriage Movement predictions, allowing same-sex couples to marry would do more to buttress than to batter the prestige of the institution, for good and for ill. After all, same-sex marriage suitors depend on the same ideals of free love, monogamy, and gender equality that the state always uses to justify prohibiting polygamy.

Readers need not be told by now that my personal family values align more comfortably with the ranks of gays, lesbians, and their allies who are fighting to expand the marital tent than with those in the U.S. Marriage Movement who have achieved recent victories to seal it shut—victories, by the way, that I predict will prove pyrrhic in the end. Full disclosure: because I believe in basic equality before the law, I have testified and submitted legal affidavits in several court cases on behalf of same-sex-marriage plaintiffs. In doing so, however, I had to squelch my serious qualms about some of the arguments that same-sex-marriage advocates make and, more importantly, about the limited vision of family diversity that the campaign fosters.

For starters, as the chapters in this book on polygamy indicate, I differ with gay-marriage advocates who deny that there are any legal parallels between bids for same-sex and for plural marriage rights. Public antipathy to polygamy is so profound that it is easy to grasp why the gay rights movement might fear guilt by association with such a pariah. Political anxiety, however, is not the only source of the disavowal. Many, perhaps most, gay-marriage fans, likely including Ossie and Harry, Shawn, Steven and Glenn, Drew and James, Eddie and Charles, and Lisa and Kat, likely share this popular aversion. The battle for same-sex marriage is a white-bread—and in fact an overwhelmingly white, assimilationist—agenda, rather than a subversive one, as queer theorists and activists long have complained.[28] Distancing itself from the taint of promiscuity that is popularly associated with gay sexual culture, the same-sex-marriage drive aspires to tame gay desire in the interests of domesticity and social respectability. However, as I discussed in the chapters on polygamy in South Africa and the United States, some contemporary polygamists legitimately draw on the same love-makes-a-family ideology that same-sex-marriage fans embrace. They also offer resonant arguments about the propriety of their brand of family values, particularly when compared with the endless parade of hypocritical married, "monogamist" Scarlet Lettermen.

Same-sex-marriage advocates are also wrong when they assert that legalizing same-sex marriage will reduce social inequality. To be sure, it would eliminate one galling and, in my view, indefensible form of discrimination against lesbians and gay men. But the upshot of opening the exclusionary gates of the marital country club to same-sex couples would be to shift more of the onus of discrimination from sex orientation to marital status, and thereby to exacerbate the latter. Marriage never has been and never will be an equal-opportunity institution. As we have seen in both the United States and South Africa, access to marriage skews especially against people from subordinate racial and class backgrounds. Making the membership rules gender inclusive will only deepen the class and race disparities.

Unhitched presents a case against the traditional marriage vows. It urges us to make peace with the inescapable fact of family diversity because the costs of our denial to individuals, families, and society are steep. The normal family ideology fosters bad faith, bad behavior, and bad public policy. A singular focus on monogamous heterosexual marriage justifies discrimination and disrespect for everyone who lives outside the charmed family circle, whether by design or by destiny. It generates infidelity, deception, desertion, high divorce rates, and family instability. It also underwrites the malignant levels of hypocrisy by the Scarlet Lettermen and their constituents. Too often these personal transgressions yield weighty political consequences, such as the impeachment of Clinton and the political demise of public figures, like John Edwards and former congressman Vito Fossella. As I write this book's conclusion in January 2010, a sensationalist, real-life "Here's to you, Mrs. Robinson" sex scandal threatens to topple the delicately assembled coalition government in Northern Ireland.[29]

What's more, the normal-family ideology does not even serve its own ends. Instead of producing uniform family values and behaviors, it unfairly burdens the lives of those who do not conform to them. More dangerous, it drives diversity underground, where exploitation, abuse, and blackmail can thrive. Gays and lesbians have now achieved too much cultural confidence and clout, however, to agree to return to the closet. Political attempts to suppress gay varieties of love, marriage, and baby carriages, such as California's Prop 8 and state bans on gay adoption, are powerless to increase the ranks of heterosexual marriages or the percentage of children who will be raised in "normal" mom-and-pop families. During the same season in 2000 when California voters approved Proposition 22, the state's first initiative against same-sex marriage, Paul and Nancy and Liza were moving into their front-house and back-house property with their first baby, Lisa and Kat and Michael and Joaquín were consummating their poly-parenting courtship, Ossie and Harry were searching for a woman willing to be a surrogate mother for their first child, Bernardo was adopting his first child,

Armando was attending L.A. County fost-adopt classes, and the Pop Luck Club in Los Angeles was growing by leaps and bounds.

What once was true for closeted gays, however, remains true for underground polygamists in the United States. Perversely, criminalizing polygamy not only shoos such families into the closet or, worse, encourages them to join outlaw compounds, but it actually increases fatherlessness and divorce. In South Africa, President Jacob Zuma continues to court and impregnate multiple women, but then to marry them publicly (well, most of them!) and to bestow on his many children access to his paternal name, attention, and property.[30] Zuma's co-wives were welcome to jointly mount the official inaugural viewing platform and hold their heads high (or drop them in slumber) as he took the oath of office (see image on page 131). But by driving polygamy underground, the United States enabled now imprisoned FLDS patriarch Warren Jeffs to appropriate more than sixty women and underage girls as his brides and to sire literally countless children, all of whom lack legal protection or the ability to choose to enter or exit his dominion.[31] Perversely too, after open polygynist Tom Green served his six-year prison sentence for a bigamy conviction, he was forbidden to reside with more than one of the four wives who still claimed to love him or to resume paternal responsibility for all of his children, as he wished to do.

In the United States, the clandestine "love-children" who some Scarlet Lettermen, like Vito Fossella and John Edwards, sire also usually become fatherless children. When their existence comes to light, it spells political downfall for their "fathers" and visits on the men's legal wives and children a torrent of public humiliation, pain, and family upheaval. Some of the aggrieved wives feel social pressure to divorce their husbands, even when they might prefer to attempt to reconcile.[32] If they do decide to split, their offspring swell the ranks of what the Marriage Movement disparagingly, and inappropriately, calls "children of divorce."[33]

In South Africa, in contrast, it was not the "first choice" of Walter Luzama's senior wife to have him take a second bride, and I doubt that she will be delighted if and when her husband and his younger bride add to the number of mouths he feels responsible to feed. Nonetheless, she consented to participate in a church wedding to share her husband rather than risk having him return to his former philandering or, worse, risk desertion or divorce. Likewise, Nobunto could agree to share her husband and Lindiwe to share her children as co-wives and co-mothers without social disapproval and without fear that the state might decide to take their children into protective custody, as Texas authorities did when they raided the YFZ ranch.

Finally, as we have seen, the normal-family ideology serves to rationalize discriminatory, hurtful policies, like the Federal Marriage Initiative, DOMA, and bans on gay adoption, that in turn stoke the exaggerated emphasis the gay rights movement places on winning the legal right to marry. Expanding access to civil marriage to same-sex couples, however, represents far too meager a vision of intimate equality or justice. A democratic society should encourage dignity, respect, and success for many modes of living, loving, and caretaking. The state should be trying to assure that citizens can freely enter supportive relationships and freely exit abusive ones. It has a legitimate interest in promoting responsible, committed care and protection for children and other dependents. These are goals that can be and are being met, or shirked, by people who are chaste, infertile, sexually impotent, adventurous, polyamorous, or just plain randy. They are within the reach of people who live in love-match or arranged marriages, whether these are monogamous, open, celibate, or polygamous. And they beckon as well to folks who live outside of matrimony in intergenerational, dual-household, or single-parent families or who reside with their lovers, housemates, beloved pets, or all alone.

A democratic state has no business dictating or even favoring any particular brand of intimacy or family life. It should value the quality and substance of relationships over their form. This demands a move beyond straight, gay, or even plural marriage. Another full disclosure: despite my support for equal marriage rights for same-sex couples, in 2006 I unhesitantly signed on to the statement, "Beyond Same-Sex Marriage: A New Strategic Vision for All Our Families and Relationships," which was authored by a group of activists, artists, scholars, and educators who want to nudge struggles for gay family rights in a more creative, inclusive direction.[34] Like many of the statement's supporters, I would like to get the state out of the marriage business entirely and return oversight of marital rituals, requisites, rewards, and sanctions to the provenance of religious and cultural communities. I agree with those political and legal theorists, as well as with a handful of politicians across the political spectrum, who favor the "disestablishment" of marriage as a civil status.[35] Civil rights, benefits, and duties should be tied to citizenship, parenthood, and guardianship, in my view. The state's mandate should be to facilitate—or at the very least not to thwart—individual commitments to give love, care, and support in however many guises they appear.

Learning from the lives, loves, and losses contained in stories about Mother Randolph's household, Ossie and Harry, the gay trio, Eddie and Charles' surrogacy-extended family, Armando Hidalgo's adoptive home, the poly-parenting agreements between lesbians and gay men, co-wives and co-mothers Nobunto and Lindiwe, the suit to allow South African whites to practice plural marriage, Jiama's four-generational, maternal Mosuo family, *tisese*, the persistent fundamentalist polygynous communities in the western United States and Canada, the Philadelphia black Muslim women seeking co-wives for their husbands, Congressman Fossella's secret family, the torrid affair that a Northern Ireland Unionist MP—an actual Mrs. Robinson—conducted with a teenage boy forty years her junior, as well as from my own untidy, intimate history, and likely some of yours too, should convince us that our erotic and domestic yearnings, abilities, and aversions are irrepressibly varied and complex.

We cannot will our desires or funnel them into a single, culturally prescribed domestic norm. But we can and should acknowledge that our needs for both eros and domesticity are often at odds. How many more times can we possibly be "shocked, *shocked!*" when another Scarlet Letterman is caught forsaking his marital vows? How much more evidence from the natural and social sciences do we need to convince us that human desires and relational capacities differ? Monogamy is not natural or even possible for everyone. But then, too, neither is "promiscuity" natural or enjoyable for everyone. Not everyone can, or wishes to, become a parent, let alone a good one. Human sexual variation, on the other hand, *is* natural, and this should be no cause for distress. That is why happy families will never be all alike.

Making our peace with sexual and family diversity does not commit us to a laissez-faire ethics of pure cultural relativism. Some family systems are clearly patriarchal, authoritarian, and even brutal, while others are more egalitarian, democratic, and humane. Some are more permissive and others prescriptive. Different family forms can be more or less child-centered, more or less cooperative, and more or less resilient. Most cultures in the world create families that favor domesticity over desire, but their ways of doing so differ. Some allot eros a much wider berth than others, typically, as we have seen, where men's urges are concerned but in rare instances for women's as well.

The modern, romantic, companionate union that both U.S. marriage movements take to be normal represents a quixotic effort to plant durable domestic turf in desire's rocky soil. History teaches that this is a utopian, or perhaps just a naive, strategy for trying to have one's cake and eat it too. If a lucky few, like Ossie and Harry, Eddie and Charles, and Barack and Michelle Obama, seem able to grasp hold of this brass ring, too many others suffer needlessly from repeated, failed rotations astride what sociologist Andrew Cherlin terms the "marriage-go-round." The normal, horse-and-carriage, family ideology can make it seem embarrassing, inauthentic, and even cowardly to remain in a passionless marriage. It can lead a sexually frustrated spouse to abandon domesticity in order to pursue desire, either by "cheating" or by fleeing the corral. The sole alternative it permits is to forfeit desire altogether.

The remarkable Mosuo family system is the only one I know that seems structurally designed to simultaneously serve those two contentious masters (or mistresses)—Desire and Domesticity. Radically separating the two Ds by ditching the "sexual family" altogether, it allows women and men alike to consume their cake and still possess it. Admittedly, the ingenious Mosuo model is not easy to imitate in the modern world. Few modern individuals are able or eager to remain in our natal homes and pool our labor, resources, and responsibilities with our maternal relatives for life.[36]

Nonetheless, we can glean hints and inspiration from the pre-modern Mosuo and from some of the post-modern gay and even polygamist family strategists in this book about ways to prevent desire from defeating domesticity and vice versa. Recall the three-parent, front-house/back-house arrangement that grew from the co-parenting agreement that Paul and Nancy drew up, as one example, or the way that "sex pig" Matt and his less frisky mate, Robert, negotiated and renegotiated ground rules to accommodate their asymmetrical libidos without jeopardizing their commitment to an enduring domestic union.

Revising Our Vows

Coming to terms with the irrepressible variety of intimacy and families in our modern world demands tough ideological concessions and political compromises from all combatants in the family wars. As in South Africa, religious and cultural conservatives must learn to tolerate equal family rights and benefits for lesbian, gay, and transgender people whose desires and practices they find sinful, repugnant, or threatening. Same-sex-marriage advocates must come to grips with the unavoidable race and class inequities that are intertwined with marriage as a legal institution and that are tellingly reflected in the social make-up of their core political constituency. Rather than fighting merely to open membership in the exclusive conjugal clubhouse to comparatively privileged lesbians and gay men, they should pitch a big family tent agenda, such as the frameworks proposed in a report, *Beyond Conjugality*, issued by the Law Commission of Canada in 2001 or in the 2006 "Beyond Same-Sex Marriage" statement in the United States. There should be enough room in that tent to shelter not only "sex pigs" and monogamous couples but also single dads and moms, polyparenting families and refuseniks, and members of plural unions, like the gay trio.

Feminists, for our part, must come to grips with unwelcome evidence that our quest for intimate equality will never speak to or for all women. We need to respond to women's myriad desires and compromises with greater empathy and nuance. Without whitewashing the painful patriarchal history of polygamy, for example, we should resist knee-jerk opposition to it. We might concede that polygamy is not *inherently* more harmful or oppressive to women than monogamous marriage or remaining unhitched. To be sure, plural marriage systems (whether polygynous or polyandrous) derive from patriarchal interests in controlling women's bodies and babies. They were designed to serve masculine erotic, domestic, and political agendas. However, the same can be said about the history of monogamous marriage. Assuring paternity and transmitting property to men's heirs were central motives for "the origins of the family, private property and the state," as the title of Engels's classic nineteenth-century book summarized. At the time that book was published, monogamously married women could not vote or own property in most of the Western world. Meanwhile, in the Utah territory, patriarchal Mormon polygamists granted women the right to vote, but they lost the suffrage when the LDS Church reluctantly repudiated polygamy in order to enter the Union.

Feminists need to respect the preferences of heterosexual women who, facing acute shortages of eligible men in their communities, would rather share a husband, children, and family than resign themselves to a life of single motherhood, like Lindiwe had experienced, or of childlessness, like Nobunto suffered, or having to forsake their desire for family. A dearth of marriageable black men is one of the toxic legacies of racial apartheid in both the United States and South Africa, the factor which served as catalyst for Moynihan's incendiary report. We have seen how some black Muslim women in Philadelphia, like some rural women in Kwa-Zulu Natal, consider polygyny to be far the less evil option, as black feminist legal critic Adrien Wing also points out. And although Johannesburg polygynist Walter Luzama is an unapologetic patriarch, he is not wrong to claim that a woman married to a man like him might find polygyny a less threatening expression of his roving libido than his philandering. In fact, some plural wives count it a blessing not to bear sole responsibility to satisfy their husband's sexual desires. Gary Tuchman interviewed fundamentalist Mormon co-wives on CNN's *Anderson Cooper 360°* in 2006 and asked the predictable question, "How is it decided which wife the husband sleeps with on a given night?" "We draw straws," one wife parried, "and the one with the short straw has to."[37]

Still, some of my feminist colleagues worry that advocating tolerance of polygyny and of other unequal varietals of intimacy relinquishes the crucial feminist insistence that the personal is political. I believe, however, that respecting the intimate choices of women who do not share feminist desires is a way to honor, rather than betray, this value. A feminist commitment to gender justice mandates promoting social conditions that make it possible for women (and men) to imagine and achieve intimate equality, if that is what they desire. It does not entitle feminists to dictate or disparage whatever else other women actually do desire. Under social conditions that enable genuine consent, women and men should be free to opt for polygyny, polyandry, or monogamy, for arranged or love-match unions, for celibacy or polyamory, or for whatever domestic arrangements sustain them and those they love.

Finally, coming to terms with our species's unruly panoply of desires and domestic arrangements would liberate us from some of the destructive burdens of bad faith and hypocrisy that we presently suffer. We could spare ourselves, for example, those political disruptions that follow each time another public figure earns his (or, less often, her) Scarlet Letter for infidelity. I favor a concept of fidelity defined to strengthen diverse family bonds rather than to impose a uniform code of sexual behavior on everyone that is unattainable and, in my view, uninspiring. If we take our lead from the Mosuo, from Matt and Robert, from Nancy, Liza, and Paul, from the gay trio, from Nobunto, Marshall, and Lindiwe Silongo, from Hendrik and Helen Van Heerden and Helen's two co-wives, as well as from strictly monogamous Ossie and Harry and President Barack and Michele Obama, we would encourage people to pledge vows of fidelity to whatever principles of intimacy and commitment they choose to negotiate and renegotiate among themselves—freely, honestly, and openly. Public policy should aim to create conditions than enable such fidelity. This includes taking measures to end discrimination against all minority forms of intimacy, to ensure consent, to prevent abuses, and to protect the rights of "the faithful" and their dependents.

No family system is ideal, and no family form can be best for everyone. In part this is because of the irresoluble tension between our needs for both eros and domesticity, in part because people (and cultures) are not and never will be all alike. Each family regime displays characteristic strengths and weaknesses; each offers distinctive satisfactions and sorrows, challenges and constraints. Every brand of family values has its fans and foes, and these are not as predictable as we so often suppose. In a liberal democracy especially, we can't possibly prevent all spouses from forsaking their vows. But we can, and we should, prevent our society from forsaking all of our other families.

Appendix

A Co-parenting Agreement

This agreement is made between Paul Finlay and Nancy Bower to express our understanding as to our rights and responsibilities as parents to our child and to each other. We fully realize that our power to make or enforce this contract is limited by state law. With this knowledge, and in the spirit of love, cooperation, and mutual respect that has developed over the course of our thirteen-year friendship, we wish to state the following to be our agreement:

1. It is our intention to jointly and equally parent our child. We will do our best to share the responsibilities involved in nurturing, feeding, clothing, loving, raising, educating, and disciplining him.
2. Each of us, in good faith, will make an effort to equally share in making all major decisions affecting our child's health, welfare, and education.
3. We agree to be jointly responsibly for our child's financial support until he is eighteen years old. We will renegotiate this to consider joint financial support until age twenty-one, depending on his educational needs and plans.
4. Our child will be given the middle name Finlay and the last name Bower. We will choose the first name cooperatively, with each of us having the power to veto a name.
5. Within ten days after the birth of our child, we will both sign a statement acknowledging that we are the biological parents, and both of our names will be put on the birth certificate..
6. We will do our best to support a healthy, loving relationship between our child and the other parent, the other parent's romantic partner, and the other parent's immediate family.
7. We will do our best to support the romantic relationships of the other parent.
8. If either of us dies while our child is still a minor, our child will be

raised by the other parent. We will each state this in our wills. The surviving parent will continue to support the child's relationships with the deceased parent's romantic partner and family (and other individuals that our child has developed a relationship with). If we both die while our child is a minor, we agree that he will be raised by the guardian named in our wills.

9. We expect that the logistics of living arrangements will be a complicated challenge, and we will attempt to be flexible in building an arrangement that works for all involved. For the first year of our child's life, we will attempt to live very close to each other. We will try to find and rent a duplex apartment or homes that are on the same street. At the end of this year we will have a better sense of what type of living arrangement will work best for all involved and we will reevaluate at that time.

10. We will generally strive to share in the day-to-day care of our child equally. If we agree in the future that it is in the best interest of the child for him to spend a greater portion of time with one of us, that parent will take all steps necessary to maximize the other parent's visitation and to help make visitation as easy as possible.

11. We will both do our best to consider the impact on our child whenever making major life decisions for ourselves. We agree if one of us decides to move out of the L.A. area while our child is still a minor, he or she will not have the right to move the child from the L.A. area with them. Instead, we agree that our child will remain with the parent located here, so as to provide continuity and stability in his environment. The parent who moves will continue to have rights and responsibilities in regard to visitation and child support as outlined in this agreement.

12. If any disputes or problems arise between us regarding our child that we cannot resolve through informal discussions, we agree to seek counseling or mediation in order to resolve them.

13. We agree to review this co-parenting agreement as needed, in order to jointly make changes to it when necessary as time passes.

14. We realize that the form of our friendship will change dramatically once our child is conceived and born, and we welcome this change. We have wanted to create a child out of the love that exists in our friendship. We will continue to give attention and nurturance to our friendship as it evolves and grows.

Notes

Notes to the Introduction

1. The Official Ingrid Bergman Web Site, http://www.ingridbergman.com/.

2. In 1950, 34,075 out of 43,554, or about 78 percent, of couples living together were married (U.S. Census Bureau, "Households by Type"). In a 2005–2007 survey, married couple families composed 49.8 percent of households, while 50.2 percent of households were non-traditional combinations (non-married couples, divorced couples (with or without children), non-married male and female head of households, etc.) (U.S. Census Bureau, "American Community Survey").

3. Human Rights Campaign, "Prop 8 Upheld."

4. See D. Popenoe, *Disturbing the Nest*; D. Popenoe, *Life without Father*; Blankenhorn, *The Future of Marriage*; Glenn, "A Plea"; and Carlson, *Conjugal America*.

5. Tolstoy, *Anna Karenina*, 1.

6. Stacey, *In the Name of the Family*; and Stacey, *Brave New Families*.

7. In a 2006 Gallup poll that asked, "When an unmarried man and woman have a child together, how important is it to you that they legally marry—very important, somewhat important, not too important, or not important at all," 76 percent of people said it was very or somewhat important (Gallup Poll, "Marriage").

On the importance of fathers, see D. Popenoe, *Life without Father*; Wilson, "The Family-Values Debate"; and Blankenhorn, *Fatherless America*.

8. Coontz, *Marriage, a History*.

9. Seth, *First Comes Marriage*.

10. Jewison, *Fiddler on the Roof*.

11. De Laclos, *Les Liaisons Dangereuses*.

12. For example, in Rwanda, Ethiopia, China, and Mayan communities in Mexico. Adekunle, *Culture and Customs of Rwanda*; "Ethiopia: Revenge of the Abducted Bride"; Stross, "Tzehal Marriage by Capture"; Adler, "China, Mongolia: Kidnapped Wives."

13. For example, among the Singapore Chinese and the Nuer tribe of Sudan. Topley, "Ghost Marriages among the Singapore Chinese"; Burton, "Ghosts, Ancestors and Individuals."

14. Tribes in Kenya, Somalia, and Nigeria, in addition to groups in India, practice levirate polygamy. Valsiner, *Culture and Human Development*; Potash, *Widows*

in African Societies; J. Anderson, *Islamic Law in Africa*; Immigration and Refugee Board of Canada, "Nigeria: Levirate Marriage Practices"; "Levirate Marriage."

15. For example, in Tibet. N. Levine, *The Dynamics of Polyandry.*

16. Sussman, *Selling Mother's Milk*; Slater, *Family Life in the Seventeenth Century*; Herdt, *Sambia Sexual Culture*; R. Popenoe, *Feeding Desire.*

17. Bilevsky, "Albanian Custom Fades"; Wekker, *The Politics of Passion*; Nanda, *Neither Man nor Woman.*

18. Missionaries imposed nuclear family life on the indigenous converts. See Richter, *The Ordeal of the Longhouse*; Kjellström, *Eskimo Marriage.*

19. Gutman, *The Black Family in Slavery and Freedom*; White, *Ar'n't I a Woman?*

20. Gordon-Reed, *Thomas Jefferson and Sally Hemings.*

21. Cogel, "The Family in Utopia."

22. Pitzer, *America's Communal Utopias.*

23. Krakauer, *Under the Banner of Heaven*, 120.

24. Goode, *World Revolution and Family Patterns.* This book is a classic work on family and modernization that was influenced by Parsons and Bales, *Family Socialization and Interaction Process.*

25. Horkheimer, *Authority and the Family*; Lasch, *Haven in a Heartless World.*

26. For analyses of postmodern changes in intimacy, see Giddens, *The Transformation of Intimacy*; Beck and Beck-Gernsheim, *The Normal Chaos of Love*; Weston, *Families We Choose*; Plummer, *Telling Sexual Stories*; Weeks, Heaphy, and Donovan, *Same-Sex Intimacies*; Stacey, *Brave New Families*; and Stacey, *In the Name of the Family.* For critics of these changes, see D. Popenoe, *Disturbing the Nest*; Waite and Gallagher, *The Case for Marriage*; Blankenhorn, *Fatherless America*; Blankenhorn, *The Future of Marriage*; Elshtain, *Public Man, Private Woman*; Glendon, "For Better or Worse?" Contemporary left-wing laments about family changes in the Frankfurt School tradition of critical theory include Bauman, *Liquid Love*; and Illouz, *Cold Intimacies.*

27. Giddens, *The Transformation of Intimacy*, 27.

28. Ibid., 58.

Notes to Chapter 1: Love, Sex, and Kinship in Gay El Lay

1. Gay Liberation Front, "Gay Revolution Comes Out."

2. Weston, *Families We Choose.*

3. Quoted in Wright, "Aside from One Little, Tiny Detail," 277.

4. On May 27, 2009, the California Supreme Court upheld Proposition 8, which overturned its own historic decision in favor of same-sex marriage the prior year. Human Rights Campaign, "Prop 8 Upheld." Since then, however, same-sex marriage advocates filed a suit challenging the constitutionality of Prop 8, which won a major first-round victory in a U.S. district court in August 2010. That decision, in turn, is under appeal, and the case appears likely ultimately to wind up

on the docket of the U.S. Supreme Court. Florida and Arizona banned same-sex marriage in 2008. McKinley and Goodstein, "Bans in 3 States on Gay Marriage." In 2008, Arkansas not only banned gay marriage but also voted to prohibit unmarried couples from adopting children. Sharples, "Ballot Initiatives." In 2009, Maine voters repealed the law allowing gay couples to wed. Goodnough, "Gay Rights Rebuke May Change Approach."

5. Stacey and Biblarz, "(How) Does the Sexual Orientation of Parents Matter." For an example of a critique of gay relationships and parenting, see Wardle, "The Potential Impact of Homosexual Parenting on Children."

6. Smith-Rosenberg, "The Female World of Love and Ritual."

7. In 1990, the first time the U.S. Census form allowed co-residing same-sex partners to declare their couple status, 14.6 percent of those who did so were interracial pairs, compared with only 5.1 percent of married heterosexual couples. In the 2000 census, 15.3 percent of same-sex male couples and 12.6 percent of lesbians, compared with 7.4 percent of married and 15 percent of unmarried heterosexual pairs, bridged racial differences. In California, more dramatically, 24 percent of same-sex couples, compared with 15 percent of married couples, were interracial. Sears, Gates, and Lau, "Race and Ethnicity of Same-Sex Couples in California"; Sears and Badgett, "Same-Sex Couples and Same-Sex Couples Raising Children in California," 7; Bell and Weinberg, *Homosexualities*, 83; Browning, *The Culture of Desire*, 23; Tarmann, "Out of the Closet"; Cohn, "Area Gay Couples Settled"; Stacey, "Cruising to Familyland."

8. During the 1980s and '90s Sullivan, a British Catholic, HIV-positive, self-described conservative gay man frequently criticized the promiscuity of gay sexual culture as a form of "libidinal pathology," and he advocated same-sex marriage partly as a way to curtail it. See Sullivan, *Virtually Normal*. His own behavior became the subject of a major gay sex scandal, therefore, when he was outed for soliciting unprotected sex on the Internet. See Goldstein, "The Real Andrew Sullivan Scandal"; P. Cameron, *The Gay 90s*.

9. Miller, "Out in the World."

10. Kenney, *Mapping Gay L.A.*, 7.

11. This was a Bravo television series that ran from 2003 to 2007 featuring "Five Gay Men. Out to make over the world. One straight guy at a time." Rocchio, "Queer Eye's 'Fab Five.'"

12. James, "Many Successful Gay Marriages Share an Open Secret."

13. For other examples, see Nimmons, *The Soul beneath the Skin*; Weeks, Heaphy, and Donovan, *Same-Sex Intimacies*.

14. Quoted in Dreyfuss, "The Holy War on Gays."

15. Shilts, *And the Band Played On*, 89.

16. M. Levine, *Gay Macho*, 79–80.

17. Warner, *The Trouble with Normal*, 128.

18. Davis and Phillips, "Debate: Gay Marriage," 17.

19. Quoted in Dreyfuss, "The Holy War on Gays."

20. Livingston, *Paris Is Burning.*

21. Weeks, Heaphy, and Donovan, *Same-Sex Intimacies,* 144.

22. Savage, "G.O.P Hypocrisy.".

23. Chauncey, *Gay New York,* 224.

24. See note 6.

25. Mann, "A Boy's Own Class," 223.

26. Ibid., 221.

27. Ibid.

28. Badgett, *Money, Myths, and Change;* Cohn, "Area Gay Couples Settled."

29. *The American Heritage Dictionary of the English Language,* 4th ed.

30. Ibid.

31. Saewyc, Pettingell, and Skay, "Hazards of Stigma."

32. See Due, *Joining the Tribe;* Russell, Franz, and Driscoll, "Same-Sex Romantic Attraction"; Russell and Joyner, "Adolescent Sexual Orientation and Suicide Risk"; Miceli, "Gay, Lesbian and Bisexual Youth."

33. Frances Beal coined the term "double jeopardy" to refer to black women's dual burden of race and gender subordination. "Triple jeopardy" soon became common parlance to reference the intersection of race, gender, and class in the lives of poor women of color. See Beal, "Double Jeopardy"; Rothenberg, *Race, Class, and Gender in the United States.*

34. Collyer, *Nuyorican Dream.*

35. Willis, *Learning to Labour.*

36. Connell, *Masculinities,* 114.

37. Stacey, *Brave New Families;* Bettie, *Women without Class;* Ortner, *New Jersey Dreaming.*

38. Cantú, "Entre Hombres/Between Men."

39. For additional examples, see Altman, *Global Sex;* Dowsett, *Practicing Desire;* Delaney, *Times Square Red, Times Square Blue.*

40. Delaney, *Times Square Red, Times Square Blue;* Chauncey, *Gay New York.*

41. Former presidential candidate John Edwards admitted on January 31, 2010, that he had an affair with Rielle Hunter and fathered her child. The scandal broke in 2008, but he did not admit paternity of the child until 2010. Ferran et al., "John Edwards Admits." Former New York State governor Eliot Spitzer resigned in 2008 after admitting to hiring escorts for sex. Silverman, "New York Governor Spitzer Resigns." His replacement, governor David Paterson, admitted before being sworn into office that both he and his wife had engaged in extramarital affairs during points in their marriage. "Governor Paterson Admits to Sex with Other Woman." Others that season included New York Republican congressman Vito Fossella, who admitted to an extramarital affair that produced one child. Barron, "Fossella Admits He Had an Extramarital Affair." Florida Democratic congressman Tim Mahoney admitted to an affair with and subsequent payoff to a former member

of his staff. Schwartz, Schwartz, and Walter, "Congressman's $121,000 Payoff." Mahoney had replaced disgraced Republican congressman Mark Foley after he was caught sending explicit messages to an underage male page. Ross, "Foley's IM Exchange with Underage Page." Detroit mayor Kwame Kilpatrick's explicit text-message exchanges with his chief of staff not only constituted an extramarital affair, but a denial in court led to a perjury charge. Bunkely, "Mayor's Amorous Texts."

Notes to Chapter 2: Gay Parenthood and the End of Paternity as We Knew It

1. I discuss the fatherlessness discourse and the history of the politics of family values in the conclusion. Also see Stacey, "Dada-ism in the Nineties."
2. Beck and Beck-Gernsheim, *The Normal Chaos of Love*, 105.
3. Lasch, *Haven in a Heartless World*.
4. Townsend, *The Package Deal.*
5. Savage, *The Kid*, 26.
6. Here too, however, gays encounter discrimination. While one national study found that 60 percent of U.S. adoption agencies accept applications from homosexual clients, only 39 percent of the agencies in this group had placed at least one child with a gay or lesbian potential parent during the target period, and only 19 percent of these agencies actively recruit prospective gay and lesbian parents. Brodzinsky, Patterson, and Vaziri, "Adoption Agency Perspectives."
7. In Florida, although two pro-LGBT parenting bills died in committee, the strict law banning "homosexual" individuals from adopting has been struck down twice at the trial-court level, but the decisions have been stayed pending review by a state appellate court. Until its decision, the law remains in effect. In Arkansas, a law passed by voters went into effect January 1, 2009, that banned unmarried couples from becoming foster or adoptive parents. The law was challenged in state court, and a trial judge ruled it unconstitutional in April 2010. As this book goes to press, the state attorney general has not decided whether to appeal the trial court decision, but the conservative Family Council that spearheaded the ballot initiative has vowed to appeal. Moritz, "Judge Strikes Down Adoption Ban." In Tennessee, for the past three years, supporters of LGBT families have brushed back attempts to ban unmarried couples from adopting children, leaving in effect an opinion by the Tennessee attorney general stating that same-sex couples can legally adopt under state law. It is expected that anti-equality Tennessee state legislators will again attempt to pass the legislation in 2010. Human Rights Campaign, "Equality from State to State 2009."
8. Compared with children of married couples, children of same-sex couples were found in one study to be twice as likely to be adopted, and children of same-sex parents were disproportionately of Hispanic and non-white race and ethnic origins. Sears and Badgett, "Same-Sex Couples and Same-Sex Couples Raising Children in California." Of the children adopted in California between October

1, 2001, and September 30, 2002, for example, 41 percent were Hispanic, 23 percent were non-Hispanic black, and only 29 percent were non-Hispanic white. U.S. Department of Health and Human Services, *The AFCARS Report.* Qualitative studies of gay fathers likewise report high percentages of cross-racial adoption. Sbordone, "Gay Men Choosing Fatherhood"; Schacher, Auerbach, and Silverstein, "Gay Fathers Expanding the Possibilities for Us All." Other, more recent studies show that gay parents are more likely to adopt non-white children, as well as children with disabilities. Gates et al., "Adoption and Foster Care by Lesbian and Gay Parents in the United States."

9. The 2000 Census reports 25,173 same-sex couples in Los Angeles County, of which 14,468 are male. With 8,015 of its reported same-sex couples raising children, Los Angeles County ranks first in the nation. Sears and Badgett, "Same-Sex Couples and Same-Sex Couples Raising Children in California." This vastly understates the incidence of gay parentage, because it does not include single parents, dual-household parents, or gay parents who did not report a same-sex partnership.

10. Growing Generations, http://www.growinggenerations.com; see also Strah and Margolis, *Gay Dads.*

11. Pop Luck Club, *Newsletter.*

12. Simmons and O'Connell, "Married-Couple and Unmarried-Partner Households: 2000," 10.

13. Twenty-four men were actively parenting children. In addition, two men were step-fathers to a partner's non-residential children; one man with his mother formerly co-foster-parented teenagers; four of the adoptive fathers had also formerly fostered teenagers, and two of these intended to resume this practice in the future; one man served as a known sperm donor for lesbian-couple friends; and one man was a genetic father who does not parent his offspring.

14. One man, a sperm dad who nicknamed himself a "spad," had facilitated a lesbian friend's desire to conceive a child with a donor willing to be an avuncular presence in her child's life. The other unwittingly impregnated a former girlfriend who chose to keep the child and agreed not to reveal its paternity.

15. Of the gay parents, five are Latino, three are black or Caribbean, and one is Asian American. Thirteen of their thirty-four children are white; nine are Latino; eight are black, Caribbean, or mixed race; and four are multi-racial Asian.

16. Nearly 40 percent of same-sex parents in the state identified themselves as black, mixed race, or of another race, compared with 28 percent of married-couple parents; 53 percent of parents in same-sex couples were white, against 58 percent of married-couple parents. According to these census data, whites are slightly over-represented among individuals in same-sex couples in California, and Asian Americans are significantly under-represented, but percentages of Hispanic, black, and mixed-race individuals are proportional to their numbers in the state. Sears and Badgett, "Same-Sex Couples and Same-Sex Couples Raising Children in California."

17. In the 2000 Census, 76 percent of children residing in male same-sex-couple households were described as their "natural-born" children. Gary Gates, Distinguished Scholar at the Williams Institute, UCLA Law School, personal communication, May 17, 2005.

18. Hertz, *Single by Chance, Mothers by Choice*.

19. Multiple births occur frequently with IVF, because physicians implant multiple embryos to increase the odds of successful gestation.

20. In fact, the surrogacy agency that Charles and Eddie used did not accept single applicants.

21. Although non-Hispanic blacks represented only 12.5 percent of the U.S. population, 37 percent of children who entered the national foster-care system in September 2001 were non-Hispanic black. Blacks, moreover, disproportionately remain in the foster-care system—45 percent of the children who exited foster care during the 2000–2001 fiscal year were non-Hispanic white, while only 30 percent were non-Hispanic black. And although there are more black than white children waiting for adoption (45 percent of the children waiting to be adopted in September 2001 were non-Hispanic black, and 34 percent were non-Hispanic white), more white than black children are adopted. Of the children adopted during the 2000–2001 fiscal year, 38 percent were white, and 35 percent were black. U.S. Department of Health and Human Services, Administration on Children, Youth, and Families, Children's Bureau, *The AFCARS Report*. Race has also been shown to affect the amount of time that children have to wait for adoption completion and legalization. Kapp, McDonald, and Diamond, "The Path to Adoption for Children of Color."

22. National cultural and institutional frameworks influence notable cross-national variations in preferred forms of gay and lesbian parenthood. Co-parenting arrangements between lesbians and gay male sperm donors, for example, appear to be more popular in Sweden than in the United States or Ireland. See Ryan-Flood, "Contested Heteronormativities."

23. A larger number (nineteen) expressed enthusiasm for parenting, while the vast majority (fifty-eight men) gave ambivalent responses. Beers, "Desire to Parent in Gay Men," 50.

24. Ibid., 49.

25. Angel's narrative provides a form of negative evidence of how a passion for parenting has come to represent primarily a search for intimacy. In direct contrast to the predestined fathers, Angel expressly seeks to avoid entering into a "pure relationship" but seeks erotic encounters that offer "purely" sex.

26. In fact, a recent national survey of eighteen- to twenty-nine-year-olds found that young men (53 percent) were as likely as young women (52 percent) to agree to the statement, "If things were different in my life, I would love to have a baby now." Kaye, Suellentrop, and Sloup, "The Fog Zone," chart 27.

27. "Love Makes a Family," unpublished speech to a gay community group, on

file with author. Additional information about this speech is withheld to protect the anonymity of my informant.

28. Ibid

29. Ibid.

30. It is important to note, however, that a situational path to parenthood does not predict an individual's emotional or behavioral response to actual parenthood. Like Glenn, many men who enter parenthood somewhat reluctantly can become "born-again" dads once they bond with their actual children. Also like Glenn, some situational fathers even come to desire or to assume a primary, at-home parenting role. Two other men in my sample exhibited this pattern, as do several men whose stories are reported in Strah and Margolis, *Gay Dads*.

31. Beers, "Desire to Parent in Gay Men," 50. Beers built upon a prior study —Sbordone, "Gay Men Choosing Fatherhood"—that compared seventy-eight gay men who chose to become fathers after they came out with eighty-three gay men who were not (yet) fathers. That study, which only allowed dichotomous responses to the question of the men's desire to parent, reported that 46 percent of the non-fathers said that they did not want to become parents.

32. Bos, *Parenting in Planned Lesbian Families*. Somewhat surprisingly, however, the mean strength of desire to have children did not differ significantly in this study between heterosexual women and men who were already parents. No gay male parents were included in this study.

33. Hertz, *Single by Chance, Mother by Choice*.

34. Data on adoptive family structure indicate how infrequently single men attempt (and/or succeed at) adoption. During the fiscal year 2001, 67 percent of adoptive families were headed by married couples, 1 percent by unmarried couples, 30 percent by single women, and 2 percent by single men. U.S. Department of Health and Human Services, *The AFCARS Report*. According to the National Committee for Single Adoptive Parents, men represent approximately one in seven of the people who contact the organization. Shireman, "Adoptions by Single Parents." Perhaps this statistic indicates these men's disproportionate need for support, given their rarity.

35. Among 9,328 same-sex couples with children randomly selected for analysis by Gary Gates, research director at the Williams Project, UCLA, 26 percent of male couples and 22 percent of female couples included an at-home parent, compared with 25 percent of heterosexual married couples with children. Bellafante, "Two Fathers, with One Happy to Stay at Home." Whereas gender differences in income may contribute to the lower incidence of full-time parenting among lesbian couples, average earnings of gay men are lower than among heterosexual men. Badgett, *Money, Myths, and Change*.

36. Furstenberg and Cherlin, *Divided Families*; Stephens, "Will Johnny See Daddy This Week?"

37. In Bell and Weinberg's classic study *Homosexualities*, 29 percent of the male

sample, compared with 75 percent of the female sample, were in stable couple relationships. Laumann et al.'s *The Social Organization of Sexuality* estimates that over a third of the men in their sample population who had only male partners in the past year were living with a partner at the time of the interview, compared to two-thirds of the men who had only female partners in the past year (p. 314).

38. Nationally in 2000, 33 percent of declared female same-sex-couple households included children under eighteen, compared with 22 percent of male same-sex-couple households and 46 percent of married-couple households. Simmons and O'Connell, "Married-Couple and Unmarried-Partner Households."

39. In *Far from Heaven*, Cathy and Frank Whitaker have a seemingly perfect life and marriage until Cathy feels her husband growing cold and distant. She discovers her husband passionately kissing another man, he seeks unsuccessful reparative therapy and turns to alcohol, and the marriage unravels. "Far from Heaven," Allmovie.com, http://www.allmovie.com/work/1:267273. Former governor of New Jersey McGreevey resigned after admitting he had an affair with a man. "New Jersey Governor Quits, Comes Out as Gay." In 2007, the former senator from Idaho, Larry Craig, resigned after pleading guilty to a misdemeanor after an undercover policeman accused him of soliciting sex in a Minneapolis airport, all the while insisting that he is not gay. Herszenhorn and Wilson, "Senator Larry Craig Is Unlikely to Finish Term."

40. Green, *The Velveteen Father*, 48.

41. See Dunne, "Opting into Motherhood"; M. Sullivan, "Rozzie and Harriet?"; Weeks, Heaphy, and Donovan, *Same-Sex Intimacies*, 107; Goldberg, *Lesbian and Gay Parents and Their Children*; Patterson, Sutfin, and Fulcher, "Division of Labor among Lesbian and Heterosexual Parenting Couples." However, Carrington interjects a more skeptical perspective on the actual level of egalitarianism achieved by the division of labor in same-sex couples' households. See Carrington, "No Place Like Home."

42. For a comprehensive review of the research on the impact of gender differences in parenting on children, see Biblarz and Stacey, "How Does the Gender of Parents Matter?"

43. *Hernandez v. Robles*, 1.

44. Bumiller, Sanger, and Stevenson, "Bush Says Iraqi Leaders Will Want U.S. Forces to Stay to Help."

45. Satinover, *Andersen et al. v. State of Washington*, 9.

46. See Biblarz and Stacey, "How Does the Gender of Parents Matter?" for a review of this literature.

47. Blankenhorn, *Fatherless America*, 1.

48. American Academy of Pediatrics, "Policy Statement: Coparent or Second-Parent Adoption by Same-Sex Couples"; Biblarz and Stacey, "How Does the Gender of Parents Matter?"; Stacey and Biblarz, "(How) Does the Sexual Orientation of Parents Matter?"; Goldberg, *Lesbian and Gay Parents and Their Children*.

49. However, as Tim Biblarz and I have argued, there are good theoretical reasons to predict that growing up with lesbian or gay parents should contribute to small average differences in adult sexual identities. Even though research suggests that most children who grow up with lesbian parents nonetheless become heterosexuals, it seems likely that a larger percentage of them than with straight parents will not. Of course, the sources of adult sexual desires remain a dark continent. After all, almost all contemporary adult lesbians and gay men grew up with heterosexual parents, and most lesbian parents seem to be raising heterosexual children.

50. In fact, when Blankenhorn testified as an expert witness in defense of Prop 8, he acknowledged that allowing same-sex couples with children to marry would be good for the couples and their children. He claimed, however, that unfortunately their interests had to be subordinated to the more important goal of preserving and strengthening heterosexual marriage. See Beck, "Blankenhorn Testifies about Marriage, Scholarship and Soul-Searching."

51. *Hernandez v. Robles*, 1.

52. For details about how the Census Bureau determines what composes a household, see U.S. Census Bureau, "America's Families and Living Arrangements."

53. Under California Family Code Ann. § 8617, adoption normally terminates the rights and responsibilities of birth parents; however, this termination is waivable, allowing for step-parent adoptions. See *Sharon S. v. Superior Court,* 561. The California Supreme Court specifically refused to hold that the ability to waive these termination rights allows for the creation of parental rights in three or more persons. Also see this case at 561 n.6: Step-parents have no clear rights to visitation or custody under California law. See *In re Kieshia E.,* 1295–1296, which held that de facto parents, including step-parents, do not gain the status of parents with visitation or custody rights. California courts are split over the constitutionality of allowing visitation rights, despite the objections of the child's parents, to close relatives who have a well-established relationship with a child. Compare *Fenn v. Sherriff,* 189, which found constitutional a statute allowing for close relatives of a deceased parent to petition for visitation with that parent's child, with *Zasueta v. Zasueta,* 252, which found the same statute unconstitutional.

Notes to Chapter 3: A South African Slant on the Slippery Slope

1. I am grateful to Tey Meadow for her co-authorship of an article I revised to compose this chapter. See Stacey and Meadow, "New Slants on the Slippery Slope."

2. "Texas Takes Custody of 400 Children after Raid on Polygamist Compound."

3. The anonymous phone call that prompted the raid, from a teenage girl who claimed to be an abuse victim, later proved to be a hoax.

4. *In re Marriage Cases,* 829.

5. *Lawrence v. Texas,* Scalia, J., dissenting, 2490; Bennett, "Bookworld: Live Discussion with William Bennett"; Kersten, "Once Same-Sex Marriage Is OK, Polygamy's Next"; "Senator Santorum Sounds Off."

6. DiGuglielmo, "Will Gay Marriage Lead to Legalized Polygamy?"

7. For example, A. Sullivan, "Idiocy of the Week."

8. For example, Bozzuti, ""The Constitutionality of Polygamy Prohibitions," 409; Chambers, "Polygamy and Same-Sex Marriage," 53; Myers, " Polygamist Eye for the Monogamist Guy," 1451; Strassberg, "Distinctions of Form or Substance," 1501; Volokh, "Same-Sex Marriage and Slippery Slopes," 1; Gher, "Polygamy and Same-Sex Marriage," 559.

9. Sapa-AFP, "TAC's Zackie Achmat Gets Married."

10. "Jacob Zuma Marries Fourth Wife."

11. Constitution of the Republic of South Africa, chap. 2, sec. 9(3).

12. See, for example, Agigian, *Baby Steps*; Benkov, *Reinventing the Family*; Cott, *Public Vows*; Kanter, *Commitment and Community*; Weston, *Families We Choose.*

13. As I discussed in chapter 1, as of this writing, same-sex marriage is legal in five states, but forty-one states have adopted constitutional amendments or legislation to prohibit same-sex marriage, including the three bans passed in November 2008 and a 2009 ballot initiative in Maine that overturned a new law that legalized same-sex marriage in that state. Human Rights Campaign, "Marriage Equality and Other Relationship Recognition Laws"; Human Rights Campaign, "Statewide Marriage Prohibitions."

14. Simon, "Legal Fights Strain Polygamist Sect"; S. Campbell, "Bigamy Charges Dismissed against Leader of Texas Sect."

15. Constitution of the Republic of South Africa, chap. 2, sec. 9(3).

16. Chambers, "Civilizing the Natives," 101; Gouws, "The Politics of State Structures," 1.

17. Author's interviews with gay activists and NHTL and Contralesa officials, June and July 2007; see Reid, "How to Be a 'Real' Gay"; Reid, " 'This Thing' and 'That Idea,' " 73.

18. See Recognition of Customary Marriage Act, sec. 7(vii)(a) and (b).

19. Ibid.

20. Sloth-Nielson and Von Heerden, "The Constitutional Family," 139.

21. Author's interviews with Constitutional Court justices, June and July 2007; see also Andrews, "Who's Afraid of Polygamy?"

22. *National Coalition for Gay and Lesbian Equality and Others v. Minister of Home Affairs and Others,* 2000 (2) SA 1 (CC), para. 50.

23. Ibid., 56.

24. Interview with Melanie Judge, Advocacy Manager at OUT, LGBT Well-Being, South Africa, Cape Town, June 25, 2007.

25. Kaoma, "The U.S. Christian Right."

26. De Vos, "A Judicial Revolution?" 161.

27. LaFraniere, "South African Parliament Approves Same-Sex Marriage."

28. Interview with Constitutional Court justice, June 12, 2007.

29. Albertyn, "Contesting Democracy," 595.

30. Sandbook, *The Politics of Africa's Economic Recovery.*

31. Seidman, "Is South Africa Different?"

32. For example, only 21.4 percent of black women and 35 percent of black men were employed in 2001, compared with 52.8 percent of white women and 70.4 percent of white men. Statistics South Africa, "Census 2001," table 2.29, p. 52; see Hassim, "Turning Gender Rights into Entitlements," 621; Seidman, "Gendered Citizenship," 287; Sloth-Nielson and Von Heerden, "The Constitutional Family," 139.

33. UNAIDS, "Annex 1 Country Profiles: South Africa"; Outwater, Abrahams, and Campbell, "Women in South Africa," 137.

34. Shisana et al., *South African National HIV Prevalence,* 38; UNICEF, "South Africa Statistics"; Cock, "Engendering Gay and Lesbian Rights," 35; The 2008 South African National HIV Survey indicated an HIV prevalence rate of 13.6 percent for Africans and only 0.3, 1.7, and 0.3% percent or whites, colored, and Indians, respectively. The HIV Survey also indicated that between the ages of fifteen and nineteen, women are three times more likely to be infected with HIV than are men; between the ages of twenty and twenty-four, they are four times more likely to be infected; and between the ages of twenty-five and twenty-nine, they are twice as likely to be infected. Shisana et al., *South African National HIV Prevalence.* Fortunately, after Mbeki was ousted in 2008, the new administration rejected denialism and initiated a serious HIV/AIDS prevention and treatment campaign, and Zuma, despite his very poor personal history on safe sex and gay rights, has committed to following World Health Organization guidelines on HIV/AIDS prevention and treatment. TAC, "Landmark Speech by President Zuma"; Hodes, "Treatment Action Campaign."

35. Statistics South Africa, "Census 2001."

36. Garenne et al., "Understanding Marital and Premarital Fertility in Rural South Africa," 279.

37. For example, due to male desires for friction during heterosexual intercourse, some South African women apply drying agents to their vaginas, causing tears and bleeding that increase their risk of HIV. Baleta, "Concern Voiced over 'Dry Sex' Practices in South Africa." Patriarchal sexual coercion and multiple partners are widespread, and many women are too subordinate to challenge men's refusal to use condoms. See Outwater, Abrahams, and Campbell, "Women in South Africa," 135–154.

38. Epprecht, *Hungochani*; Roscoe and Murray, *Boy-Wives and Female Husbands.*

39. C. Anderson, "The Persistence of Polygyny," 99–112.

40. "Who's Your Daddy?"

41. Clayton, "Profile: Zuma Charmed Wives and Nation."

42. Republic of South Africa Primary Census Data, 2001, tables 6.2 and 6.4. (The 1996 census did not include a separate category for polygamous marriages.)

43. Gouws, "The Politics of State Structures"; Mbatha, "Reforming the Customary Law of Succession"; Pieterse, "It's a 'Black Thing'"; Van der Vliet, "Traditional Husbands, Modern Wives?"

44. Quoted in Van der Vliet, "Traditional Husbands, Modern Wives?" 231.

45. Gouws, "The Politics of State Structures"; see also Mbatha, "Reforming the Customary Law of Succession"; Pieterse, "It's a 'Black Thing.'"

46. Epprecht, *Hungochani*; Roscoe and Murray, *Boy-Wives and Female Husbands*; Bonthuys, *The Civil Union Act.*

47. Van der Vliet, "Traditional Husbands, Modern Wives?"; Bonthuys, "The Civil Union Act."

48. Quoted in Reid, "'This Thing' and 'That Idea,'" 84.

49. Quoted in Tucker, *Queer Visibilities*, 111.

50. Pieterse, "It's a 'Black Thing.'"

51. In fact, during my 2007 field research, I could find no interest or conversations among gay activists and lawyers to consider an appeal for gender-neutral polygamy. However, in 2009, a South African colleague informed me that a feminist listserv discussion had emerged on this very topic. She reported that in June 2009, one feminist on the list posted a call for three or four women to volunteer to become a test case for same-sex multiple-partner marriages. Shireen Hassim, personal communication.

52. Cock, "Engendering Gay and Lesbian Rights," 38..

53. "South Africans Disapprove of Homosexuals, Abortion."

54. Cock, "Engendering Gay and Lesbian Rights," 40–41.

55. According to law professor Pierre de Bos, approximately one thousand same-sex couples married during the first year that it was legal. Personal communication, Montreal, June 2008.

56. Judge, Manion, and de Waal, introduction to *To Have and to Hold*, 12.

57. Winnie Mandela justified kidnapping four youths in Soweto in 1988 (one of whom was murdered) because of the alleged homosexuality of the priest with whom they were staying. Trewhela, "Mbeki and AIDS in Africa"; see also Holmes, "White Rapists Made Coloureds (and Homosexuals)."

58. Espera, "Jacob Zuma Draws Fire for Anti-gay Speech."

59. Trewhela claims that Mbeki "endorses an Africanist myth of a pure and primal Africa contaminated by a sinful West." Scholars debate the role of homosexuality and homophobia in African cultures and whether the West imposed either. For example, see Yarbrough, "We Thee Wed"; Hoad, "Tradition, Modernity and Human Rights"; Epprecht, *Hungochani*; Roscoe and Murray, *Boy-Wives and Female Husbands.*

60. IRIN, "Murder of Young Lesbian Sparks Homophobia Concerns."

61. Ibid. Ironically, some scholars indicate that butch/femme is a dominant practice among blacks and coloreds in South Africa, which only heightens the racial hostility. Cock, "Engendering Gay and Lesbian Rights," 43.

62. IRIN, "Murder of Young Lesbian Sparks Homophobia Concerns."

63. Human Rights Watch, "South Africa: Lesbians Targeted for Murder"; author's interviews with David Bilchitz and Pierre de Vos, Montreal, June 2008.

64. Outwater, Abrahams, and Campbell, "Women in South Africa," 140; IRIN, "Murder of Young Lesbian Sparks Homophobia Concerns."

65. CIET, "Beyond Victims and Villains."

66. Outwater, Abrahams, and Campbell, "Women in South Africa," 142.

67. IRIN, "Murder of Young Lesbian Sparks Homophobia Concerns"; Robins, "Sexual Rights and Sexual Cultures."

68. Meyer, "Parenthood in a Time of Transition."

69. For example, Utah Child Welfare Law § 78-30-9(3)(a)); Human Rights Campaign, "Equality from State to State 2009."

70. Appleton, "Presuming Women."

71. *In re Marriage Cases* (but note that the Maine electorate overturned the legislative victory in November 2009).

72. A number of black gay intellectuals and activists criticize the insensitive ways in which many white gay activists draw superficial analogies between homophobia and racism and the struggles against both. See, for example, Farrow, "Is Gay Marriage Anti-Black?"

73. For exceptions, see Chambers, "Civilizing the Natives"; Franke, "Becoming a Citizen."

74. Cott, *Public Vows.*

75. Ertman, "Race Treason."

76. Cott, *Public Vows,* 4.

77. Myers, "Polygamist Eye for the Monogamist Guy"; see also Ertman, "The Story of *Reynolds v. United States.*"

78. Quoted in Chambers, "Civilizing the Natives," 68.

79. Weisbrod and Sheingorn, "*Reynolds v. United States,*" 828, n.6.

80. Burgett, "On the Mormon Question"; Iversen, *The Antipolygamy Controversy in U.S. Women's Movements.*

81. Chambers, "Civilizing the Natives," 66.

82. Bigamy is a misdemeanor in thirteen states. For examples of felon statutes, see the bigamy statutes of Massachusetts: "Polygamy," M.G.L. c272 §1; New York: "Unlawfully Purporting a Marriage," N.Y.G.L §255.10 (misdemeanor), and "Bigamy," N.Y.G.L. §255.15 (felony); and Utah: "Bigamy," UT.G.L. §76-7-101 (third-degree felony).

83. Strassberg, "Distinctions of Form or Substance."

84. The 2001 Tom Green case, *State v. Green,* sparked national interest. Green, a self-proclaimed Mormon polygamist, was the only individual prosecuted for

bigamy by Utah between 1953 and 2003. Green was released from prison on August 2007 after serving six years of his five-year-to-life sentence. Associated Press, "Utah: Polygamist Freed After 6 Years."

85. *State v. Holm*, 778.

86. See Stacey, *Brave New Families*; Stacey, *In the Name of the Family*; Weston, *Families We Choose*.

87. Rich, "Compulsory Heterosexuality and Lesbian Existence."

88. Ware, *Prejudice and the People of God*, 94.

89. Quoted in Manson, "FLDS Added to List of Hate Groups."

90. In 2001, 41.9 percent of black women and 43 percent of black men over the age of fifteen had never married, compared with 20.7 percent of white non-Hispanic women and 27.4 percent of white non-Hispanic men; the comparable rates for Asians and Hispanics were 33.4 percent of Asian men, 40 percent of Hispanic men, 25.3 percent of Asian women, and 29.7 percent of Hispanic women. U.S. Census Bureau, "Table 1: Marital History for People 15 Years and Over."

91. Prominent gay author Andrew Sullivan posted a blog entry that inflamed racial tensions: "No ethnic community is as homophobic in America as African-Americans." A. Sullivan, "Young Evangelicals and Gay Couples." For an example of a retort, see Coates, "Andrew on Black Homophobia." After Prop 8 passed in California, some prominent white gays blamed its victory on homophobic African American voters. See, for example, gay columnist Savage, "Black Homophobia."

92. Farrow, "Is Gay Marriage Anti-Black?"

93. I discuss this history in the conclusion.

94. Boykin, *One More River to Cross*; Mosk, "Gay Unions Fracture MD's Black Caucus."

95. Brumbaugh et al., "Attitudes toward Gay Marriage in States Undergoing Marriage Law Transformation."

96. Egan, "California's Proposition 8."

97. Beyondmarriage.org, "Beyond Same-Sex Marriage"; Farrow, "Is Gay Marriage Anti-Black?"

98. See note 69 and accompanying text.

99. Volokh, "Changing Attitudes about Homosexuality."

100. A 2006 survey reported 21 percent of lesbians and 5 percent of gay men currently have a child living at home. Two-thirds of lesbians said they plan to have a child in the next three years; one-third of male couples plan to raise kids. Shapiro, "Gay Families Growing."

101. See, for example, Agigian, *Baby Steps*; Mohler and Frazer, *A Donor Insemination Guide*; M. Sullivan, *The Family of Woman*.

102. Volokh, "Changing Attitudes about Homosexuality."

103. Jones, "Majority of Americans Continue to Oppose Gay Marriage."

104. A 2009 Gallop Poll found that 59 percent of eighteen- to twenty-nine-year-olds supported gay marriage, compared to 37 percent of fifty- to sixty-four-year-

olds. Ibid. A 2006 California poll found that 54 percent of respondents aged eighteen to twenty-nine support gay marriage, compared to 29 percent of those aged sixty-five and over. Religioustolerance.org, "Single U.S. Public Opinion Polls"; see also Loftus, "America's Liberalization in Attitudes toward Homosexuality." See also Carroll, "Society's Moral Boundaries Expand Somewhat This Year."

105. Turley, "Polygamy Laws Expose Our Hypocrisy"; Turley's quip refers to the names of two TV programs that were popular at the time—*Queer Eye for the Straight Guy* and *Everyone Loves Raymond*.

106. Carroll, "Society's Moral Boundaries Expand Somewhat This Year." There is no sign of any significant change of heart in the public aversion to polygamy in the United States since 2005. "A Gallup poll of 1,015 adults nationwide—conducted in May 2009 just before we were treated to the saucier details of the lives of South Carolina's Republican governor and Nevada's Republican senator—found that 92 percent of Americans think it is morally wrong for a married man or woman to have a fling. . . . Only one behavior came close to the disapproval of adultery in the Gallup poll. Polygamy—deemed wrong by 91 percent of Americans." Porter, "Tales of Republicans, Bonobos and Adultery."

107. "Mark Olsen and Will Scheffer, Feeling the 'Big Love.'"

108. In an early episode, for example, a school friend of one of the Henrickson children shrieks, "Oh my god, Sarah has three mommies!" As if to underscore the reference to the children's book about lesbian parenthood, *Heather Has Two Mommies,* the friend's name is Heather. "Big Love: Plot Trivia and Quotes."

109. See Tapestry Against Polygamy, "By 3rd Anniversary of 'Lawrence'—Polygamy Rights Accelerating," which quotes a sound-bite from Mark Henkel of TruthBearer.org, proposing, "the solution to end the so-called 'same sex marriage' debate once and for all: true limited government by getting government out of defining and 'abominating' marriage altogether."

110. Dobner, "Teens Defend Polygamy at Utah Rally."

111. American Civil Liberties Union, "In re Texas Department of Family & Protective Services."

112. Chambers, "Civilizing the Natives"; Goodwyn, Berkes, and Walters, "Warren Jeffs and the FLDS."

113. Chambers, "Civilizing the Natives," 70–71.

114. Former wives, Lost Boys, and men who flee or are cast out of these sects populate many of the anti-polygamy groups, such as Tapestry Against Polygamy, which publicize abuses and excoriate officials who fail to prosecute polygynists. See www.polygamy.org. For examples and discussion of some of the appalling abuses of the FLDS, see Krakauer, *Under the Banner of Heaven*; Wall and Pulitzer, *Stolen Innocence.*

115. "Beyond Same-Sex Marriage"; Duggan, "Holy Matrimony"; Warner, *The Trouble with Normal.*

116. Kurtz, "Beyond Gay Marriage."

117. Kersten, "Once Same-Sex Marriage Is OK, Polygamy's Next."

118. Kurtz, "Big Love from the Set."

119. Harrie, "A GOP Lawmaker Says Polygamists Deserve an Apology."

120. Tapestry Against Polygamy, "Tapestry Against Polygamy Calls Elder Russell M. Nelson 'Serial Polygamist.'"

121. Giddens, *The Transformation of Intimacy*, 27.

122. Burgett, "On the Mormon Question," 77; see also Cott, *Public Vows*.

123. See Pro-Polygamy.com, "Anti-Polygamy Is the Real 'Slippery Slope.'"

124. Ertman, "Race Treason."

125. Cherlin, "The Deinstitutionalization of American Marriage"; Coontz, *Marriage, a History*; Cott, *Public Vows*.

Notes to Chapter 4: Paradoxes of Polygamy and Modernity

1. Prominent examples of right-wing political and/or evangelical Christian clergy caught in "sexcapades" include Larry Craig, Mark Foley, Newt Gingrich, Jimmy Swaggart, Jim Bakker, Ted Haggard, and most recently Mark Sanford and John Ensign. Of course, Republicans do not hold a monopoly on extra-marital transgressions or sexual hypocrisy. John Edwards, Elliot Spitzer, Bill Clinton, and Jim McGreevey have all done their part to maintain bipartisanship in at least this arena.

2. Grace and Moore, "Fossella Shuns His Gay Sister — Source."

3. Spitzer was caught making recurrent use of a high-price prostitution agency. John Edwards vehemently denied the extra-marital affair he was conducting and paternity of the child he sired while seeking the Democratic Party nomination for president. Unlike Fosello and the other right-wing family values sinners, Spitzer and Edwards are both liberal Democrats. However, Spitzer, who built his political career as a vigorous, righteous prosecutor, had helped to pass a law to increase penalties against prostitution. Edwards, whose wife, Elizabeth, had been diagnosed with terminal cancer, arranged to have a loyal campaign aide falsely claim paternity of his child.

4. See the discussion of this subject in chapter 3, as well as in Cott, *Public Vows*; Gordon, *The Mormon Question*; and Coontz, *Marriage, a History*.

5. Barash and Lipton, *Strange Bedfellows*, 41. George P. Murdock's *Ethnographic Atlas* recorded the marital composition of 1,231 societies. Among those, 186 were monogamous. 453 had occasional polygyny, 588 had more frequent polygyny, and 4 had polyandry.

6. "Court Sets Deadline for Participants in Polygamy Case"; Katbamna, "Half a Good Man Is Better than None at All."

7. Sizwe Samayende, "Sharing Hubbie across the Line."

8. Dyanti, "Two Wives Better than One for Some South Africa Men."

9. Zeitzen, *Polygamy*; Van Wichelen, "Polygamy Talk and the Politics of Femi-

nism"; White and Burton, "Causes of Polygyny"; Bergstrom, "Economics of Polygyny."

10. As I revise this chapter in January 2010, President Zuma himself just vindicated Nobunto's cynicism by acknowledging an extra-marital affair (or perhaps, given his three wives at the time, it is more accurate to label it a triple extra-marital affair) and paternity of his twentieth child as a result. "South Africa's Prez Zuma Apologizes for Another Sexual Affair"; "S. Africa's Zuma Apologizes for Sexual Affair."

11. See Epprecht, *Hungochani*; Roscoe and Murray, *Boy-Wives and Female Husbands*.

12. For example, see Lan, *Global Cinderellas*; Hondagneu-Sotelo, *Doméstica*; Parreñas, *Servants of Globalization*.

13. Reid, "How to Be a Real Gay," 46–47.

14. Anthony Costa, quoted in Pieterse, "It's a 'Black Thing,'" 364.

15. Landman, "Polygamy Beats Divorce."

16. Ibid.

17. Ibid.; see also Yarbrough, "We Thee Wed," 26.

18. Landman, "Polygamy Beats Divorce."

19. These are pseudonyms. Despite the officially public character of the filed lawsuit, I have chosen to protect the privacy of the plaintiffs.

20. Quoted in Krakauer, *Under the Banner of Heaven*, 252.

21. TruthBearer.org, "Love-Not-Force."

22. PolygamyDay.com home page, http://www.polygamyday.com/.

23. 2Wives.com home page, http://www.2wives.com/.

24. Pro-polygamy.com home page, http://www.pro-polygamy.com/.

25. Stacey, *In the Name of the Family*, 73.

26. The women identified additional benefits they perceived in polygyny that echo claims made by many fundamentalist Mormon co-wives: "She could fill something that even a husband couldn't fill. It was a cross between a sister and a friend and a co-worker." Hagerty, "Philly's Black Muslims Increasingly Turn to Polygamy."

27. Wing, "Polygamy from Southern Africa to Black Britannia to Black America"; Wing, "Polygamy in Black America," 186.

28. In fact, some poor black and Latina women seem to be reaching this conclusion. For example, see Brown and Hamilton, "From Pain, Family," A1.

29. Bernstein, "In Secret, Polygamy Follows Africans to N.Y."

30. See Liberated Christians, "Multiple Intimate Relationships."

31. See Polyamory Society, "Introduction to Polyamory: What Is Polyamory?"

32. Klesse, *The Spectre of Promiscuity*.

33. Unitarian Universalists for Polyamory Awareness, "Mission."

34. Unitarian Universalists for Polyamory Awareness, "Polyamory and the Unitarian Universalist Association Principles and Purposes."

35. For astute personal confessional and social commentary on recent political sex scandals, see Weiss, "The Affairs of Men."

36. See chap. 3, note 82, for information on bigamy laws and penalties in the United States.

37. Sullum, "Attacking Pluralism"; see also Turley, "Polygamy Laws Expose Our Hypocrisy."

38. Adams, "Polygamist Tom Green Out of Prison: Now What?"

39. For example, see Emens, "Monogamy's Law."

40. Campbell et al., *Polygamy in Canada*.

41. Bailey et al., "Expanding Recognition of Foreign Polygamous Marriages."

42. For example, see Emens, "Monogamy's Law"; Sigman, "Everything Lawyers Know about Polygamy Is Wrong"; Ertman, "Race Treason."

43. Wing, "Polygamy from Southern Africa to Black Britannia to Black America."

44. "Court Sets Deadline for Participants in Polygamy Case."

45. Religioustolerance.org, "The LDS Restorationist Movement, Including the Mormon Churches."

46. Neff and Manson, "Court Rejects Polygamy Defense."

47. "Big Love Forums and News: Discussion."

48. Porter, "Tales of Republicans, Bonobos and Adultery."

49. Berger, "Racing down the Slippery Slope."

50. Van der Vliet, "Traditional Husbands, Modern Wives?"; Andrews, "Who's Afraid of Polygamy?"

51. Tierney, "Who's Afraid of Polygamy?"

52. Reported in personal communication from Shireen Hassim, June 12, 2009.

53. Most accounts date Smith's fateful revelation about polygyny on July 12, 1843, but some sources date it back to 1830.

Notes to Chapter 5: Unhitching the Horse from the Carriage

1. Giddens, *The Transformation of Intimacy*, 27.

2. Ibid., 58.

3. Shih, "Genesis of Marriage among the Moso and Empire-Building in Late Imperial China."

4. Harrell, *Ways of Being Ethnic in Southwest China*; Walsh, "The Mosuo — Beyond the Myths of Matriarchy."

5. Scholars are not certain how distinctive the Mosuo kinship and sexual system was compared with other Naxi and nearby ethnic groups, particularly the Pumi. McKhann speculates that the Naxi cultures were once more similar and overlapped with bilateral, bilineal practices generally but that they evolved in different directions. See McKhann, "Naxi, Rerkua, Moso, Meng."

6. Shih, "*Tisese* and Its Anthropological Significance," 704.

7. Shih, "The Yongning Moso"; Walsh, "The Mosuo—Beyond the Myths of Matriarchy."

8. This is at least true with respect to their heterosexual desires. I have been unable to locate any data or even scholarly discussion about homosexuality in Mosuo culture, and my repeated attempts to ask questions about it during my visit were met with uniform denials of its existence within the culture. That in itself is worthy of investigation.

9. Shih, "The Yongning Moso."

10. Shih and Jenike, "A Cultural-Historical Perspective on the Depressed Fertility among the Matrilineal Moso in Southwest China," 38.

11. Hinton, "Small Happiness: Women of a Chinese Village."

12. Huashang, "Tisese: A Documentary on Three Moso Women."

13. Namu and Mathieu, *Leaving Mother Lake*.

14. Ibid., 53.

15. Shih, "The Yongning Moso"; Shih, "Genesis of Marriage among the Moso and Empire-Building in Late Imperial China."

16. Bai Hua, *The Remote Country of Women*.

17. Cai Hua. *A Society without Fathers or Husbands*.

18. See Walsh, "From Nu Guo to Nu'er Guo"; Namu's early memoir, *The Kingdom of Daughters*, has not been translated into English.

19. "Lijiang"; "Mosuo Matriarchy"; "The Woman's Kingdom"; "China's 'Kingdom of Women.'"

20. "The Woman's Kingdom."

21. Mackie, "The Lake of Free Love."

22. Twitchell, review of *The Remote Country of Women*, 167.

23. Schein, "Gender and Internal Orientalism in China."

24. I have assigned pseudonyms to Gezo and all of the other individuals I name in this chapter.

25. In addition to Gezo, who arranged the visits and translated from Mosuo to Mandarin, my retinue included three others who also served as translators, guides, and companions: my driver, Mr. Li, a thirty-year-old married Bai man with one daughter who lives in Lijiang; Wang Fen, a twenty-three-year-old female graduate student in anthropology from a university in Kunming who was hired to translate between Mandarin and English; and Ron Cho, my fortuitous seatmate during my flight from Shanghai to Lijiang. Ron was a twenty-seven-year-old software engineer who was taking a week's vacation and who turned out to be a semi-closeted gay man, a born anthropologist, and an enthusiastic volunteer research assistant and translator who agreed to join my journey to Lugu Lake.

26. Scholars disagree over whether *tisese* was the original universal form of Mosuo kinship that was later modified to incorporate marriage, or whether a mixed system, with patrilineal marriage for rulers, was present from the outset. See, for

example, Shih, "The Yongning Moso," which claims that the Mosuo were matrilineal and practiced non-conjugal kinship all the way back to the Han period; McKhann believes that the Mosuo were originally bilineal, and the matrilineal non-marriage system was a later strategic adaptation to the caste system and a means to maintain power by elites. McKhann, "Naxi, Rerkua, Moso, Meng," 34–35.

27. Shih, "Genesis of Marriage among the Moso and Empire-Building in Late Imperial China."

28. Engels, *Origins of the Family, Private Property, and the State*; Morgan, *Ancient Society*.

29. Ruxian, "A Living Fossil of the Family," 61.

30. Walsh, "The Mosuo—Beyond the Myths of Matriarchy."

31. Namu and Mathieu, *Leaving Mother Lake*, 94.

32. Ibid.

33. Bai Hua, *The Remote Country of Women*, 7–8.

34. Shih, "Tisese and Its Anthropological Significance."

35. Ibid.

36. Knodel, "Yongning Moso."

37. Ibid.

38. Namu and Mathieu, *Leaving Mother Lake*, 94; Knodel, "Yongning Moso"; Shih, "*Tisese* and Its Anthropological Significance."

39. Knodel, "Yongning Moso."

40. Shih, "*Tisese* and Its Anthropological Significance," 701.

41. Shih, "The Yongning Moso."

42. Walsh, "From Nu Guo to Nu'er Guo," 457.

43. Knodel, "Yongning Moso," 58.

44. Bai Hua, *The Remote Country of Women*, 29.

45. Walsh, "The Mosuo—Beyond the Myths of Matriarchy."

46. Walsh, "From Nu Guo to Nu'er Guo," 459.

47. Forney, "Minority Report."

48. Walsh, "From Nu Guo to Nu'er Guo," 472.

49. Ibid.

50. Zhou and Hoffman, "The Women's Kingdom."

51. Walsh, "From Nu Guo to Nu'er Guo," 469.

52. Cai Hua claimed in *A Society without Fathers or Husbands*, quite implausibly, that multiple furtive visits were practiced "without exception" even by those who were in "conspicuous" long-term visiting relationships. I encountered substantial hostility toward Cai Hua and his account of Mosuo culture and later discovered that his faculty position at Beijing University has come under threat due to charges of plagiarism and inaccuracies and distortions in his data. See Liu, "Research on the Na and Academic Integrity." Gezo Ita and Wang Fen both claimed that Cai Hua is not welcome to visit at any of his field sites.

53. Walsh, "The Mosuo—Beyond the Myths of Matriarchy"; Shih, "*Tisese* and Its Anthropological Significance"; Harrell, *Ways of Being Ethnic in Southwest China*.

54. The state runs "Yunnan Folk Culture Villages" in Kunming, and additional cultural villages have been set up in the province.

55. Walsh, "The Mosuo—Beyond the Myths of Matriarchy."

56. Ibid.; Walsh "From Nu Guo to Nu'er Guo."

57. Knodel, "Yongning Moso."

58. Walsh, "The Mosuo—Beyond the Myths of Matriarchy"; Walsh "From Nu Guo to Nu'er Guo."

59. Qi, "Family Planning among Ethnic Minorities."

60. Fineman, *The Neutered Mother*.

61. Namu and Mathieu, *Leaving Mother Lake*, 7.

62. Cai Hua, *A Society without Fathers or Husbands*; Shih and Jenike, "A Cultural-Historical Perspective on the Depressed Fertility among the Matrilineal Moso in Southwest China"; Walsh, "The Mosuo—Beyond the Myths of Matriarchy"; Ruxian, "A Living Fossil of the Family."

63. Shih and Jenike, "A Cultural-Historical Perspective on the Depressed Fertility among the Matrilineal Moso in Southwest China."

64. Namu and Mathieu, *Leaving Mother Lake*, 69.

65. My translators, Ron Cho and Wang Fen, claimed that extreme anxiety and gold-digging now is common among Chinese professional women, who hope to find husbands to liberate them from full-time employment.

66. Shih and Jenike, "A Cultural-Historical Perspective on the Depressed Fertility among the Matrilineal Moso in Southwest China."

Notes to the Conclusion

1. Sinatra divorced his first wife after a volatile, very public adulterous affair with movie star and pin-up Ava Gardner, who became his second wife. Mia Farrow was twenty-one years old in 1966, when she became the fifty-year-old singer's third wife. Frankie kept the tabloids sizzling with stories that he'd set JFK up with Marilyn Monroe and the like. Summers and Swan, "Sex, Sinatra and the Women Who Fell for Him."

2. Goode, *World Revolution and Family Patterns*.

3. Giddens, *The Transformation of Intimacy*.

4. For example, see Lasch, *Haven in a Heartless World*; Bauman, *Liquid Love*; Illouz, *Cold Intimacies*; D. Popenoe, *Disturbing the Nest*.

5. As I write in February 2010, the Ugandan legislature has been actively considering a law to punish homosexuality with a life sentence and to allow execution of "repeat offenders."

6. Moynihan, *The Negro Family*.

7. See, for example, Staples, *The Black Family*, 124–133; Stack, *All Our Kin*.

8. Murray, "Rediscovering the Underclass"; Cosby, "Dr. Bill Cosby Speaks"; Patterson, *Rituals of Blood*; H. Cooper, "Barack Obama, Father-in-Chief"; Obama, "We Need Fathers to Step Up."

9. Moynihan, *The Negro Family*, chap. 4.

10. Garfinkel and McLanahan, *Single Mothers and Their Children*.

11. Ribuffo, "Family Policy Past as Prologue."

12. Phyllis Schlafly warned that the ERA would cause women to lose preferential child custody and support after divorce and would lead to gay rights, unisex toilets, and women in combat. Although such arguments stirred sufficient fears to defeat the ERA, most of these predictions have come to pass nonetheless. See Schlafly, *Feminist Fantasies*; Schlafly, "Stop ERA."

13. "Republican Contract with America." For a critique, see Borosage, "A *Real* Contract with America."

14. Giloff, *The Jesus Machine*; Reyes, "Jerry Falwell Is Gone."

15. "Dan Quayle vs. Murphy Brown."

16. I personally received one of these campaign fundraising letters. The same quote appears in Moynihan, "Defining Deviancy Down," 26.

17. Blankenhorn, *Fatherless America*, 1.

18. The personnel and boards of many of these institutes are interlocking, with David Blankenhorn, David Popenoe, and Maggie Gallagher playing central roles in most of them. Related institutes and advocacy projects include the late sociologist Steven Nock's Marriage Matters at the University of Virginia, Gallagher's National Organization for Marriage, and Don Browning's Religion, Family and Culture Project at the University of Chicago.

19. For example, one of the recommendations in a Council on Families in America report on marriage in America: "Don't glamorize unwed motherhood, marital infidelity, alternative lifestyles and sexual promiscuity. Imagine depicting divorce and unwed childbearing as frequently and as approvingly as you currently depict smoking and littering." In Popenoe et al., *Promises to Keep*, 313.

20. For a description and analysis of the extra-academic realm of virtual social science publications on family, see "Virtual Social Science and the Politics of Family Values," chapter 4 in my book *In the Name of the Family*.

21. I discuss the fatherlessness discourse in Stacey, "Dada-ism in the Nineties."

22. Kranish, "In Bully Pulpit, Preaching Values," 17.

23. For an in-depth look at DOMA by state, see MarriageWatch.org, "State Defense of Marriage Acts."

24. DeWitt, "Moynihan, Welfare Reform and the Myth of 'Benign Neglect.'"

25. The bill passed by a vote of 85–14 in the Senate and 342–67 in the House and was signed into law by President Clinton on September 21, 1996.

26. "Obama's Father's Day Speech."

27. Obama, "We Need Father's to Step Up."

28. See, for example, Warner, *The Trouble with Normal*; Duggan, "Holy Mat-

rimony"; Polikoff, *Beyond (Straight and Gay) Marriage*; Farrow, "Is Gay Marriage Anti-Black?"; BeyondMarriage.org, "Beyond Same-Sex Marriage."

29. Formerly known as a fundamentalist Christian, Member of Parliament Iris Robinson, wife of Northern Ireland's First Minister Peter Robinson was discovered to have had an affair with a nineteen-year-old boy. The First Minister stepped down so that the sex scandal and related financial scandals could be investigated. This threatened the fragile balance of power in the Northern Ireland governing coalition. Clarke, "And Here's to You, Mrs. Robinson . . ."

30. Hughes, "Zuma's Woes."

31. Estimates of the number of Jeffs's wives and children vary greatly, ranging from forty to eighty wives and as many as 250 children. See, for example, Goodwyn, Berkes, and Walters, "Warren Jeffs and the FLDS"; and Colby, "FOX Facts: Warren Jeffs."

32. In the wake of the Tiger Woods ultra–Scarlet Letterman expose, for example, it became newsworthy when his wife had second thoughts about divorcing him. As one typical news story began, "Ever since the news broke of Tiger Woods' viral infidelities, it's been kind of a common assumption that his wife Elin Nordegren would soon file for divorce. But she apparently has other ideas." McMullen, "People: Hold Everything, Tiger Woods' Wife Doesn't Want a Divorce."

33. Not only does the label imply that parental divorce is automatically among the most important determinants of a child's development, identity, and fate, but constant use of the term itself contributes to the negative effects of divorce on children. Note that when a marriage with young children ends because one or both parents die, we don't refer to their offspring as "children of death." In the news story about Tiger Woods, his wife was reported to want to protect her children from being a "child of divorce" who felt slighted by their father as she had. See ibid.

34. The document and signatories are available at www.beyondmarriage.org.

35. For theorists calling for the disestablishment of marriage, see, for example, Metz, *Untying the Knot*; Garrett, "Marriage Unhitched from the State"; and Culbertson, "Arguments against Marriage Equality." During the Massachusetts legislature's debate over same-sex marriage, Republican assemblyman Paul Loscocco, who opposes same-sex marriage, proposed eliminating the term *marriage* and providing equal civil union benefits to all couples. Deborah Glick, a lesbian Democratic state senator in New York made a similar proposal. Stacey, "Can Marriage Be Saved?" 8.

36. However, the economic crisis is forcing vast numbers of young adults to remain in or return to the family "nests" they expected to leave behind.

37. A. Cooper, "Hiding in Plain Sight."

Bibliography

Adams, Brooke. 2007. "Polygamist Tom Green Out of Prison: Now What?" *Salt Lake Tribune*, August 8. http://www.rickross.com/reference/polygamy/polygamy679.html.

———. 2006. "Polygamists' Children Speak." *Salt Lake Tribune*, August 20.

Adekunle, Julius. 2007. *Culture and Customs of Rwanda*. Westport, CT: Greenwood.

Adler, Martin, producer. "China, Mongolia: Kidnapped Wives." Insight News TV. http://www.insightnewstv.com/d08/.

Agigian, Amy. 2004. *Baby Steps: How Lesbian Alternative Insemination Is Changing the World*. Middletown, CT: Wesleyan University Press.

Albertyn, Catherine. 2003. "Contesting Democracy: HIV/AIDS and the Achievement of Gender Equality in South Africa." *Feminist Studies* 29:595–615.

Altman, Dennis. 2001. *Global Sex*. Chicago: University of Chicago Press.

American Academy of Pediatrics. 2002. "Policy Statement: Coparent or Second-Parent Adoption by Same-Sex Couples." *Pediatrics* 109 (2): 339–340.

American Civil Liberties Union. 2008. "In re Texas Department of Family & Protective Services: Brief of Amici Curiae in Opposition to Relator's Petition for Mandamus." May 29. http://www.aclu.org/religion-belief/re-texas-department-family-protective-services-brief-amici-curiae-opposition-relator.

Anderson, Connie M. 2000. "The Persistence of Polygyny as an Adaptive Response to Poverty and Oppression in Apartheid South Africa." *Cross Cultural Research* 34 (2): 99–112.

Anderson, J. Norman D. 1970. *Islamic Law in Africa*. New impression ed. New York: Routledge.

Andrews, Penelope. 2009. "Who's Afraid of Polygamy? Exploring the Boundaries of Family, Equality and Custom in South Africa." *Utah Law Review* 2009 (2): 351–379.

Appleton, Susan F. 2006. "Presuming Women: Resisting the Assumption of Legitimacy in the Same-Sex Couples Era." *Boston University Law Review* 86:227–297.

Associated Press. 2007. "Utah: Polygamist Freed after 6 Years." *New York Times*, August 8. http://www.nytimes.com/2007/08/08/us/08brfs-POLYGAMISTFR_BRF.html.

Associated Press. 2006. "Fate of Polygamy Sect Unclear as Leader Held." *USA Today,* August 29.

———. 2004. "Tom Green to Be Paroled in August '07." August 28.

Badgett, M. V. Lee. 2001. *Money, Myths, and Change: The Economic Lives of Lesbians and Gay Men.* Chicago: University of Chicago Press.

Bai Hua. 1994. *The Remote Country of Women.* Trans. Qingyun Wu and Thomas O. Beebee. Honolulu: University of Hawaii Press. Originally published 1988.

Bailey, Martha Jane, Beverley Baines, Bita Amani, and Amy Kaufman. 2006. "Expanding Recognition of Foreign Polygamous Marriages: Policy Implications for Canada." Queen's University Legal Studies Research Paper No. 07-12. http://ssrn.com/abstract=1023896.

Baleta, A. 1998. "Concern Voiced over "Dry Sex" Practices in South Africa." *Lancet* 352:1292.

Barash, David P., and Judith Eve Lipton. 2009. *Strange Bedfellows: The Surprising Connection between Sex, Evolution and Monogamy.* New York: Bellevue Literary Press.

Barron, James. 2008. "Fossella Admits He Had an Extramarital Affair." *New York Times,* May 9. http://www.nytimes.com/2008/05/09/nyregion/09fossella.html?_r=2.

Bauman, Zygmunt. 2003. *Liquid Love: On the Frailty of Human Bonds.* Malden, MA: Blackwell.

Beal, Frances M. 2003. "Double Jeopardy: To Be Black and Female." In *Sisterhood Is Powerful,* ed. Robin Morgan. New York: Washington Square. Originally published 1970.

Beck, Amanda. 2010. "Blankenhorn Testifies about Marriage, Scholarship and Soul-Searching." *Prop 8 on Trial,* January 31. http://prop8.berkeleylawblogs.org/2010/01/31/blankenhorn-testifies-about-marriage-scholarship-and-soul-searching/.

Beck, Ulrich, and Elizabeth Beck-Gernsheim. 1995. *The Normal Chaos of Love.* Cambridge, UK: Polity.

Beers, James Robert. 1996. "Desire to Parent in Gay Men." Ph.D. diss., Columbia University, Teachers College.

Bell, Alan P., and Martin S. Weinberg. 1978. *Homosexualities: A Study of Diversity among Men and Women.* New York: Simon and Schuster.

Bellafante, Ginia. 2004. "Two Fathers, with One Happy to Stay at Home." *New York Times,* January 12, A1, A12.

Benkov, Laura. 1995. *Reinventing the Family: The Emerging Story of Lesbian and Gay Parents.* New York: Random House.

Bennett, William. 2006. "Bookworld: Live Discussion with William Bennett." *Washington Post,* June 9.

Berger, Knute. 2004. "Racing down the Slippery Slope." *Seattle Weekly,* June 23.

http://www.seattleweekly.com/2004-06-23/news/racing-down-the-slippery
-slope.php.

Bergstrom, Theodore C. 1994. "Economics of Polygyny." University of Michigan Center for Research on Economic and Social Theory, Working Paper Series 94-11, University of Michigan, August 25. http://www.econ.ucsb.edu/~tedb/ Evolution/polygyny3.pdf.

Bernstein, Nina. 2007. "In Secret, Polygamy Follows Africans to N.Y." *New York Times,* March 23. http://www.nytimes.com/2007/03/23/nyregion/23polygamy .html?ex=1332388800&en=634614e51ada09f3&ei=5124&partner=permalink& exprod=permalink.

Bettie, Julie. 2003. *Women without Class: Girls, Race, and Identity.* Berkeley: University of California Press.

Beyondmarriage.org. 2006. "Beyond Same-Sex Marriage: A New Strategic Vision for All Our Families and Relationships."

Bhe and Others v. The Magistrate, Khayelitsha and Others; Shibi v. Sithole and Others; South African Human Rights Commission and Another v. President of the Republic of South Africa. 2004. Case CCT 49-03. http://www.saflii.org/za/cases/ ZACC/2004/17.html.

Biblarz, Timothy, and Judith Stacey. 2010. "How Does the Gender of Parents Matter?" *Journal of Marriage and Family* 72:3–22.

"Big Love Forums and News: Discussion." n.d. Website for HBO series *Big Love.* http://www.hbo.com/big-love/talk.html#/big-love/talk/index.html.

"Big Love: Plot Trivia and Quotes." n.d. TV.com. http://www.tv.com/big-love/ pilot/episode/356488/trivia.html.

Bilevsky, Dan. 2008. "Albanian Custom Fades: Woman as Family Man." *New York Times,* June 25. http://www.nytimes.com/2008/06/25/world/europe/25 virgins.html?_r=3.

"Birth Parents' Responsibilities toward Child; Cessation." 2004. California Family Code, Ann. §8617. St. Paul, MN: Thomson West.

Blankenhorn, David. 2009. *The Future of Marriage.* New York: Encounter Books.

———. 1995. *Fatherless America: Confronting Our Most Urgent Social Problem.* New York: Basic Books.

Bonthuys, Elsje. 2008. "The Civil Union Act: More of the Same." In *To Have and to Hold: The Making of Same-Sex Marriage in South Africa,* ed. Melanie Judge, Anthony Manion, and Shuan de Waal, 171–181. Auckland Park, South Africa: Fanele.

Borosage, Robert L. 2005. "A *Real* Contract with America." *Nation,* October 6. http://www.thenation.com/doc/20051024/borosage.

Bos, Henny. 2004. *Parenting in Planned Lesbian Families.* Amsterdam: Vossiuspers UvA.

Boykin, Kevin. 1996. *One More River to Cross: Black and Gay in America.* New York: Anchor Books.

Bozzuti, Joseph. 2004. "The Constitutionality of Polygamy Prohibitions after *Lawrence v. Texas*: Is Scalia a Punchline or a Prophet?" *Catholic Lawyer* 43:409–442.

Brodzinsky, David, Charlotte J. Patterson, and Mahnoush Vaziri. 2002. "Adoption Agency Perspectives on Lesbian and Gay Prospective Parents: A National Study." *Adoption Quarterly* 5 (3): 5–23.

Brooks, David. 2003. "The Power of Marriage." *New York Times*, November 22.

Brown, Tina, and Elizabeth Hamilton. 2006. "From Pain, Family: Seeking Stability amid the Chaos, More Poor Women of Color Are Turning to Each Other." *Hartford Courant*, April 30, A1.

Browning, Frank. 1993. *The Culture of Desire: Paradox and Perversion in Gay Lives Today*. New York: Random House.

Brumbaugh, Stacey M., Laura A. Sanchez, Steven L. Nock, and James D. Wright. 2008. "Attitudes toward Gay Marriage in States Undergoing Marriage Law Transformation." *Journal of Marriage and Family* 70:345–359.

Bumiller, E., D. E. Sanger, and R. W. Stevenson. 2005. "Bush Says Iraqi Leaders Will Want U.S. Forces to Stay to Help." *New York Times*, January 28, A1.

Bunkely, Nick. 2008. "Mayor's Amorous Texts Lead to Perjury Inquiry." *New York Times*, January 26. http://www.nytimes.com/2008/01/26/us/26detroit.html.

Burgett, Bruce. 2005. "On the Mormon Question: Race, Sex and Polygamy in the 1850s and the 1990s." *American Quarterly* 57:75–102.

Burton, John W. 1978. "Ghosts, Ancestors and Individuals among the Atuot of the Southern Sudan." *Man* (Royal Anthropological Institute of Great Britain and Ireland), new series, 13 (4): 600–617.

Cai Hua. 2001. *A Society without Fathers or Husbands: The Na of China*. Trans. Asti Hustvedt. New York: Zone Books. Originally published 1997.

Cameron, Edwin. 1993. "Sexual Orientation and the Constitution: A Test Case for Human Rights." *South African Legal Journal* 110:450–472.

Cameron, Paul. 1993. *The Gay 90s: What the Empirical Evidence Reveals about Homosexuality*. Franklin, TN: Adroit.

Campbell, Angela, et al. 2005. *Polygamy in Canada: Legal and Social Implications for Women and Children*. Status of Women Canada's Policy Research Fund. http://www.vancouversun.com/pdf/polygamy_021209.pdf.

Campbell, Steve. 2009. "Bigamy Charges Dismissed against Leader of Texas Sect." *Fort Worth Star-Telegram*, October 30. http://www.mcclatchydc.com/crime/story/78103.html.

Cantú, Lionel. 2000. "Entre Hombres/Between Men: Latino Masculinities and Homosexualities." In *Gay Masculinities*, ed. Peter Nardi, 224–246. Thousand Oaks, CA: Sage.

Carlson, Allan. 2007. *Conjugal America: On the Public Purposes of Marriage*. New Brunswick, NJ: Transaction.

Carrington, Christopher. 1999. *No Place Like Home: Relationships and Family Life among Lesbians and Gay Men*. Chicago: University of Chicago Press.

Carroll, Joseph. 2005. "Society's Moral Boundaries Expand Somewhat This Year." Gallop Poll, May 16. http://www.gallup.com.

Chambers, David L. 2000. "Civilizing the Natives: Marriage in Post-Apartheid South Africa." *Daedalus* 129 (4): 101–124.

———. 1997. "Polygamy and Same-Sex Marriage." *Hofstra Law Review* 26:53–83.

Chauncey, George. 1994. *Gay New York: Gender, Urban Culture and the Making of the Gay Male World*. New York: Basic Books.

Cherlin, Andrew J. 2010. *The Marriage-Go-Round: The State of Marriage and Family in America Today*. New York: Knopf.

———. 2004. "The Deinstitutionalization of American Marriage." *Journal of Marriage and the Family* 66:848–861.

"China's 'Kingdom of Women.'" 2008. *National Geographic*. Video. June 17. http://news.nationalgeographic.com/news/2008/06/080617-mosuo-video-ap.html.

CIET. 2000. "Beyond Victims and Villains: Sexual Violence, South Johannesburg (1997–2000)." Summary Report, SR-ZA-sv-00. http://www.ciet.org/en/documents/projects_library_docs/2006224131250.pdf.

Clark, Brigitte. 2002. "Families and Domestic Partnerships." *South African Law Journal* 119:634–649.

Clarke, Liam. 2010. "And Here's to You, Mrs. Robinson . . ." *New York Times,* January 10. http://www.timesonline.co.uk/tol/news/world/ireland/article6982377.ece.

Clayton, Jonathan. 2007. "Profile: Zuma Charmed Wives and Nation." *Australian,* December 9. http://www.theaustralian.com.au/news/profile-zuma-charmed-wives-and-nation/story-e6frg6uf-1111115152426.

Coates, Ta-Nehisi. 2008. "Andrew on Black Homophobia." *Atlantic,* October 1. http://ta-nehisicoates.theatlantic.com/archives/2008/10/andrew_on_black_homophobia.php.

Cock, Jacklyn. 2002. "Engendering Gay and Lesbian Rights: The Equality Clause in the South African Constitution." *Women's Studies International Forum* 26: 35–45.

Cogel, Metin M. 2000. "The Family in Utopia: Celibacy, Communal Child Rearing and Continuity in a Religious Commune." *Journal of Family History* 25 (4): 491–503.

Cohn, D'Vera. 2003. "Area Gay Couples Settled, Middle-Aged, Study Finds." *Washington Post,* June 13, B1.

Colby, Jamie. 2006. "FOX Facts: Warren Jeffs." FOX Online w/ Jamie Colby, August 31. http://www.foxnews.com/story/0,2933,210981,00.html.

Collyer, Laurie, director. 2000 *Nuyorican Dream*. Film. Big Mouth Productions.

Connell, R. W. 1995. *Masculinities*. Berkeley: University of California Press.

Constitution of the Republic of South Africa. 1996. http://www.acts.co.za/constitution/index.htm.

Coontz, Stephanie. 2005. *Marriage, a History: From Obedience to Intimacy, or How Love Conquered Marriage*. London: Penguin.

Cooper, Anderson. 2006. "Hiding in Plain Sight." *Anderson Cooper 360°*. CNN. Aired May 10. http://transcripts.cnn.com/TRANSCRIPTS/0605/10/acd.02.html.

Cooper, Helene. 2009. "Barack Obama, Father-in-Chief." *New York Times*, July 19. http://thecaucus.blogs.nytimes.com/2009/06/19/barack-obama-father-in-chief/.

Cosby, Bill. "Dr. Cosby Speaks at the 50th Anniversary Commemoration of Brown v. Topeka Board of Education." http://www.eightcitiesmap.com/transcript_bc.htm.

Cott, Nancy F. 2001. *Public Vows: A History of Marriage and the Nation*. Cambridge, MA: Harvard University Press.

"Court Sets Deadline for Participants in Polygamy Case." 2010. *News Ahead,* January 28. http://www.newsahead.com/preview/2010/01/28/canada-28-jan-2010-court-sets-deadline-for-participants-in-polygamy-case/index.php.

Culbertson, Tucker. 2007. "Arguments against Marriage Equality: Commemorating and Reconstructing *Loving v. Virginia*." *Washington University Law Review* 85:575.

"Dan Quayle vs. Murphy Brown." 1992. *Time*, June 1. http://www.time.com/time/magazine/article/0,9171,975627,00.html.

Davis, Evan, and Melanie Phillips. 1999. "Debate: Gay Marriage." *Prospect Magazine* 40 (April): 16–20.

de Laclos, Choderlos. 1961. *Les Liaisons Dangereuses*. New York: Penguin Putnam. Originally published 1782.

Delany, Samuel. 1999. *Times Square Red, Times Square Blue*. New York: NYU Press.

De Vos, Pierre. 2008. "A Judicial Revolution? The Court-Led Achievement of Same-Sex Marriage in South Africa." *Utrecht Law Review* 4 (2): 161–174.

DeWitt, Larry. 2005. "Moynihan, Welfare Reform and the Myth of 'Benign Neglect.'" Larry DeWitt's personal website, October. http://www.larrydewitt.net/Essays/Moynihan.htm.

DiGuglielmo, Joey. 2008. "Will Gay Marriage Lead to Legalized Polygamy? Legal Experts Respond to Arguments of Conservative Activists." *Washington Blade*, June 6.

Dobner, Jennifer. 2006. "Teens Defend Polygamy at Utah Rally." *Washington Post*, August 20. http://www.washingtonpost.com/wpdyn/content/article/2006/08/20115/AR2006082000113.html.

Dobson, James. 2005. "An Open Letter to South Africans on Same-Sex Marriage." *Christians for Truth,* November. http://www.cft.org.za/articles/dobson_gay_marriage_sa.htm.

———. n.d. "Same Sex Marriage Talking Points." *Truth News.* http://www
.truenews.org/Homosexuality/same_sex_marriage_talking_points.html.

DOMAwatch.org. 2009. "Marriage Amendment Summary." October 15. http://
www.domawatch.org/amendments/amendmentsummary.html.

Dowsett, Gary W. 1996. *Practicing Desire: Homosexual Sex in the Era of AIDS.* Stanford, CA: Stanford University Press.

Dreyfuss, Robert. 1999. "The Holy War on Gays." *Rolling Stone,* March 18, 38–41.

Due, Linnea. 1996. *Joining the Tribe: Growing Up Gay and Lesbian in the '90s.* New York: Doubleday.

Duggan, Lisa. 2004. "Holy Matrimony." *Nation,* February 26. http://www.the
nation.com/doc/20040315/duggan.

Dunne, Gilliane. 2000. "Opting into Motherhood: Lesbians Blurring the Boundaries and Transforming the Meaning of Parenthood and Kinship." *Gender and Society* 14(1):11–35.

Dyanti, Aurelia. 2003. "Two Wives Better than One for Some South Africa Men." *Star,* July 16. http://www.polygamyinfo.com/intnalmedia%20plyg%20192star
.htm.

Egan, Patrick. 2009. "California's Proposition 8: What Happened, and What Does the Future Hold?" *The Task Force,* January 6. http://www.thetaskforce.org/
reports_and_research/prop8_analysis.

Elder, Sean. 2004. "Why My Wife Won't Sleep with Me: Confessions of a Dependent Male." *New York Magazine,* April 5, 43.

Elshtain, Jean Bethke. 1981. *Public Man, Private Woman.* Princeton, NJ: Princeton University Press.

Emens, Elizabeth F. 2004. "Monogamy's Law: Compulsory Monogamy and Polyamorous Existence." *New York University Law Review of Law and Social Change* 29:277.

Engels, Friedrich. 1952. *The Origin of the Family, Private Property, and the State.* Moscow: Foreign Languages Publishing House. Originally published 1884.

Epprecht, Marc. 2004. *Hungochani: The Story of a Dissident Sexuality in Southern Africa.* London: McGill-Queen's University Press.

Ertman, Martha M. 2010. "Race Treason: The Untold Story of America's Ban on Polygamy." *Columbia Journal of Gender and Law* 19:287–366.

———. 2007. "The Story of *Reynolds v. United States*: Federal 'Hell Hounds' Punishing Mormon Treason." In *Family Law Stories,* ed. Carol Sanger. Eagan, MN: Thomson Reuters West.

Espera, Troy. 2006. "Jacob Zuma Draws Fire for Anti-gay Speech." *GMax,* September 28. http://www.gmax.co.za/look06/09/28-SAzuma.html.

"Ethiopia: Revenge of the Abducted Bride." 1999. BBC News. June 13. http://news
.bbc.co.uk/2/hi/africa/371944.stm.

"Far from Heaven." 2002. Allmovie.com. http://www.allmovie.com/work/1:267273.

Farrow, Kenyon. 2004. "Is Gay Marriage Anti-Black?" *Chickenbones: A Literary Journal.* http://www.nathanielturner.com/isgaymarriageantiblack.htm.

Fenn v. Sherriff. 2001. California Court of Appeals, 3rd District. Cal. Rpts. 3d, 1:185, 189.

Ferran, Lee, Brian Ross, Nadine Shubailat, and Chris Francescani. 2010. "John Edwards Admits He Fathered Rielle Hunter's Child." ABCNews.com, January 21. http://abcnews.go.com/GMA/john-edwards-admits-fathered-rielle-hunter -child-affair/story?id=9620812.

Fineman, Martha Albertson. 1995. *The Neutered Mother, the Sexual Family, and Other Twentieth-Century American Tragedies.* New York: Routledge.

Flaks, David K. 1994. "Gay and Lesbian Families: Judicial Assumptions, Scientific Realities." *William and Mary Bill of Rights Journal* 3.

Flanagan, Caitlin. 2003. "The Wifely Duty." *Atlantic* 291 (1) (January–February).

Forney, Matthew. 2002. "Minority Report: The Mosuo, a Small Matrilineal Tribe in Central China Are Preserving Their Traditions by Exploiting Them." *Time Asia,* November 11. http://www.time.com/time/asia/features/china_cul_rev/ minorities.html.

Franke, Katherine. 1999. "Becoming a Citizen: Reconstruction Era Regulation of African American Marriages." *Yale Journal of Law and the Humanities* 11:251– 309.

Friedan, Betty. 1997. *The Feminine Mystique.* New York: Norton. Originally published 1963.

Freud, Sigmund. 1989. *Civilization and Its Discontents.* New York: Norton. Originally published 1930.

Furstenberg, Frank, Jr., and Andrew J. Cherlin. 1991. *Divided Families: What Happens to Children When Parents Part?* Cambridge, MA: Harvard University Press.

Gallagher, Maggie. 1992. "An Unwed Mother for Quayle." *New York Times,* September 24, A29.

Gallup Poll. 2006. "Marriage." http://www.gallup.com/poll/117328/marriage.aspx.

Garenne, Michel, Stephen Tollman, Kathleen Kahn, Terri Collins, and Shirley Ngwenya. 2001. "Understanding Marital and Premarital Fertility in Rural South Africa." *Journal of Southern African Studies* 27:277–290.

Garfinkel, Irwin, and Sara S. McLanahan. 1986. *Single Mothers and Their Children: A New American Dilemma.* Washington, DC: Urban Institute Press.

Garrett, Jeremy. 2009. "Marriage Unhitched from the State: A Defense." *Public Affairs Quarterly* 23 (2) (April): 161–180.

Gates, Gary, Lee M. V. Badgett, Jennifer Ehrle Macomber, and Kate Chambers. 2007. "Adoption and Foster Care by Lesbian and Gay Parents in the United States." Urban Institute, March 23. http://www.urban.org/publications/411437 .html.

Gay Liberation Front. 1969. "Gay Revolution Comes Out." *Rat,* August, 12–16.

Gevisser, Mark, and Edwin Cameron, eds. 1995. *Defiant Desires: Gay and Lesbian Lives in South Africa*. New York: Routledge.

Gher, Jaime M. 2008. "Polygamy and Same-Sex Marriage—Allies or Adversaries within the Same-Sex Marriage Movement." *William and Mary Journal of Women and Law* 14:559–603.

Giddens, Anthony. 1993. *The Transformation of Intimacy: Sexuality, Love and Eroticism in Modern Societies*. Stanford, CA: Stanford University Press.

Giloff, Dan. 2007. *The Jesus Machine: How James Dobson, Focus on the Family and Evangelical America Are Winning the Culture War*. New York: St. Martin's Griffin.

Glendon, Mary Ann. 2004. "For Better or Worse?" *Wall Street Journal*, February 25.

Glenn, Norval D. 1993. "A Plea for Objective Assessment of the Notion of Family Decline." *Journal of Marriage and Family* 55 (3): 542–544.

Goldberg, Abbie E. 2009. *Lesbian and Gay Parents and Their Children: Research on the Family Life Cycle*. Washington, DC: American Psychological Association.

Goldstein, Richard. 2001. "The Real Andrew Sullivan Scandal." *Village Voice*, June 19. http://www.villagevoice.com/2001-06-19/news/the-real-andrew-sullivan-scandal/1.

Goode, William J. 1963 *World Revolution and Family Patterns*. New York: Free Press.

Goodnough, Abby. 2009. "Gay Rights Rebuke May Change Approach." *New York Times*, November 4. http://www.nytimes.com/2009/11/05/us/05marriage.html.

Goodridge v. Department of Health. 2003. Supreme Judicial Court of Massachusetts. 798 N.E.2d. 941.

Goodwyn, Wade, Howard Berkes, and Amy Walters. 2005. "Warren Jeffs and the FLDS." NPR.org, May 3. http://www.npr.org/templates/story/story.php?storyId=4629320.

Gordon, Sarah Barringer. 2002. *The Mormon Question: Polygamy and Constitutional Conflict in Nineteenth-Century America*. Chapel Hill: University of North Carolina Press.

Gordon-Reed, Annette. 1997. *Thomas Jefferson and Sally Hemings: An American Controversy*. Charlottesville: University of Virginia Press.

Gouws, Amanda. 2004. "The Politics of State Structures: Citizenship and the National Machinery for Women in South Africa." *Feminist Africa* 3:1–15.

"Governor Paterson Admits to Sex with Other Woman for Years." 2008. *New York Daily News*, March 18. http://www.nydailynews.com/news/2008/03/17/2008-03-17_gov_paterson_admits_to_sex_with_other_wo.html.

Grace, Melissa, and Tina Moore. 2008. "Fosella Shuns His Gay Sister—Source." *Daily News*, May 11. http://www.nydailynews.com/news/2008/05/12/2008-05-12_fossella_shuns_his_gay_sister__source.html.

Green, Jesse. 1999. *The Velveteen Father: An Unexpected Journey to Fatherhood.* New York: Villard.

Gutman, Herbert G. 1977. *The Black Family in Slavery and Freedom, 1750–1925.* New York: Vintage.

Hagerty, Barbara Bradley. 2008. "Philly's Black Muslims Increasingly Turn to Polygamy." NPR.org, June 2. www.npr.org/templates/story/story.php?storyId=90886407&sc=emaf.

Harrell, Steven. 2001. *Ways of Being Ethnic in Southwest China.* Seattle: University of Washington Press.

Harrie, Dan. 1999. "A GOP Lawmaker Says Polygamists Deserve an Apology." *Salt Lake Tribune,* October 12.

Hartley, Wyndham. 2006. "MPs Dig in Their Heels against Same-Sex Unions." *Johannesburg Business Day,* September 14.

Hartmann, Heidi. 1981. "The Unhappy Marriage of Marxism and Feminism: A Debate on Class and Patriarchy." In *Women and Revolution: A Discussion of the Unhappy Marriage of Marxism and Feminism,* ed. Lydia Sargent, 1–42. Cambridge, MA: South End.

Hassim, Shireen. 2005. "Turning Gender Rights into Entitlements: Women and Welfare Provision in Postapartheid South Africa." *Social Research* 72:621–646.

Hawthorne, Nathaniel. 1968. *The Scarlet Letter.* Cambridge: Cambridge University Press. Originally published 1850.

Herdt, Gilbert. 1999. *Sambia Sexual Culture: Essays from the Field.* Chicago: University of Chicago Press.

Heritage Foundation. "Marriage in the Fifty States." http://www.heritage.org/Research/Family/Marriage50/.

Hernandez v. Robles. 2006. New York Court of Appeals. 855 N.E.2d 1.

Herszenhorn, David M., and Duff Wilson. 2007. "Senator Larry Craig Is Unlikely to Finish Term, Spokesman Says." *New York Times,* September 6. http://www.nytimes.com/2007/09/06/world/americas/06iht-06craig.7408519.html?pagewanted=2&_r=1&sq=Larry%20Craig&st=cse&scp=4.

Hertz, Rosanna. 2008. *Single by Chance, Mothers by Choice: How Women Are Choosing Parenthood without Marriage and Creating the New American Family.* Oxford: Oxford University Press.

Hinton, Carma, director. 1984. "Small Happiness: Women of a Chinese Village." Film. New York: New Day Films.

Hoad, Neville. 1998. "Tradition, Modernity and Human Rights: an Interrogation of Contemporary Gay and Lesbian Rights Claims in Southern African Nationalist Discourses." *Development Update Quarterly Journal of the South African National NGO Coalition and INTERFUND* 2:32.

Hodes, Rebecca. 2008. "Treatment Action Campaign and the State's Response to HIV/AIDS." AllAfrica.com, December 4. http://allafrica.com/stories/200812040771.html.

Holmes, Rachel. 1995. "'White Rapists Made Coloureds (and Homosexuals)': The Winnie Mandela Trial and the Politics of Race and Sexuality." In *Defiant Desires: Gay and Lesbian Lives in South Africa*, ed. Mark Gevisser and Edwin Cameron, 284–294. New York: Routledge.

Hondagneu-Sotelo, Pierrette. 2001. *Doméstica: Immigrant Workers Cleaning and Caring in the Shadows of Affluence*. Berkeley: University of California Press.

Horkheimer, Max. 2002. *Authority and the Family*. New York: Continuum.

Hsu, Elisabeth. 1998. "Mosuo and Naxi: The House." In *Naxi and Moso Ethnography*, ed. Michael Oppitz and Elisabeth Hsu, 47–65. Zurich: University of Zurich Press.

Huashang, Zhou, director. 2001. "Tisese: A Documentary on Three Moso Women." Film. Asian Educational Media Service.

Hughes, Dana. 2010. "Zuma's Woes: 3 Wives, 1 Fiancé and an Out-of-Wedlock Child." ABCNews.com, February 8. http://abcnews.go.com/International/ south-african-president-jacob-zumas-sex-scandal/story?id=9781141.

Human Rights Campaign. 2010a. "Marriage Equality and Other Relationship Recognition Laws." http://www.hrc.org/documents/Relationship_Recognition_ Laws_Map.pdf.

———. 2010b. "Prop 8 Upheld." http://www.hrc.org/10459.htm.

———. 2010c. "Statewide Marriage Prohibitions." http://www.hrc.org/documents/ marriage_prohibitions_2009.pdf.

———. 2009. "Equality from State to State 2009." http://www.hrc.org/documents/ HRC_States_Report_09.pdf.

Human Rights Watch. 2007. "South Africa: Lesbians Targeted for Murder; A Climate of Violent Homophobia Mars South Africa's Celebration of Women's Day." August 9. http://hrw.org/english/docs/2007/08/08/safric16617.htm.

Illouz, Eva. 2007. *Cold Intimacies: The Making of Emotional Capitalism*. Malden, MA: Polity.

Immigration and Refugee Board of Canada. 2006. "Nigeria: Levirate Marriage Practices among the Yoruba, Igbo and Hausa-Fulani; Consequences for a Man or Woman Who Refuses to Participate in the Marriage; Availability of State Protection (February 2006)." NGA101045.E. March 16. http://www.unhcr.org/ refworld/topic,463af2212,469f2db72,45f1478811,0.html.

In re Kieshia E. 1993. Supreme Court of California. 859 P.2d 1290.

In re Marriage Cases. 2008. Supreme Court of California. 43 Cal.4th 757.

IRIN. 2006. "Murder of Young Lesbian Sparks Homophobia Concerns." *Mail and Guardian*, February 21. http://www.irinnews.org/report.aspx?reportid=58200.

Iversen, Joan S. 1997. *The Antipolygamy Controversy in U.S. Women's Movements, 1880–1925: A Debate on the American Home*. New York: Garland.

"Jacob Zuma Marries Fourth Wife." 2008. *Pan-African News Wire*. http://panafrican news.blogspot.com/2008/01/jacob-zuma-marries-fourth-wife.html.

James, Scott. 2010. "Many Successful Gay Marriages Share an Open Secret." *New*

York Times, January 28. http://www.nytimes.com/2010/01/29/us/29sfmetro
.html.

Jewison, Norman, director. 1971. *Fiddler on the Roof.* Film. Cartier Productions.

Jones, Jeffrey. 2009. "Majority of Americans Continue to Oppose Gay Marriage."
Gallup Poll, May 27. http://www.gallup.com/poll/118378/Majority-Americans
-Continue-Oppose-Gay-Marriage.aspx.

Judge, Melanie, Anthony Manion, and Shaun de Waal, eds. 2008. *To Have and to
Hold: The Making of Same-Sex Marriage in South Africa.* Auckland Park, South
Africa: Fanele.

Kamerman, Sheila B., and Alfred J. Kahn. 1989. *Privatization and the Welfare State.*
Princeton, NJ: Princeton University Press.

Kanter, Rosabeth Moss. 1972. *Commitment and Community: Communes and Utopias in Sociological Perspective.* Cambridge, MA: Harvard University Press.

Kaoma, Rev. Kapya. 2009. "The U.S. Christian Right and the Attack on Gays in
Africa." *Huffington Post,* December 10. http://www.huffingtonpost.com/rev
-kapya-kaoma/the-us-christian-right-an_b_387642.html.

Kapp, Stephen, Thomas P. McDonald, and Kandi L. Diamond. 2001. "The Path to
Adoption for Children of Color." *Child Abuse and Neglect* 25 (2): 215–229.

Katbamna, Mira. 2009. "Half a Good Man Is Better than None at All." *Guardian,*
October 27. http://www.guardian.co.uk/education/2009/oct/27/polygamy
-study-russia-central-asia.

Kaye, Kelleen, Katherine Suellentrop, and Corinna Sloup. 2009. "The Fog Zone:
How Misperceptions, Magical Thinking and Ambivalence Put Young Adults at
Risk for Unplanned Pregnancy." Washington, DC: National Campaign to Pre-
vent Teen and Unplanned Pregnancy.

Kenney, Moira Rachel. 2001. *Mapping Gay L.A.: The Intersection of Place and Politics.* Philadelphia: Temple University Press.

Kersten, Katherine. 2006. "Once Same-Sex Marriage Is OK, Polygamy's Next."
Star Tribune, April 6.

Kjellström, Rolf. 1973. *Eskimo Marriage: An Account of Traditional Eskimo Courtship and Marriage.* Solna: Nordiska Museet.

Klesse, Christian. 2007. *The Spectre of Promiscuity: Gay Male and Bisexual Non-
monogamies and Polyamories.* Burlington, VT: Ashgate.

Knodel, Susanne. 1998. "Yongning Moso: Kinship and Chinese State Power." In
Naxi and Moso Ethnography, ed. Michael Oppitz and Elisabeth Hsu, 47–65. Zurich: University of Zurich Press.

Krakauer, Jon. 2003. *Under the Banner of Heaven: A Story of a Violent Faith.* New
York: Random House.

Kranish, Michael. 2009. "In Bully Pulpit, Preaching Values." *Boston Globe,* December 10.

Kurtz, Stanley. 2006. "Big Love from the Set." *National Review Online.* http://www
.nationalreview.com/kurtz/kurtz200603130805.asp.

————. 2003. "Beyond Gay Marriage: The Road to Polyamory." *Weekly Standard* 8 (45) (August 4–11). http://www.weeklystandard.com/Content/Public/Articles/000/000/002/938xpsxy.asp.

LaFraniere, Sharon. 2006. "South African Parliament Approves Same-Sex Marriage." *New York Times,* November 15.

Lan, Pei-Chia. 2006. *Global Cinderellas: Migrant Domestics and Newly Rich Employers in Taiwan.* Durham, NC: Duke University Press.

Landman, Christina. 1999. "Polygamy Beats Divorce, Afrikaner Academic Says." *Victoria Times-Colonist,* January 16, A8.

Lasch, Christopher. 1995. *Haven in a Heartless World: The Family Besieged.* New York: Norton.

Laumann, Edward O., John H. Gagnon, Robert T. Michael, and Stuart Michaels. 2000. *The Social Organization of Sexuality: Sexual Practices in the United States.* Chicago: University of Chicago Press.

Law Commission of Canada. 2001. *Beyond Conjugality: Recognizing and Supporting Close, Personal Adult Relationships.* Available online at http://www.lcc.gc.ca.

Lawrence v. Texas. 2003. U.S. Supreme Court. 123 S.Ct. 2472.

Levine, Martin P. 1998. *Gay Macho: The Life and Death of the Homosexual Clone.* New York: NYU Press.

Levine, Nancy E. 1989. *The Dynamics of Polyandry: Kinship, Domesticity, and Population on the Tibetan Border.* Chicago: University of Chicago Press.

"Levirate Marriage." n.d. *New World Encyclopedia.* http://www.newworld encyclopedia.org/entry/Levirate_Marriage.

Liberated Christians. 1999. "Multiple Intimate Relationships: A Summary of Liberated Christians' Views." http://www.libchrist.com/bible/polygamy.html.

"Lijiang." 2005. CCTV television broadcast. April 5.

Lithwick, Dahlia. 2004. "Slippery Slop: The Maddening 'Slippery Slope' Argument against Gay Marriage." *Slate,* May 19. http://www.slate.com/id/2100824/.

Liu, Xiaoxing. 2008. "Research on the Na and Academic Integrity." *Critique of Anthropology* 28 (3): 297–320.

Livingston, Jennie, director. 1990. *Paris Is Burning.* Film. Miramax Films.

Loftus, Jeni. 2001. "America's Liberalization in Attitudes toward Homosexuality, 1973 to 1998." *American Sociological Review* 66:762–782.

"Love Makes a Family." n.d. First person account of gay fatherhood published in a local gay community newspaper on file with author. Identifying information withheld to protect the privacy of my research subject.

Loving v. Virginia. 1967. United States Supreme Court. 388 U.S. 1.

Mabena v. Letsaolo. 1998. 2 SA 1068 (T).

Mackie, Nick. 2007. "The Lake of Free Love." *LonelyPlanet.tv.* Video. http//www .lonelyplanet.tv/Clip.aspx?key=A1A45082E248670C.

Mann, William J. 1997. "A Boy's Own Class." In *Queerly Classed: Gay Men and Lesbians Write about Class,* ed. Susan Raffo, 217–226. Boston: South End.

Manson, Pamela. 2005. "FLDS Added to List of Hate Groups." *Salt Lake Tribune,* April 21.

"Mark Olsen and Will Scheffer, Feeling the 'Big Love.'" 2007. *Fresh Air,* NPR, October 1. http://www.npr.org/templates/story/story.php?storyId=12421072.

MarriageWatch.org. 2005. "State Defense of Marriage Acts." June 27. http://marriagelaw.cua.edu/Law/states/doma.cfm.

Mbatha, Likhapha. 2002. "Reforming the Customary Law of Succession." *South African Journal of Human Rights* 18:259–286.

McKhann, Charles. 1998. "Naxi, Rerkua, Moso, Meng: Kinship, Politics and Ritual on the Yunnan-Sichuan Frontier." In *Naxi and Moso Ethnography,* ed. Michael Oppitz and Elisabeth Hsu. Zurich: University of Zurich Press.

McKinley, Jesse, and Laurie Goodstein. 2008. "Bans in 3 States on Gay Marriage." *New York Times,* November 5. http://www.nytimes.com/2008/11/06/us/politics/06marriage.html.

McMullen, Randy. 2010. "People: Hold Everything, Tiger Woods' Wife Doesn't Want a Divorce." *Mercury News,* January 26.

Melendez, Michaele M. 2004. "Young Americans More Likely to Support Gay Marriage, Polls Suggest." Newhouse News Service, March 11.

Metz, Tamara. 2010. *Untying the Knot: Marriage, the State, and the Case for Their Divorce.* Princeton, NJ: Princeton University Press.

Meyer, David D. 2006. "Parenthood in a Time of Transition: Tensions between Legal, Biological and Social Conceptions of Parenthood." *American Journal of Comparative Law* 54:125.

Miceli, Melinda S. 2002. "Gay, Lesbian and Bisexual Youth." In *Handbook of Lesbian and Gay Studies,* ed. Diane Richardson and Steven Seidman, 199–214. London: Sage.

Miller, Neil. 1993. *Out in the World: Gay and Lesbian Life from Buenos Aires to Bangkok.* New York: Random House.

Minister of Home Affairs and Another v. Fourie and Another. 2004. (6) SA 121 (CC), paragraph 50.

Mohler, Marie, and Lacy Frazer. 2002. *A Donor Insemination Guide: Written by and for Lesbian Women.* Binghamton, UK: Harrington Park.

Morgan, Lewis H. 1965. *Ancient Society.* Cambridge, MA: Belknap Press of Harvard University Press. Originally published 1877.

Moritz, Rob. 2010. "Judge Strikes Down Adoption Ban." *Arkansas News,* April 16. http://arkansasnews.com/2010/04/16/judge-strikes-down-adoption-ban/.

Mosk, Matthew. 2006. "Gay Unions Fracture MD's Black Caucus: Civil Rights Pull as Strong as Church's." *Washington Post,* January 28, A01.

"Mosuo Matriarchy." 2002. *ABC Evening News with Peter Jennings.* Aired May 13.

Moynihan, Daniel Patrick. 1993. "Defining Deviancy Down." *American Scholar,* Winter, 17–30.

———. 1965. *The Negro Family: The Case for National Action* (*The Moynihan Report*).

Office of Policy Planning and Research, U.S. Department of Labor. http://www
.dol.gov/oasam/programs/history/webid-meynihan.htm.

Mthembu v. Letsela and Another. 1997. (2) SA 936.

Murdock, George P. 1967. *Ethnographic Atlas.* Pittsburgh: University of Pittsburgh
Press.

Murray, Charles. 2005. "Rediscovering the Underclass." American Enterprise Institute for Public Policy Research, October 7. http://www.aei.org/issue/23313.

Myers, Michael G. 2006. "Polygamist Eye for the Monogamist Guy: Homosexual
Sodomy . . . Gay Marriage . . . Is Polygamy Next?" *Houston Law Review* 2006:
1451–1486.

Namu, Yang Erche, and Christine Mathieu. 2004. *Leaving Mother Lake: A Girlhood
at the Edge of the World.* New York: Back Bay Books.

Nanda, Serena. 1998. *Neither Man nor Woman: The Hijras of India.* Cincinnati, OH:
Wadsworth.

*National Coalition for Gay and Lesbian Equality and Others v. Minister of Home Af-
fairs and Others.* 2000. (2) SA 1 (CC).

Neff, Elizabeth, and Pamela Manson. 2006. "Court Rejects Polygamy Defense."
Salt Lake Tribune, May 17.

"New Jersey Governor Quits, Comes Out as Gay." 2004. CNN.com, August 13.
http://www.cnn.com/2004/ALLPOLITICS/08/12/mcgreevey.nj/.

Nieves, Evelyn. 2006. "S.D. Abortion Bill Takes Aim at Roe." *Washington Post,* February 23, A01.

Nimmons, David. 2002. *The Soul beneath the Skin: The Unseen Hearts and Habits of
Gay Men.* New York: St. Martin's.

Obama, Barack. 2009. "We Need Fathers to Step Up." *Parade,* June 21. http://www
.parade.com/export/sites/default/news/2009/06/barack-obama-we-need
-fathers-to-step-up.html.

"Obama's Father's Day Speech." 2008. *CNN ElectionCenter2008,* June 27. http://
www.cnn.com/2008/POLITICS/06/27/obama.fathers.ay/.

Oppitz, Michael, and Elisabeth Hsu, eds. 1998. *Naxi and Moso Ethnography: Kin,
Rites, Pictographs.* Zurich: University of Zurich Press.

Ortner, Sherry. 2003. *New Jersey Dreaming: Capital, Culture, and the Class of '58.*
Durham, NC: Duke University Press.

Outwater, Anne, Naeema Abrahams, and Jacquelyn C. Campbell. 2005. "Women
in South Africa: Intentional Violence and HIV/AIDS." *Journal of Black Studies*
35 (4): 135–154.

Palmore v. Sidoti. 1984. United States Supreme Court. 466 U.S. 429.

Parreñas, Rhacel Salazar. 2001. *Servants of Globalization: Women, Migration, and
Domestic Work.* Stanford, CA: Stanford University Press.

Parsons, Talcott, and Robert F. Bales. 1956. *Family Socialization and Interaction
Process.* London: Routledge.

Patterson, C. J., E. L. Sutfin, and M. Fulcher. 2004. "Division of Labor among

Lesbian and Heterosexual Parenting Couples: Correlates of Specialized versus Shared Patterns." *Journal of Adult Development* 11:179–189.

Patterson, Orlando. 1999. *Rituals of Blood: Consequences of Slavery in Two American Centuries.* New York: Basic Books.

Pear, Robert, and David. D. Kirkpatrick. 2004. "Bush Plans $1.5 Billion Drive for Promotion of Marriage." *New York Times,* January 14, A1.

Peter v. the Minister of Law and Order. 1990 (4) SA 6 (E).

Pierson, Christopher, and Francis G. Castles. 2000. *The Welfare State Reader.* Malden, MA: Blackwell.

Pieterse, Marius. 2001. "It's a 'Black Thing': Upholding Culture and Customary Law in a Society Founded on Nonracialism." *South African Journal of Human Rights* 17:364–391.

Pitzer, Donald E. 1997. *America's Communal Utopias.* Chapel Hill: University of North Carolina Press.

Plummer, Ken. 1995. *Telling Sexual Stories: Power, Change and Social Worlds.* New York: Routledge.

Polikoff, Nancy. 2008. *Beyond (Straight and Gay) Marriage: Valuing All Families under the Law.* Boston: Beacon.

Polyamory Society. n.d. "Introduction to Polyamory: What Is Polyamory?" http://www.polyamorysociety.org/page6.html.

Popenoe, David. 1996. *Life without Father.* Cambridge, MA: Harvard University Press.

———. 1988. *Disturbing the Nest: Family Change and Decline in Modern Societies.* New Brunswick, NJ: Transaction.

Popenoe, Rebecca. 2003. *Feeding Desire: Fatness, Beauty and Sexuality among a Saharan People.* New York: Routledge.

Popenoe, David, Jean Bethke Elshtain, and David Blankenhorn, eds. 1996. *Promises to Keep: Decline and Renewal of Marriage in America.* Lanham, MD: Rowman and Littlefield.

Pop Luck Club. 2002. *Newsletter,* August. http://www.popluckclub.org/.

Porter, Eduardo. 2009. "Tales of Republicans, Bonobos and Adultery." *New York Times,* July 2, A20.

Potash, Betty. 1986. *Widows in African Societies: Choices and Constraints.* Stanford, CA: Stanford University Press.

Principle Voices. n.d. "FAQs about Mormon Polygamy." http://principlevoices .org/diversity-of-fundamentalist-mormons.

Pro-Polygamy.com. 2008. "Obama's Historic Election Gives Hope to Polygamous Americans." November 7. http://www.pro-polygamy.com/articles.php?news= 0063.

———. 2004. "Anti-Polygamy Is the Real 'Slippery Slope.'" April 16. http://www .pro-polygamy.com/articles.php?news=0016.

Qi, Fu. 2009. "Family Planning among Ethnic Minorities: A Review." *China*

Human Rights. http://www.chinahumanrights.org/CSHRS/Magazine/Text/t20090115_406184.htm.

Recognition of Customary Marriages Act. 1998. Act no. 120 of the South African Parliament. http://www.acts.co.za/custom_marriages/index.htm.

Reid, Graeme. 2007. "How to Be a 'Real' Gay: Emerging Gay Spaces in Small-Town South Africa." Ph.D. diss., University of Amsterdam.

———. 2009. " 'This Thing' and 'That Idea': Traditionalist Responses to Homosexuality and Same-Sex Marriage." In *To Have and to Hold: The Making of Same-Sex Marriage in South Africa,* ed. Melanie Judge, Anthony Manion, and Shaun de Waal, 73–86. Auckland Park, South Africa: Fanele.

Religioustolerance.org. 2006. "Single U.S. Public Opinion Polls: Same-Sex Marriages and Civil Unions." http://www.religioustolerance.org/hom_marp.htm.

———. n.d. "The LDS Restorationist Movement, Including the Mormon Churches." http://www.religioustolerance.org/lds_poly2.htm.

"Republican Contract with America." House of Representatives website. http://www.house.gov/house/Contract/CONTRACT.html.

Reyes, Robert Paul. 2007. "Jerry Falwell Is Gone, but James Dobson Still Preaching Intolerance." *American Chronicle,* May 18. http://www.americanchronicle.com/articles/view/27498.

Ribuffo, Leo P. 2006. "Family Policy Past as Prologue: Jimmy Carter, the White House Conference on Families, and the Mobilization of the New Christian Right." *Review of Policy Research* 23 (2): 311–338.

Rich, Adrienne. 1983. "Compulsory Heterosexuality and Lesbian Existence." *Signs: A Journal of Culture and Society* 5:631–660.

Richter, Daniel K. 1992. *The Ordeal of the Longhouse: The Peoples of the Iroquois League in the Era of European Colonization.* Chapel Hill: University of North Carolina Press.

Risman, Barbara J., ed. 2009. *Families as They Really Are.* New York: Norton.

Roberts, Michelle. 2008. "Man Arrested in Polygamy Compound Raid." *Huffington Post,* April 7.

Robertson et al. v. Minister of Home Affairs. 2007. South Africa Constitutional Court. This suit was dismissed on procedural grounds. I received a copy of the plaintiffs' affidavit from SA Constitutional Court librarian.

Robins, Steven. 2006. "Sexual Rights and Sexual Cultures: Reflections on 'The Zuma Affair' and 'New Masculinities' in the New South Africa." *Horizontes Antropológicos,* Porto Alegre, 12 (26): 149–183.

Rocchio, Christopher. 2007. "Queer Eye's 'Fab Five' Members Discuss Show's Legacy and Impact." *Reality TV World,* October 1. http://www.realitytvworld.com/news/queer-eye-fab-five-members-discuss-show-legacy-and-impact-5850.php.

Rofes, Eric. 1998. *Dry Bones Breathe: Gay Men Creating Post-AIDS Identities and Cultures.* New York: Harrington Park.

Roscoe, Will, and Stephen O. Murray. 1998. *Boy-Wives and Female Husbands: Studies in African Homosexualities*. New York: Palgrave Macmillan.

Ross, Brian. 2006. "Foley's IM Exchange with Underage Page." ABCNews.com, September 29. http://abcnews.go.com/wnt/brianross/story?id=2509586&page=1.

Rothenberg, Paula. 2007. *Race, Class, and Gender in the United States: An Integrated Study*. New York: Worth.

Russell, Stephen T., Brian T. Franz, and Anne K. Driscoll. 2001. "Same-Sex Romantic Attraction and Experiences of Violence in Adolescence." *American Journal of Public Health* 91 (6): 903–906.

Russell, Stephen T., and Kara Joyner. 2001. "Adolescent Sexual Orientation and Suicide Risk: Evidence from a National Study." *American Journal of Public Health* 91 (8): 1276–1281.

Ruxian, Yan. 1982. "A Living Fossil of the Family: A Study of the Family Structure of the Naxi Nationality in the Lugu Lake Region." *Social Sciences in China* 4: 60–83.

Ryan-Flood, Rolsin. 2005. "Contested Heteronormativities: Discourses of Fatherhood among Lesbian Parents in Sweden and Ireland." *Sexualities* 8 (2): 189–204.

Saewyc, E., S. Pettingell, and C. Skay. 2004. "Hazards of Stigma: The Sexual and Physical Abuse of Gay, Lesbian, and Bisexual Adolescents in the U.S. and Canada." *Journal of Adolescent Health* 34 (2): 115–116.

"S. Africa's Zuma Apologizes for Sexual Affair." 2010. *VOA News*, February 6. http://www1.voanews.com/english/news/africa/S-Africas-Zuma-Apologizes -for-Sexual-Affair-83728012.html.

Sage, Alexandria. 2004. "Utah Polygamy Ban Challenged." CBSNews.com, January 27. http://www.cbsnews.com/stories/2004/01/27/national/main596268 .shtml.

Sandbook, Richard. 1993. *The Politics of Africa's Economic Recovery*. Cambridge: Cambridge University Press.

Sapa-AFP. 2008. "TAC's Zackie Achmat Gets Married." *Mail and Guardian Online*, January 6. http://www.mg.co.za/article/2008-01-06-tacs-zackie-achmat-gets -married.

Satinover, J. B. 2004. "Declaration of Jeffrey B. Satinover in Support of Intervenors' Response to Plaintiffs' Motion for Summary Judgment." *Andersen et al. v. State of Washington*. No. 04-2-04964-4 SEA. Filed June 24.

Savage, Dan. 2000. *The Kid: What Happened after My Boyfriend and I Decided to Go Get Pregnant*. New York: Penguin.

———. 2003. "G.O.P. Hypocrisy." *New York Times*, April 25. http://www.nytimes .com/2003/04/25/opinion/25SAVA.html.

———. 2008. "Black Homophobia." *Stranger*, November 5. http://slog.thestranger .com/2008/11/black_homophobia.

Sbordone, Albert. 1993. "Gay Men Choosing Fatherhood." Ph.D. diss., City University of New York.

Schacher, Stephanie J., Carl F. Auerbach, and Louise B. Silverstein. 2005. "Gay Fathers Expanding the Possibilities for Us All." *Journal of GLBT Family Studies* 1 (3): 31–52.

Schein, Louisa. 1997. "Gender and Internal Orientalism in China." *Modern China* 23 (1): 69–98.

Schlafly, Phyllis. 2003. *Feminist Fantasies*. Dallas: Spence.

———. 1978. "Stop ERA." *Smithsonian Source,* December 6. http://www.smithsonian source.org/display/primarysource/viewdetails.aspx?PrimarySourceId=1159.

Schwartz, Emma, Rhonda Schwartz, and Vic Walter. 2008. "Congressman's $121,000 Payoff to Alleged Mistress." ABCNews.com, October 13. http://abcnews.go .com/Blotter/Politics/story?id=5997043&page=1%29.

Sears, R. Bradley, and M. V. Lee Badgett. 2004. "Same-Sex Couples and Same-Sex Couples Raising Children in California: Data from Census 2000." Williams Project on Sexual Orientation and the Law, UCLA Law School.

Sears, R. Bradley, Gary Gates, and Holning Lau. 2006. "Race and Ethnicity of Same-Sex Couples in California: Data from Census 2000." Williams Institute, UCLA Law School.

Seidman, Gay W. 1999a. "Is South Africa Different? Sociological Comparisons and Theoretical Contributions from the Land of Apartheid." *Annual Review of Sociology* 25:419–440.

———. 1999b. "Gendered Citizenship: South Africa's Democratic Transition and the Construction of a Gendered State." *Gender and Society* 13:287–307.

"Senator Santorum Sounds Off." 2003. Editorial. *New York Times,* April 22.

Seth, Reva. 2008. *First Comes Marriage: Modern Relationship Advice from the Wisdom of Arranged Marriages*. New York: Fireside.

Shapiro, Beth. 2006. "Gay Families Growing." 365Gay.com, April 25. http://365 .com/Newscon06/04/042506family.htm.

Sharon v. Superior Court. 2003. California Supreme Court. 73 P.3d 554, 561.

Sharples, Tiffany. 2008. "Ballot Initiatives: No to Gay Marriage, Anti-abortion Measures." *Time,* November 5. http://www.time.com/time/politics/article/ 0,8599,1856820,00.html.

Shih, Chuan-kang. 2001. "Genesis of Marriage among the Moso and Empire-Building in Late Imperial China." *Journal of Asian Studies* 60 (2): 381–412.

———. 2000. "*Tisese* and Its Anthropological Significance: Issues around the Visiting Sexual System among the Moso." *L'Homme* 154–155:697–704.

———. 1993. "The Yongning Moso: Sexual Union, Household Organization, Gender and Ethnicity in a Matrilineal Duolocal Society in Southwest China." Ph.D. diss., Stanford University.

Shih, Chuan-kang, and Mark R. Jenike. 2002. "A Cultural-Historical Perspective

on the Depressed Fertility among the Matrilineal Moso in Southwest China."
Human Ecology 30 (1): 21–47.

Shilts, Randy. 1987. *And the Band Played On: Politics, People and the AIDS Epidemic.*
New York: St. Martin's.

Shireman, Joan F. 1995. "Adoptions by Single Parents." *Marriage and Family Review*
20:367–387.

Shisana, O., T. Rehle, L. C. Simbayl, et al. 2005. *South African National HIV Prev-*
alence, Incidence, Behavior and Communication Survey 2008: A Turning Tide
among Teenagers? Cape Town: HSRC. http://www.hsrc.ac.za/Media_Release
-379.phtml.

Sigman, Shayna M. 2006 "Everything Lawyers Know about Polygamy Is Wrong."
Cornell Journal of Law and Public Policy 16 (1): 101–186.

Silverman, Stephen M. 2008. "New York Governor Spitzer Resigns amid Sex Scandal." *People*, March 12. http://www.people.com/people/article/0,,20183518,00
.html.

Simmons, Tavia, and Martin O'Connell. 2003. "Married-Couple and Unmarried-
Partner Households: 2000." U.S. Census Bureau, February.

Simon, Stephanie. 2009. "Legal Fights Strain Polygamist Sect." *Wall Street Journal,*
May 11, A5. http://online.wsj.com/article/SB124200435765305371.html.

Sizwe Samayende. 2002. "Sharing Hubbie across the Line." *News 24,* April 28.
http://www.news24.com/Content/SouthAfrica/Politics/1057/0412ff4515f2474
ba8368c8f1aca1e31/28-04-2002-01-33/Sharing_hubbie_across_the_line.

Slater, Miriam. 1984. *Family Life in the Seventeenth Century: The Verneys of Claydon*
House. New York: Routledge and Kegan Paul.

Sloth-Nielson, Julia, and Belinda Von Heerden. 2003. "The Constitutional Family:
Developments in South African Family Law Jurisprudence under the 1996 Constitution." *International Journal of Law, Policy and the Family* 17 (2): 121–146.

Smith-Rosenberg, Carole. 1975. "The Female World of Love and Ritual: The
Relationships between Women in Nineteenth-Century America." *Signs* 1 (1): 1–
29. http://links.jstor.org/sici?sici=0097-9740%28197523%291%3A1%3C1%3ATF
WOLA%3E2.0.CO%3B2-H.

"South Africans Disapprove of Homosexuals, Abortion." 2004. *Afrol News,* October 21. http://www.afrol.com/articles/14605.

"South Africa's Prez Zuma Apologizes for Another Sexual Affair; Married to 3
Women; 4th Wife in a Few Months." 2010. *USAfricaOnline,* February 7. http://
www.usafricaonline.com/zuma-sex-affair-child-wives-201/.

Stacey, Judith. 2004b. "Can Marriage Be Saved? A Forum." *Nation,* July 5. http://
www.thenation.com/doc/20040705/forum2/8.

———. 2004b. "Cruising to Familyland: Gay Hypergamy and Rainbow Kinship."
Current Sociology 52 (2): 181–197.

———. 1998a. *Brave New Families: Stories of Domestic Upheaval in Late-Twentieth-*
Century America. Berkeley: University of California Press.

———. 1998b. "Dada-ism in the Nineties: Getting Past Baby Talk about Father-lessness." In *Lost Fathers: The Politics of Fatherlessness*, ed. Cynthia Daniels. New York: St. Martin's.

———. 1996. *In the Name of the Family: Rethinking Family Values in the Postmodern Age*. Boston: Beacon.

———. 1994. "Scents, Scholars and Stigma: The Revisionist Campaign for Family Values." *Social Text* 40 (Autumn): 51–75.

Stacey, Judith, and Timothy J. Biblarz. 2001. "(How) Does the Sexual Orientation of Parents Matter?" *American Sociological Review* 66 (2): 159–183.

Stacey, Judith, and Tey Meadow. 2009. "New Slants on the Slippery Slope: The Politics of Polygamy and Gay Family Rights in South Africa and the U.S." *Politics and Society* 37 (2): 167–202.

Stack, Carol B. 1997. *All Our Kin: Strategies for Survival in a Black Community*. New York: Basic Books.

Staples, Robert. 1978. *The Black Family*. Belmont, CA: Wadsworth.

State v. Green. 2004. Utah Supreme Court. 99 P.3d 820.

State v. Holm. 2006. Utah Supreme Court. 137 P.3d 726.

Statistics South Africa. 2003. "Census 2001: Census in Brief." http://www.statssa .gov.za/census01/html/C2001Censusbrief.asp.

Stephens, Linda S. 1996. "Will Johnny See Daddy This Week? An Empirical Test of Three Theoretical Perspectives of Post-divorce Contact." *Journal of Family Issues* 17 (4): 466–494.

Strah, David, and Susanna Margolis. 2003. *Gay Dads*. New York: J. T. Tarcher/ Putnam.

Strassberg, Maura L. 1997. "Distinctions of Form or Substance: Monogamy, Po-lygamy and Same-Sex Marriage." *North Carolina Law Review* 75:1501–1624.

Stross, Brian. 1974. "Tzethal Marriage by Capture." *Anthropological Quarterly* 47 (3): 328–346.

Stuever, Hank. 2000. "Is Gay Mainstream?" *Washington Post*, April 27, C1.

Summers, Anthony, and Robbyn Swan. 2005. "Sex, Sinatra and the Women Who Fell for Him." *Times Online*, May 9. http://entertainment.timesonline.co.uk/ tol/arts_and_entertainment/books/article520603.ece.

Sullivan, Andrew. 2008. "Young Evangelicals and Gay Couples." *Daily Dish*, Sep-tember 30. http://andrewsullivan.theatlantic.com/the_daily_dish/2008/09/ young-evangelic.html.

———. 2003a. "The Conservative Case for Gay Marriage." *Time*, June 22. http:// www.time.com/time/magazine/article/0,9171,460232,00.html.

———. 2003b. "Idiocy of the Week." *Salon*, April 22. http://dir.salon.com/story/ opinion/sullivan/2003/04/22/santorum/index.html.

———. 1995. *Virtually Normal: An Argument about Homosexuality*. New York: Knopf.

Sullivan, Maureen. 2004. *The Family of Woman: Lesbian Mothers, Their Children, and the Undoing of Gender*. Berkeley: University of California Press.

Sullivan, Maureen. 1996. "Rozzie and Harriet? Gender and Family Patterns of Lesbian Coparents." *Gender and Society* 10 (6): 747–767.

Sullum, Jacob. 2001. "Attacking Pluralism." *Reason Online,* May 29. http://reason.com/archives/2001/05/29/attacking-pluralism.

Sussman, George D. 1982. *Selling Mother's Milk: The Wet Nurse Business in France, 1715–1914.* Urbana: University of Illinois Press.

Tapestry Against Polygamy. 2006a. "By 3rd Anniversary of 'Lawrence'—Polygamy Rights Accelerating." Pro-Polygamy.com, June 26. http://www.pro-polygamy.com/articles.php?news=0044.

———. 2006b. "Tapestry Against Polygamy Calls Elder Russell M. Nelson 'Serial Polygamist,' Denounces Hypocrisy." Press release. *Affirmation,* June 7. http://www.affirmation.org/news/2006_76.shtml.

Tarmann, Allison. 2002. "Out of the Closet and onto the Census Long Form." *Population Today,* 30 (4): 1.

Tasker, Fiona. 2005. "Lesbian Mothers, Gay Fathers, and Their Children: A Review." *Developmental and Behavioral Pediatrics* 26:224–240.

Taylor, Paul. 2006. "Wedge Issues on the Ballot: Can State Initiatives on Gay Marriage, Minimum Wage Affect Candidate Races?" Pew Research Center. July 26.

"Texas Takes Custody of 400 Children after Raid on Polygamist Compound." 2008. *New York Times,* April 8. http://www.nytimes.com/2008/04/08/world/americas/08iht-texas.1.11761542.html.

Tierney, John. 2006. "Who's Afraid of Polygamy?" *New York Times,* March 11. http://select.nytimes.com/2006/03/11/opinion/11tierney.html?_r=1&scp=2&sq=john+tierney&st=nyt.

Topley, Marjorie. 1955. "Ghost Marriages among the Singapore Chinese." *Man* 55 (February): 29–30.

Tolstoy, Leo. 2004. *Anna Karenina.* New York: Penguin. Originally published 1899.

Townsend, Nicholas. 2002. *The Package Deal: Marriage, Work, and Fatherhood in Men's Lives.* Philadelphia: Temple University Press.

Treatment Action Campaign (TAC). 2009. "Landmark Speech by President Zuma." October 30. http://www.tac.org.za/community/node/2767.

Trewhela, Paul. 2000. "Mbeki and AIDS in Africa: A Comment." *New York Review of Books* 47 (16).

TruthBearer.org. 1999. "Love-Not-Force." July 13. http://www.truthbearer.org/love-not-force/.

Tucker, Andrew. 2009. *Queer Visibilities: Space, Identity and Interactions in Cape Town.* Chichester, UK: Wiley-Blackwell.

Turley, Jonathan. 2004. "Polygamy Laws Expose Our Hypocrisy." *USA Today,* October 4.

Turnbull, Lornet. 2004. "Family Is . . . Being Redefined All the Time." *Seattle Times.* Reprinted in the *Indianapolis Star,* May 31.

Twitchell, Jeffrey. 1995. Review of *The Remote Country of Women*, by Bai Hua. *Chinese Literature: Essays, Articles, Reviews* 17 (December): 167–169.

UNAIDS. 2006. "Annex 1 Country Profiles: South Africa." In *2006 Report on the Global AIDS Epidemic*, 455. http://www.unaids.org/en/KnowledgeCentre/HIVData/GlobalReport/2006/default.asp.

UNICEF. n.d. "South Africa Statistics." http://www.unicef.org/infobycountry/southafrica_statistics.html.

Unitarian Universalists for Polyamory Awareness. n.d. "Polyamory and the Unitarian Universalist Association Principles and Purposes." http://www.uupa.org/Literature/polyprinciples.html.

———. n.d. "Mission." http://www.uupa.org/index#mission.

U.S. Census Bureau. 2005–2007. "American Community Survey." http://factfinder.census.gov/servlet/ADPTable?_bm=y&-geo_id=01000US&-qr_name=ACS_2007_3YR_G00_DP3YR2&-ds_name=ACS_2007_3YR_G00_&-_lang=en&-_sse=on.

———. 2005. "Table 1: Marital History for People 15 Years and Over, by Age, Sex, Race, and Hispanic Origin: 2001." February 1. http://www.census.gov/population/socdemo/marital-hist/p70-97/tab01-hispanic.xls.

———. 2009.. "America's Families and Living Arrangements." http://www.census.gov/population/www/socdemo/hh-fam.html.

———. 1950. "Households by Type." http://www.census.gov/population/www/socdemo/hh-fam.html.

U.S. Department of Health and Human Services, Administration for Children and Families, Administration on Children, Youth, and Families, Children's Bureau. 2003. *The AFCARS Report*. http://www.acf.hhs.gov/programs/cb/publications/afcars/report8.pdf.

Valsiner, Jaan. 2000. *Culture and Human Development*. London: Sage.

Van der Vliet, Virginia. 1991. "Traditional Husbands, Modern Wives? Constructing Marriages in a South African Township." In *Tradition and Transition in Southern Africa*, ed. Andrew D. Spiegel and Patrick A. McAllister. New Brunswick, NJ: Transaction.

Van Wichelen, Sonja. 2009. "Polygamy Talk and the Politics of Feminism: Contestations over Masculinity in a New Muslim Indonesia." *Journal of International Women's Studies* 11 (1): 173–188.

Volokh, Eugene. 2006. "Same-Sex Marriage and Slippery Slopes." *Hofstra Law Review* 34:1–40.

———. 2005. "Changing Attitudes about Homosexuality." *Volokh Conspiracy*. http://www.volokh.com/posts/1124468214.shtml.

Volks NO v. Robinson, 2005 (5) BCLR 446 (CC); 2005. SACLR LEXIS 3, 21/02.2005.

Waite, Linda, and Maggie Gallagher. 2000. *The Case for Marriage: Why Married*

People Are Happier, Healthier and Better Off Financially. New York: Random House.

Wall, Elissa, and Lisa Pulitzer. 2008. *Stolen Innocence: My Story of Growing Up in a Polygamous Sect, Becoming a Teenage Bride and Breaking Free of Warren Jeffs.* New York: HarperCollins.

Walsh, Eileen Rose. 2005. "From Nu Guo to Nu'er Guo: Negotiating Desire in the Land of the Mosuo." *Modern China* 31 (4): 448–486.

———. 2001. "The Mosuo—Beyond the Myths of Matriarchy: Gender Transformation and Economic Development 10–12." Ph.D. diss., Temple University.

Wardle, Lynn D. 1997. "The Potential Impact of Homosexual Parenting on Children." *University of Illinois Law Review* 1997:833–919.

Ware, Charles. 2001. *Prejudice and the People of God: How Revelation and Redemption Lead to Reconciliation.* Grand Rapids, MI: Kregel.

Warner, Michael. 1999. *The Trouble with Normal: Sex, Politics, and the Ethics of Queer Life.* New York: Free Press.

Weeks, Jeffrey, Brian Heaphy, and Catherine Donovan. 2001. *Same-Sex Intimacies: Families of Choice and Other Life Experiments.* London: Routledge.

Weisbrod, Carol, and Pamela Sheingorn. 1978. "*Reynolds v. United States*: Nineteenth-Century Forms of Marriage and the Status of Women." *Connecticut Law Review* 10:828–858.

Weiss, Philip. 2008. "The Affairs of Men: The Trouble with Sex and Marriage." *New York,* May 18. http://nymag.com/relationships/sex/47055/.

Wekker, Gloria. 2006. *The Politics of Passion: Women's Sexual Culture in the Afro-Surinamese Diaspora.* New York: Columbia University Press.

Weston, Kath. 1997. *Families We Choose.* New York: Columbia University Press.

White, Deborah Gray. 1999. *Ar'n't I a Woman? Females Slaves in the Plantation South.* New York: Norton.

White, Douglas R., and Michael L. Burton. 1988. "Causes of Polygyny: Ecology, Economy, Kinship and Warfare." *American Anthropological Association,* December, 871–887. http://links.jstor.org/sici?sici=0002-7294%28198812%292%3A90%3A4%3C871%3ACOPEEK%3E2.0.CO%3B2-I.

Whitehead, Barbara Dafoe. 1993. "Dan Quayle Was Right." *Atlantic,* April, 47ff.

"Who's Your Daddy?" 2007. *Saturday Star,* June 16, 1.

Willis, Paul. 1981. *Learning to Labour.* New York: Columbia University Press.

Wilson, James Q. 1993. "The Family-Values Debate." *Commentary,* April.

Wing, Adrien Katherine, ed. 2003a. *Critical Race Feminism: A Reader,* 2nd ed. New York: NYU Press.

———. 2003b. "Polygamy in Black America." In *Critical Race Feminism: A Reader,* 2nd ed., ed. Adrien Katherine Wing, 186–194. New York: NYU Press.

———. 2001. "Polygamy from Southern Africa to Black Britannia to Black America: Global Critical Race Feminism as Legal Reform for the Twenty-First Century." *Journal of Contemporary Legal Issues* 11:811.

Winslow, Ben. 2008. "Texas Attorney General Hints at Bigamy Prosecutions." *Deseret News*, April 17.

Wright, Janet M. 2001. "'Aside from One Little, Tiny Detail, We Are So Incredibly Normal': Perspectives of Children in Lesbian Step Families." In *Queer Families, Queer Politics: Challenging Culture and the State*, ed. Mary Bernstein and Renate Reimann. New York: Columbia University Press.

"The Woman's Kingdom." 2006. *Frontline*. PBS broadcast, June 27.

Yarbrough, Michael W. 2005. "We Thee Wed: Marriage Law, Culture, and Subjectivity in Post-apartheid South Africa." Comparative Research Workshop, Yale University.

Zasueta v. Zasueta. California Court of Appeals, Fifth District. 126 Cal. Rpts. 2d 245.

Zeitzen, Miriam Koktvedgaard. 2008. *Polygamy: A Cross-Cultural Analysis*. Oxford, UK: Berg.

Zhou, Xiaoli, and Brent E. Hoffman, producers. 2006. "The Women's Kingdom." Film. German Camera Productions.

Index

Debates ⟶   y/n/no?

1. Should the US gov't promote marriage.

2. Can diff family systems co-exist in the same society?

3. If sexuality is partially socially constructed would women be as polyandrous as men.

About the Author

Judith Stacey is Professor of Social and Cultural Analysis and Sociology at New York University. Her published books include *In the Name of the Family: Rethinking Family Values in the Postmodern Age* (1996), *Brave New Families: Stories of Domestic Upheaval in Late Twentieth-Century America* (1990, reissued in 1998), and *Patriarchy and Socialist Revolution in China* (1983).

writing style
audience
evidence & how presented/used

* Kinship
Sex
love
patriarchal culture -
      what does this entail
      where -
      when
      why -

Transpose

* deep cup   lower sound
  shallow cup   crisp

ER) - SIT
    feet flat on
          floor

* put mirror in
        business

be bop

Aat 7
5

3

5